LONGMAN LINGUISTICS LIBRARY

PRINCIPLES OF PRAGMATICS

LONGMAN LINGUISTICS LIBRARY

Principles of Pragmatics

Geoffrey Leech

LONGMAN

LONDON AND NEW YORK

Longman Group UK Limited
Longman House, Burnt Mill, Harlow
Essex CM20 2JE, England
and Associated Companies throughout the world

*Published in the United States of America
by Longman Inc., New York*

© *Longman Group Limited 1983*

*First published 1983
Seventh impression 1990*

British Library Cataloguing in Publication Data

Leech, Geoffrey
Principles of pragmatics: (Longman linguistics
library; 30)
1. Pragmatics   2. Language-Philosophy
I. Title
401   P99.4.P72

ISBN 0-582-55110-2

Library of Congress Cataloging in Publication Data

Leech, Geoffrey N.
Principles of pragmatics.
(Longman linguistics library; no. 30)
Bibliography: p.
Includes index.
1. Pragmatics.   I. Title.   II. Series.
P99.4.P72L43   1983   410   82-22850
ISBN 0-582-55110-2 (pbk.)

Set in 10/11 pt Linotron 202 Times
Produced by Longman Singapore Publishers (Pte) Ltd.
Printed in Singapore

To Tom and Camilla

Contents

Preface

Pragmatics can be usefully defined as the study of how utterances have meanings in situations. In this book I present a *complementarist* view of pragmatics within an overall programme for studying language as a communication system. Briefly, this means studying the use of a language as distinct from, but complementary to, the language itself seen as a formal system. Or more briefly still: grammar (in its broadest sense) must be separated from pragmatics. To argue this, it is not sufficient to define pragmatics negatively, as that aspect of linguistic study which cannot be accommodated in linguistics proper. Rather, one must develop theories and methods of description which are peculiar to pragmatics itself, and show that these have to be different from those which are appropriate to grammar. The domain of pragmatics can then be defined so as to delimit it from grammar, and at the same time to show how the two fields combine within an integrated framework for studying language.

Up to now, the strongest influences on those developing a pragmatic paradigm have been the formulation of a view of meaning in terms of illocutionary force by Austin and Searle, and of a view of meaning in terms of conversational implicature by Grice. These have also been the strongest influences on the ideas I present here. But my approach to pragmatics is by way of the thesis that communication is problem-solving. A speaker, *qua* communicator, has to solve the problem: 'Given that I want to bring about such-and-such a result in the hearer's consciousness, what is the best way to accomplish this aim by using language?' For the hearer, there is another kind of problem to solve: 'Given that the speaker said such-and-such, what did the speaker mean me to understand by that?' This conception of communication leads to a rhetorical approach to pragmatics, whereby the speaker is seen as trying to achieve his aims within constraints imposed by principles and maxims of 'good communicative behaviour'. In this not only Grice's Cooperative Principle, but other principles such as those of Politeness and Irony play an important role. To sum up: pragmatics differs from grammar in that it is essentially goal-directed and evaluative. I hope that, through this orientation, this book will help to bring about a new *rapprochement* between grammar and rhetoric.

Chapter 1 sketches the historical and intellectual background to the present study, and proposes a set of postulates which are enlarged upon in Chapters 2 and 3. Chapter 3 advocates a combination of formalist and functionalist viewpoints in the philosophy of linguistics. Chapter 4 begins a more descriptive part of the book, which develops the application of the maxims of Grice's Cooperative Principle within the more general framework of an Interpersonal Rhetoric. Chapters 5 and 6 concentrate on other maxims of the Interpersonal Rhetoric, notably maxims of politeness. The framework which has been elaborated in these three chapters is then put to descriptive use in an account of how a limited area of English grammar – the grammar of certain negative and interrogative sentence types – is pragmatically implemented in English. The title 'Communicative Grammar' has been reasonably applied to a linguistic description which, like this one, relates grammatical forms to their various pragmatic utilizations. After this practical demonstration, Chapters 8 and 9 return to more polemical matters. They argue that a rhetorical view of pragmatics requires us to take a different view of performatives and of illocutionary acts from that which is familiar in the 'classical' speech-act formulations of Austin and Searle. The view is put forward that Searle's taxonomy of illocutionary acts should be reinterpreted as a semantic taxonomy of speech-act verbs.

I have benefited from many discussions of these issues with colleagues and with audiences both in Britain and overseas. I am particularly grateful to a group of postgraduate students at Lancaster who discussed the first draft of this book with me: they include Susan George, Andrew McNab, Dilys Thorp, and last but not least, Jennifer Thomas, to whom I am also indebted for subsequent discussions and criticisms. A colleague at Lancaster, R. L. V. Hale, has done me the favour of casting a searching but friendly philosophical eye over several chapters, and suggesting a number of improvements. My co-editor of the Longman Linguistics Library, Professor R. H. Robins, has also kindly given me the benefit of his comments on the final manuscript. The customary disclaimer that I alone am responsible for the shortcomings of this book is particularly appropriate here: on a subject so controversial as the present one, even my most benevolent critics have found – and no doubt will find – enough cause for disagreement.

I acknowledge with thanks the permission granted by John Benjamins, B. V., Amsterdam, to reprint, as part of Chapter 7 of the present work, part of the paper 'Pragmatics and conversational rhetoric' which I contributed to Herman Parret, Marina Sbisà, and Jef Verschueren, eds, *Possibilities and Limitations of Pragmatics*, Amsterdam: John Benjamins, 1981.

University of Lancaster
May 1982   G. N. L.

A note on symbols

The symbols *s* and *h* are used throughout the book to symbolize 'speaker(s) or writer(s)' and 'hearer(s) or reader(s)' respectively. A subscript added to one of these symbols indicates that the person referred to is a participant in the primary speech situation, secondary speech situation, etc. For example, s_1 means 'primary speaker', s_2 means 'secondary speaker'.

The symbols $\uparrow s$, $\uparrow h$, $\downarrow s$, and $\downarrow h$ are interpreted as follows:

$\uparrow s$ = 'desirable for the speaker'
$\uparrow h$ = 'desirable for the addressee'
$\downarrow s$ = 'undesirable for the speaker'
$\downarrow h$ = 'undesirable for the addressee'

Additional abbreviations are:
CP = 'Cooperative Principle'
PP = 'Politeness Principle'
IP = 'Irony Principle'

Chapter 1

Introduction

The aim of science is increase of verisimilitude
[Karl R. Popper, *Objective Knowledge*, p. 71]

In a broad sense, this book is about the nature of human language. In a narrower sense, it is about one aspect of human language, which I believe is important for understanding human language as a whole. This aspect I shall call GENERAL PRAGMATICS.

1.1 Historical preamble

The subject of 'pragmatics' is very familiar in linguistics today. Fifteen years ago it was mentioned by linguists rarely, if at all. In those far-off-seeming days, pragmatics tended to be treated as a rag-bag into which recalcitrant data could be conveniently stuffed, and where it could be equally conveniently forgotten. Now, many would argue, as I do, that we cannot really understand the nature of language itself unless we understand pragmatics: how language is used in communication.

How has this change come about?[1] In part, the whole of the recent history of linguistics can be described in terms of successive discoveries that what has gone headlong into the rag-bag can be taken out again and sewed and patched into a more or less presentable suit of clothes. To the generation which followed Bloomfield, linguistics meant phonetics, phonemics, and if one was daring–morphophonemics; but syntax was considered so abstract as to be virtually beyond the horizon of discovery. All this changed after Chomsky, in the later 1950s, discovered the centrality of syntax; but like the structuralists, he still regarded meaning as altogether too messy for serious contemplation. In the earlier 1960s (for by this time the pace of linguistic advance had quickened) Katz and his collaborators (Katz and Fodor 1963; Katz and Postal 1964; Katz 1964) began to find out how to incorporate meaning into a formal linguistic theory, and it was not long before the 'California or bust' spirit led to a colonization of pragmatics. Lakoff, with others, was soon arguing (1971) that syntax could not be legitimately separated from the study of language use. So pragmatics was henceforth on the linguistic map. Its colonization was only the last stage of a wave-by-wave expansion of linguistics from a narrow discipline dealing with the physical data of speech, to a broad discipline taking in form, meaning, and context.

But this is only part of the story. First, all the names mentioned in the preceding paragraph are American, for it describes the progress of mainstream American linguistics. It is probably more true of linguistics than of other subjects that its dominating influences have been American; but we should not forget that many influential scholars, both in the USA and elsewhere, have continued to work outside the 'American mainstream'. We should not overlook independent thinkers such as Firth, with his early emphasis on the situational study of meaning, and Halliday, with his comprehensive social theory of language. And equally important, we should not overlook the influences of philosophy. When linguistic pioneers such as Ross and Lakoff staked a claim in pragmatics in the late 1960s, they encountered there an indigenous breed of philosophers of language who had been quietly cultivating the territory for some time. In fact, the more lasting influences on modern pragmatics have been those of philosophers; notably, in recent years, Austin (1962), Searle (1969), and Grice (1975).

The widening scope of linguistics involved a change in the view of what language is, and how linguistics should define its subject. The American structuralists were happiest with the idea that linguistics was a physical science, and therefore did their best to rid the subject of appeals to meaning.[2] But by accepting ambiguity and synonymy as among the basic data of linguistics, Chomsky opened a door for semantics. Subsequently, Chomsky's disaffected pupils in the generative semantics school went a stage further in taking semantics to be base for their linguistic theories. But once meaning has been admitted to a central place in language, it is notoriously difficult to exclude the way meaning varies from context to context, and so semantics spills over into pragmatics. In no time the generative semanticists found they had bitten off more than they could chew. There is a justifiable tendency in scientific thought to assume that an existing theory or paradigm works until it is shown to fail. On this basis, the generative semanticists tried to apply the paradigm of generative grammar to problems – such as the treatment of presuppositions and of illocutionary force – which most people would now regard as involving pragmatics. The attempt failed: not in the spectacular way in which theories are supposed to fail on account of a crucial falsifying observation, but in the way in which things tend to happen in linguistics, through a slowly accumulating weight of adverse arguments.[3]

I should explain that I am using the term PARADIGM roughly in Kuhn's sense, not as a synonym for 'theory', but as a more general term referring to the set of background assumptions which one makes about the nature and limits of one's subject-matter, the method of studying it, and what counts as evidence, and which determines the form that theories take.[4] For example, the paradigm term 'generative grammar' in practice refers to a whole set of theories which share certain assumptions: that language is a mental phenomenon, that it can be studied. through the algorithmic specifications of rules operating according to certain conventions, that the data for such theories are available through intuition, that languages consist of sets of sentences, etc.

While the generative semanticists were exploring the outer limits of this paradigm in semantics and pragmatics, Chomsky himself, with others of similar views, was interested in a narrower definition of the scope of this paradigm, that of the so-called Extended Standard Theory, which then evolved into a narrower Revised Extended Standard Theory. These versions of generative grammar have maintained the centrality of syntax; semantics has been relegated to a peripheral position in the model, and has to some extent been abandoned altogether.[5] Pragmatics does not enter into the model at all, and indeed Chomsky has strongly maintained the independence of a grammar, as a theory of a 'mental organ' or 'mental faculty', from consideration of the use and functions of language.[6]

This more limited definition of the scope of linguistic theory is, in Chomsky's own terminology, a 'competence' theory rather than a 'performance' theory. It has the advantage of maintaining the integrity of linguistics, as within a walled city, away from contaminating influences of use and context. But many have grave doubts about the narrowness of this paradigm's definition of language, and about the high degree of abstraction and idealization of data which it requires.

One result of this limitation of generative grammar to a strict formalism is that, since about 1970, it has been progressively losing its position as the dominant paradigm of linguistics. More and more linguists have found their imagination and intellect engaged by approaches more wide-ranging than those allowed for in generative grammar. These approaches do not yet add up to an integrated paradigm for research, but they have had the effect collectively of undermining the paradigm of Chomsky. Sociolinguistics has entailed a rejection of Chomsky's abstraction of the 'ideal native speaker/hearer'. Psycholinguistics and artificial intelligence place emphasis on a 'process' model of human language abilities, at the expense of Chomsky's disassociation of linguistic theory from psychological process. Text linguistics and discourse analysis have refused to accept the limitation of linguistics to sentence grammar. Conversational analysis has stressed the primacy of the social dimension of language study. To these developments may be added the attention that pragmatics – the main subject of this book – has given to meaning in use, rather than meaning in the abstract.

Cumulatively these approaches, and others, have led to a remarkable shift of direction within linguistics away from 'competence' and towards 'performance'. This shift is welcome from many points of view, but the resulting pluralism has meant that no comprehensive paradigm has yet emerged as a successor to generative grammar. A unified account of what language is has, I believe, been lost. Hence the purpose of this book is to argue in favour of a fresh paradigm. This does not mean that the ideas I shall present are highly original: paradigms emerge over a period and decay over a period, and the ideas put forward here have seemed to me to be 'in the air' in a way which makes it difficult to pin down their origin in particular authors.[7] Neither will this book attempt an overall account of language: instead, it will concentrate on arguing the validity of a particular view of the distinction between grammar and pragmatics. This argument, however, will have fundamental implications for the way one looks at language. In essence, the claim will be that grammar (the abstract formal system of language) and pragmatics (the principles of language use) are complementary domains within linguistics. We cannot understand the nature of language without studying both these domains, and the interaction between them. The consequences of this view include an affirmation of the centrality of formal linguistics in the sense of Chomsky's 'competence', but a recognition that this must be fitted into, and made answerable to, a more comprehensive framework which combines functional with formal explanations.

At this point, I shall merely state the major postulates of this 'formal–functional' paradigm. In the next chapter I shall examine them and argue their *prima-facie* plausibility; in the remaining chapters, I shall try to justify them in more detail through analysis of particular descriptive problems. The postulates are:

P1: The semantic representation (or logical form) of a sentence is distinct from its pragmatic interpretation.

P2: Semantics is rule-governed (= grammatical); general pragmatics is principle-controlled (= rhetorical).

P3: The rules of grammar are fundamentally conventional; the principles of general pragmatics are fundamentally non-conventional, *ie* motivated in terms of conversational goals.

P4: General pragmatics relates the sense (or grammatical meaning) of an utterance to its pragmatic (or illocutionary) force. This relationship may be relatively direct or indirect.

P5: Grammatical correspondences are defined by mappings; pragmatic correspondences are defined by problems and their solutions.

P6: Grammatical explanations are primarily formal; pragmatic explanations are primarily functional.

P7: Grammar is ideational; pragmatics is interpersonal and textual.

P8: In general, grammar is describable in terms of discrete and determinate categories; pragmatics is describable in terms of continuous and indeterminate values.

The effect of these postulates is to define two separate domains, and two separate paradigms of research, making up a single 'complex' paradigm for linguistics. Arguments in favour of this paradigm are based on the simplicity and naturalness of the explanations it offers. There is no clear way of testing the validity of scientific paradigms: they exist on a more abstract plane than the scientific method which Popper described as 'the method of bold conjectures and ingenious and severe attempts to refute them'. Nevertheless, by exploring, formulating, and refining paradigms of research, we are determining the background assumptions on which the search for truth about language will proceed with increased understanding.

1.2 Semantics and pragmatics

In practice, the problem of distinguishing 'language' (*langue*) and 'language use' (*parole*) has centred on a boundary dispute between semantics and pragmatics. Both fields are concerned with meaning, but the difference between them can be traced to two different uses of the verb *to mean*:

[1] What does *X* mean?   [2] What did you mean by *X*?

Semantics traditionally deals with meaning as a dyadic relation, as in [1], while pragmatics deals with meaning as a triadic relation, as in [2]. Thus meaning in pragmatics is defined relative to a speaker or user of the language, whereas meaning in semantics is defined purely as a property of expressions in a given language, in abstraction from particular situations, speakers, or hearers. This is a rough-and-ready distinction which has been refined, for particular purposes, by philosophers such as Morris (1938, 1946) or Carnap (1942).[8] I shall redefine pragmatics for the purposes of linguistics, as the study of meaning in relation to speech situations (see 1.4 below).

The view that semantics and pragmatics are distinct, though complementary and interrelated fields of study, is easy to appreciate subjectively, but is more difficult to justify in an objective way. It is best supported negatively, by pointing out the failures or weaknesses of alternative views. Logically, two clear alternatives are possible: it may be claimed that the uses of meaning shown in [1] and [2] are both the concern of semantics; or that they are both the concern of pragmatics. The three views I have now mentioned may be diagrammed and labelled as shown in Fig. 1.1.

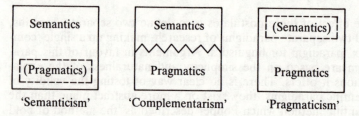

FIGURE 1.1

Because of difficulties of terminology and definition, it is hard to pin down clear cases of semanticism and pragmaticism. In practice, one notices a preference of a semantic type of explanation to a pragmatic one, or vice versa. In a modified sense, therefore, the labels 'semanticist' and 'pragmaticist' may be applied to those who assimilate as much of the study of meaning to one position as possible.

Examples of each position are the following. In the philosophy of language, there has been an influential tradition of philosophers, such as Wittgenstein, Austin, Alston, and Searle, who have been sceptical of traditional approaches to meaning in terms of abstract mental entities such as concepts, and who have in one way or another assimilated semantics to pragmatics. For example, Searle (1969:17) argues for an approach which views the theory of meaning (and in fact the whole of language) as a sub-part of a theory of action; thus meaning is defined in terms of what speech acts speakers perform relative to hearers. On the other hand, in generative semantics in the earlier 1970s, there was an effort to assimilate pragmatics to semantics, particularly by arguing for the PERFORMATIVE HYPOTHESIS (Ross 1970), in terms of which a sentence, in its deep structure or semantic representation, is a performative sentence such as *I state to you that X, I order you to Y*. In this way, the illocutionary or pragmatic force of an utterance was encapsulated in its semantic structure.[9]

The two opposed positions of Searle (1969) and Ross (1970) appear to be very close together, because of the significance they both attach to performative sentences (see 8.2, 8.6). But in fact, they are at opposite poles, as one can see by reading Searle's critique of the performative hypothesis (Searle 1979:162–79). The contrast can also be studied in two contrasting approaches to indirect illocutions such as *Can you pass the salt*: the approach taken by Searle (1979 [1975b]:30–57), and that taken by Sadock (1974, esp. 73–95).

The third viewpoint, that of complementarism, is the one I shall support. The arguments for this position will take the following form. Any account of meaning in language must (a) be faithful to the facts as we observe them, and (b) must be as simple and generalizable as possible. If we approach meaning entirely from a pragmatic point of view, or entirely from a semantic point of view, these requirements are not met; however, if we approach meaning from a point of view which combines semantics and pragmatics, the result can be a satisfactory explanation in terms of these two criteria.

1.2.1 An example: the Cooperative Principle of Grice

My argument will be in favour of the study of pragmatics by means of CONVERSATIONAL PRINCIPLES of the kind illustrated by H. P. Grice's Cooperative Principle (1975:45–6). I shall want to introduce into pragmatics not only a Cooperative Principle (CP), but other principles, such as a Politeness Principle (PP).[10] The interaction between these two principles, the CP and the PP, will in fact be one of the major concerns of this book, particularly in Chapters 4–7.

The CP has been often quoted and discussed in the past few years, but since it will be an important starting-point for the arguments of this book, I cite it again here. Under this principle, four categories of MAXIMS are distinguished:

The Cooperative Principle (abbreviated to CP)

QUANTITY: Give the right amount of information: *ie*
1. Make your contribution as informative as is required.
2. Do not make your contribution more informative than is required.

QUALITY: Try to make your contribution one that is true: *ie*
1. Do not say what you believe to be false.
2. Do not say that for which you lack adequate evidence.

RELATION: Be relevant.

MANNER: Be perspicuous; *ie*
1. Avoid obscurity of expression.
2. Avoid ambiguity.
3. Be brief (avoid unnecessary prolixity).
4. Be orderly.

[Adapted from Grice 1975]

The kind of constraint on linguistic behaviour exemplified by Grice's CP differs from the kind of rule normally formulated in linguistics, or for that matter, in logic, in a number of ways (see below, 2.2). (I shall not, for the present, distinguish between 'principles' and 'maxims', since the latter are simply, according to Grice's usage, a special manifestation of the former).

(a) Principles/maxims apply variably to different contexts of language use.
(b) Principles/maxims apply in variable degrees, rather than in an all-or-nothing way.
(c) Principles/maxims can conflict with one another.
(d) Principles/maxims can be contravened without abnegation of the kind of activity which they control.

The last of these statements amounts to a claim that, in Searle's terminology (1969:33ff), conversational principles and maxims are 'regulative' rather than 'constitutive'. The rules of a language (*eg* the rules for forming tag-questions in English) normally count as an integral part of the definition of that language, but maxims do not. Hence if one tells a lie in English, one breaks one of Grice's maxims (a Maxim of Quality); but this does not mean that one fails in any way to speak the English language. In fact, it has been claimed that part of the definition of human languages is that they can be used to deceive or misinform (see Lyons 1977:83 –4; Thorpe 1972:33). On the other hand, if one breaks the rule for tag-questions by saying *We've met before, isn't it?* rather than *We've met before, haven't we?* one thereby fails in some particular to speak the English language.

One element, although it is part of the everyday interpretation of the terms 'principle' and 'maxim', has been carefully omitted from the above definition. This is the implication that such constraints are of a moral or ethical nature. The requirement to tell the truth might, indeed, be regarded as a moral imperative; but the reason for including it in a scientific account of language is descriptive rather than prescriptive. The maxims form a necessary part of the description of linguistic meaning in that they explain how it is that speakers often 'mean more than they say': an explanation which, in Grice's terms, is made by means of pragmatic implications called CONVERSATIONAL IMPLICATURES. For example, in strictly logical terms,

[3] Many of the delegates opposed the motion

is not inconsistent with the proposition that

[4] All the delegates opposed the motion.

In most contexts, however, it will normally be interpreted as excluding that possibility, on the grounds that if the speaker knew that all of the delegates opposed the motion, the first Maxim of Quantity ('Make your contribution as informative as is required') would have obliged him to be informative enough to say so. In this sense, [3] CONVERSATIONALLY IMPLICATES [5]:

[5] Not all the delegates opposed the motion.

But the implicature holds only if certain premisses or 'enabling assumptions' hold. These include first the assumption (which may or may not be supported by contextual evidence) that the speaker knows whether all the delegates opposed the motion, and secondly the assumption that the speaker is observing the CP. It is quite open to the speaker to opt out of the CP, for example for the purpose of wantonly deceiving the hearer. One can tell lies in English or in any other language, but the point about the CP is that if speakers told lies randomly and indiscriminately, we should no longer be able to communicate by means of language.

In saying that people normally follow the CP, then, one is by no means taking a moral stance. But one thing that cannot be denied is that principles introduce communicative values, such as truthfulness, into the study of language. Traditionally, linguists have avoided referring to such values, feeling that they undermine one's claim for objectivity. But so long as the values we consider are ones we suppose, on empirical grounds, to be operative in society, rather than ones we impose on society, then there is no reason to exclude them from our inquiry.

The distinction I have just drawn between 'principles'/'maxims' and 'rules' will be developed and modified as this book proceeds. As it stands, it is too absolute. Rules are not always so clear-cut in their application as has been implied, nor can the comp- lementary roles of semantics and pragmatics be made so precise as it appears in examples [3] and [4]; but the CP is exemplary in that it shows a division of labour between the SENSE of an utter- ance and its FORCE. Taking this simple example, we may see in it the semantics/pragmatics distinction as a special case of Saus- sure's distinction between *langue* and *parole* (1959 [1916]:11–13), or Chomsky's distinction between competence and performance (1965:3–9). Both these distinctions, however, have been used to define language, for the purposes of linguistics, in an abstract way, effectually excluding the data of language use from con- sideration. For this reason and for others, I shall avoid these fam- iliar dichotomies; instead, I shall refer to the formal language system as GRAMMAR, in opposition to PRAGMATICS, which may also, in a more general sense, be regarded as part of the domain of linguistics. This use of *grammar*, although broad, actually corre- sponds to a current use of the term to mean the study of the whole language system, as in 'transformational grammar'.

1.3 General pragmatics

I have mentioned that my principal subject in this book is GENERAL PRAGMATICS. By this term I mean to distinguish the study of the general conditions of the communicative use of lan- guage, and to exclude more specific 'local' conditions on language use. The latter may be said to belong to a less abstract field of SOCIO-PRAGMATICS, for it is clear that the Cooperative Principle and the Politeness Principle operate variably in different cultures or language communities, in different social situations, among different social classes, etc.[11] One has only to think of the school- boy taboo against 'telling tales' (*ie* the inopportune telling of the truth!), or the way in which politeness is differently interpreted in (say) Chinese, Indian, or American societies, to realize that pragmatic descriptions ultimately have to be relative to specific social conditions. In other words, socio-pragmatics is the socio- logical interface of pragmatics. Much of the work which has taken place in conversational analysis has been limited in this sense, and has been closely bound to local conversational data.[12] The term PRAGMALINGUISTICS, on the other hand, can be applied to the study of the more linguistic end of pragmatics – where we consider the particular resources which a given language provides for conveying particular illocutions[13] (Fig. 1.2).

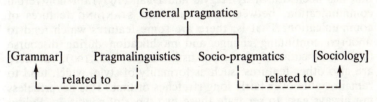

FIGURE I.2

In contrast, general pragmatics, as studied here, is a fairly abstract study. Of course, we do need detailed pragmalinguistic studies which are language-specific, and detailed socio-pragmatic studies which are culture-specific. At the same time, we also need studies at the more general level as a necessary stage of abstraction between the study of language in total abstraction from situation, and the study of more socially specialized uses of language.

My definition of 'general pragmatics' will be further restricted to the study of linguistic communication in terms of conversational principles. It will be limited, that is, to a RHETORICAL model of pragmatics. This means that certain topics which may justly be considered part of pragmatics will be put into the background. First, I shall take little account of what Grice has called CONVENTIONAL IMPLICATURES, *ie* pragmatic implications which are derived directly from the meanings of words, rather than via conversational principles.[14] (For example, in the sentence *She was poor, but she was honest*, the word *but* carries the implicature that for a person to be poor is a good reason for supposing him not to be honest. The meanings of 'pragmatic particles' such as *de* in Classical Greek, *ja* in German, and *sitä* in Finnish may be placed in the same category.)[15] Another exclusion is the attitudinal function of intonation, and of non-verbal communication through gestures and paralanguage. More relevant, but still peripheral to my present concern, is the study of what may be called REFERENTIAL PRAGMATICS, *ie* the assignment of reference to referential expressions in a given utterance: these include indexical elements such as personal pronouns and the tense of the verb.

One further field which might be included in pragmatics, and which is only touched on here, is the study of relatively permanent parameters of situation in relation to language choice, such as those which have been included by Halliday (*eg* 1978) and others under the heading of REGISTER, and which still others have studied under the heading of STYLE (Crystal and Davy 1969). The distinction between pragmatics and register corrresponds to one that has been drawn by Argyle and Dean (1965) for non-verbal communication, between DYNAMIC and STANDING features of communication. That is, there are some features which tend to undergo continuing change and modification during discourse (such as illocutionary force in Austin's sense, 1962:100); but there are also other features, such as formality of style, which tend to remain stable over fairly long stretches of time. It is nevertheless not always easy to separate these two types of condition. Politeness, for instance, is often a function of both: standing features such as the social distance between participants interact with dynamic features such as the kind of illocutionary demand the speaker is making on the hearer (request, advice, command, etc.) to produce a degree of politeness appropriate to the situation (see 5.7).

Having narrowed the field in this way, I shall now present a diagram (Fig. 1.3) designed to capture the distinction implied between semantics (as part of the grammar) and general pragmatics (as part of the use of the grammar). I am taking for granted here a familiar and well-established tripartite model of the language system (grammar), consisting of semantics, syntax, and phonology. These levels can be regarded as three successive coding systems whereby 'sense' is converted into 'sound' for the purposes of encoding a message (PRODUCTION), or whereby 'sound' is converted into 'sense' for the purposes of decoding one (INTERPRETATION). Figure 1.3 shows that the grammar interacts with pragmatics via semantics. This view, although a useful start-

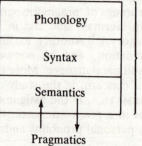

FIGURE 1.3

ing-point, is not the whole story; we may note, as an exception, that pragmatically related aspects of phonology (*eg* the polite use of a rising tone) interact directly with pragmatics, rather than indirectly, via syntax and semantics.

1.4 Aspects of speech situations

The question inevitably arises: how do we know we are dealing with pragmatic, rather than with semantic phenomena? Since pragmatics studies meaning in relation to speech situation, reference to one or more of the following aspects of the speech situation will be a criterion.

(i) *Addressers or addressees*
Following the practice of Searle and others, I shall refer to addressers and addressees, as a matter of convenience, as *s* ('speaker') and *h* ('hearer'). These will be a shorthand for 'speaker(s)/writer(s)' and 'hearer(s)/reader(s)'. Thus the use of the abbreviations *s* and *h* does not restrict pragmatics to the spoken language. A significant distinction can be made (*cf* Lyons 1977:34) between a receiver (a person who receives and interprets the message) and an addressee (a person who is an *intended* receiver of the message). A receiver, that is, might be a bystander or an eavesdropper, rather than an addressee. This distinction is relevant to the present inquiry, in that the analyst of pragmatic meaning is best thought of as a receiver: a proverbial 'fly on the wall' who tries to make sense of the content of a discourse according to whatever contextual evidence is available. The use of the symbol *h*, however, will always signify one or more addressees, or persons to whom the utterance is *addressed* by *s*.

(ii) *The context of an utterance*
CONTEXT has been understood in various ways, for example to include 'relevant' aspects of the physical or social setting of an utterance. I shall consider context to be any background knowledge assumed to be shared by *s* and *h* and which contributes to *h*'s interpretation of what *s* means by a given utterance.

(iii) *The goal(s) of an utterance*
I shall often find it useful to talk of a *goal* or *function* of an utterance, in preference to talking about its *intended* meaning, or *s*'s intention in uttering it (see further 2:3.3.1). The term *goal* is more neutral than *intention*, because it does not commit its user

to dealing with conscious volition or motivation, but can be used generally of goal-oriented activities. The term *intention* can be misleading on this score.

(iv) The utterance as a form of act or activity: a speech act

Whereas grammar deals with abstract static entities such as sentences (in syntax) and propositions (in semantics), pragmatics deals with verbal acts or performances which take place in particular situations, in time. In this respect, pragmatics deals with language at a more concrete level than grammar.

(v) The utterance as a product of a verbal act

There is another sense in which the word 'utterance' can be used in pragmatics: it can refer to the *product* of a verbal act, rather than to the verbal act itself. For instance, the words *Would you please be quiet?*, spoken with a polite rising intonation, might be described as a sentence, or as a question, or as a request. However, it is convenient to reserve terms like *sentence* and *question* for grammatical entities derived from the language system, and to reserve the term *utterance* for *instances* of such entities, identified by their use in a particular situation. Hence an utterance may be a sentence-instance, or sentence-token; but strictly speaking, it cannot be a sentence. In this second sense, utterances are the elements whose meaning we study in pragmatics. In fact, we can correctly describe pragmatics as dealing with utterance meaning, and semantics as dealing with sentence meaning. However, there is no need to assume that all utterances are sentence-tokens. We may wish to isolate as an utterance a piece of language which is either too short or too long to be classified as a single sentence.

The meaning of *utterance* in (iv) and the meaning of *utterance* in (v) can be easily confused: there is a difference, but not a particularly marked one, between describing *Would you please be quiet?* as an utterance (as in (v)), and describing the *act* of uttering *Would you please be quiet?* as an utterance (as in (iv)).[16] Fortunately, the confusion can be alleviated, since it is generally convenient to say that 'utterance' in the sense of (iv) corresponds to 'speech act', or more precisely to ILLOCUTIONARY ACT, in the sense of that term employed by Austin (1962:100). This means we can use *illocutionary act* or *illocution* for the utterance-action as described in (iv), and can keep the term *utterance* for the linguistic product of that act. When we try to work out the meaning of an utterance, this can be thought of as an attempt to reconstruct what act, considered as a goal-directed communication, was it a goal of the speaker to perform in producing the utterance.

Thus the meaning of an utterance, in this sense, can be called its ILLOCUTIONARY FORCE. (Austin in fact distinguished illocutionary acts from other kinds of acts, notably locutionary and perlocutionary acts. But the other kinds of act (see further 9.1) can be largely discounted in an account of pragmatics).

From the above-mentioned elements of (i) addresser and addressee, (ii) context, (iii) goals, (iv) illocutionary act, and (v) utterance, we can compose a notion of a SPEECH SITUATION, comprising all these elements, and perhaps other elements as well, such as the time and the place of the utterance. Pragmatics is distinguished from semantics in being concerned with *meaning in relation to a speech situation*.

1.5 Rhetoric

Earlier I characterized the present approach to pragmatics as 'rhetorical'. This use of the term 'rhetorical' is very traditional, referring to the study of the effective use of language in communication. But whereas rhetoric has been understood, in particular historical traditions, as the art of using language skilfully for persuasion, or for literary expression, or for public speaking, I have in mind the effective use of language in its most general sense, applying it primarily to everyday conversation, and only secondarily to more prepared and public uses of language. The point about the term *rhetoric*, in this context, is the focus it places on a goal-oriented speech situation, in which s uses language in order to produce a particular effect in the mind of h.

I shall also use the term RHETORIC as a countable noun, for a set of conversational principles which are related by their functions. Using a distinction familiar in the work of Halliday, I shall distinguish two rhetorics, the INTERPERSONAL and the TEXTUAL rhetorics (Fig. 1.4) (see also 3.3). Each of the two rhetorics (whose functions will be explained later) consists of a set of principles, such as the CP and the PP already mentioned. The principles, in turn, consist of a set of maxims, in accordance with Grice's terminology. Grice's 'maxim', however, I shall call a 'sub-maxim', thereby introducing another level into the hierarchy. But I do not wish to insist too rigidly on this four-level hierarchy, since it is not always clear to what level a given precept belongs. For example, of Grice's two Maxims of Quality (which I call sub-maxims), the second seems to be a predictable extension of the first:

Maxim 1: Do not say what you believe to be false.

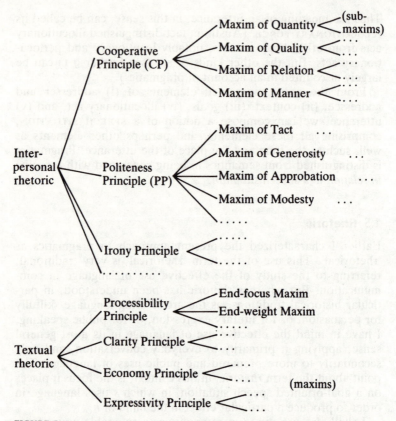

FIGURE 1.4

Maxim 2: Do not say that for which you lack adequate evidence.

If we say something for which we lack adequate evidence, we do not know whether what we say is true or false. Therefore Maxim 2 simply says 'Do not put yourself in a position where you risk breaking Maxim 1'; and both can be summarized in the precept 'Avoid telling untruths'. The taxonomic lay-out of Fig. 1.4 is merely a way of sketching out in advance some of the territory to be covered in this book (especially in Chs 4–6). It is not meant to be definitive.

The rhetorical principles socially constrain communicative behaviour in various ways, but they do not (except in the case of 'purely social' utterances such as greetings and thanks) provide the main motivation for talking. Cooperation and politeness, for instance, are largely regulative factors which ensure that, once conversation is under way, it will not follow a fruitless or disruptive path. It is therefore necessary to distinguish between illocutionary goals and social goals, or equivalently between the illocutionary force of an utterance and its RHETORICAL FORCE – *ie* the meaning it conveys regarding *s*'s adherence to rhetorical principles (*eg* how far *s* is being truthful, polite, ironic). Together, the illocutionary force and the rhetorical force of an utterance make up its PRAGMATIC FORCE.

The distinction between SENSE (meaning as semantically determined) and FORCE (meaning as pragmatically, as well as semantically determined) is essential to this study. But it is also essential to realize the bond between the two: force *includes* sense, and is also pragmatically *derivable* from it in a way to be elucidated in Chapter 2.

Notes

1. See Newmeyer (1980) for a readable book-length account of the events to which this paragraph alludes.
2. Bloomfield's famous dismissal of meaning as the 'weak point in language study' (1933/35:140) was followed by attempts to exclude meaning altogether from the techniques of linguistics – see especially Harris (1951:7).
3. The rise and decline of the performative hypothesis (see 8.6) is particularly instructive from this point of view. The controversy over presuppositions also raged through the 1970s, with Wilson (1975), Kempson (1975), and Gazdar (1979) against the logical (*ie* semanticist) account of presupposition which was current in linguistics in the late 1960s.
4. Kuhn's 'paradigm' (1962), and Lakatos's 'research programme' (1970, 1978) are in this respect more illuminating, as a scientific model for linguistics, than the doctrine of the crucial experiment.
5. See Chomsky (1976:306), and Chomsky and Ronat (1979:56–7).
6. See Chomsky's controversy with Searle on the functional basis of language (1976:55–77).
7. Among many influences and parallel developments, I should mention the authors cited in note 3 above, as well as Harnish (1976) Holdcroft (1978), Bach and Harnish (1979), Givón (1979), and Edmondson (1981).
8. For an account of these earlier philosophical approaches, see Lyons (1977:115).
9. The generative semantics approach did not distinguish between the deep syntactic structure and the semantic structure of a sentence. See especially McCawley (1968) and Lakoff (1971).

10. Grice (1975:47) himself notes the importance of politeness as a factor in the account of conversational meaning. Earlier accounts of politeness in terms of rhetorical principles and maxims are to be found in Leech (1980:9–30, 79–116).
11. Thus socio-pragmatics would involve the assignment of variant values to the principles and maxims. But are the CP and the PP universal? It would be surprising if they did not operate in some form or other in all societies. Counter-examples have been reported – *eg* Keenan (1976) cites the case of Malagasy speakers who habitually disregard the Maxim of Quantity – but as Harnish points out (1976:340, note 29), these are not true counter-examples, since there is no claim that the CP is observed categorically.
12. *Eg* in the work of Gumperz, Schegloff and Sacks, Labov and Fanshel. A useful survey of research in this area is Corsaro (1981).
13. I am indebted to Thomas (1981) for formulating the pragmalinguistic/socio-pragmatic distinction (also Thomas, forthcoming).
14. Grice (1975:44). For further discussions of conventional implicature, see Harnish (1976:331–340) and Karttunen and Peters (1979).
15. On *ja, doch* and other 'modal particles' in German, see Bublitz (1978); on *sitä*, see Hakulinen (1975).
16. The two senses of *utterance* are distinguished in French by the terms *énonciation* and *énoncé*. For discussion, see Lyons (1977:26).

Chapter 2

A set of postulates

The most useful thing about a principle is that it can always be sacrificed to
expediency

[Somerset Maugham, *The Circle*, Act I]

To clarify the distinction that is being proposed between semantics and pragmatics, I shall give in this and the following chapters
some explanation of the postulates listed on page 5. These postulates will be repeated in small capitals under each heading of
this chapter. Although I shall argue that the postulates have
prima-facie plausibility, more detailed arguments in their support
will be presented later, in the descriptive chapters.

2.1 Semantic representation and pragmatic interpretation

P1: THE SEMANTIC REPRESENTATION (OR LOGICAL FORM) OF AN
UTTERANCE IS DISTINCT FROM ITS PRAGMATIC INTER-
PRETATION.

My face-value reason for accepting this complementarist view
(see *p* 6) is that contrary views have in the past led to implausible, if not absurd, accounts of language.

Let us look first at an example of implausibility in the
SEMANTICIST position: an attempt to assimilate pragmatic
phenomena to semantics. According to the PERFORMATIVE
HYPOTHESIS put forward by the generative semantics school in
the early 1970s (see further 8.6), every sentences S in a language is
in its deep or semantic structure a performative sentence roughly
of the form *I state/declare/ask/etc. S*. By this means the illocutionary force of an utterance was given a place in its semantic representation (which, since this school did not distinguish semantic
representations from syntactic ones, was also its deep syntactic
representation). The most absurd manifestation of this approach
I have met was S. R. Levin's proposal that the deep structure of
every poem (for example, of every one of the 154 *Sonnets* of

Shakespeare) begins with a deleted performative which reads: *I imagine myself in and invite you to conceive of a world in which* ... (1976:150). But without considering such exotica as this, one can appreciate the implausibility of the performative hypothesis by merely considering that one of its consequences is the following. In a piece of expository written prose (say, an encyclopaedia article), every single sentence will have, in its underlying structure, a performative preface such as *I state that...* which has undergone deletion; so that a 100-sentence article will presumably have the same prefixed clause (or a similar one) repeated 100 times. Moreover, to make it more implausible, this performative will include a reference to the writer (*I*), even in formal expository prose of the kind in which first person reference is avoided for stylistic reasons.[1] The performative hypothesis was an apparently inadvertent attempt to 'grammaticize' pragmatic phenomena (*ie* illocutionary forces), and could, I believe, only have been entertained by those for whom the grammatical paradigm of generative grammar was considered all-sufficient. Only in this way could they have tried to ignore the obvious: *viz* that language takes place in situations.[2] (I shall elaborate this view of the performative hypothesis in 8.6).

On the other hand, there have been rather implausible attempts to state everything about meaning, if not about language in general, in terms of speech acts and speech situations. This attempt reached something of an extreme in Alston's proposal to define word meaning in terms of a word's contribution to illocutionary force:

> A meaning of W_1 is $W_2 =_{df.}$ In most sentences in which W_2 occurs, W_1 can be substituted for it without changing the illocutionary-act potential of the sentence.
>
> [Alston 1964:38]

Alston defines synonymy of words (W_1, W_2, etc) as a matter of the similar illocutionary-act potential of the sentences in which they occur; but since words do not normally constitute illocutionary acts in isolation, he has no way of explaining how words have meanings in themselves. The meaning of *cow*, for him, will not depend on any idea or definition of a cow as a bovine milk-giving animal, but will be a function of all the illocutionary acts we can perform using the word *cow*.

A better-known example of pragmaticism is Searle's speech-act theory (1969), summarized in his suggestion that 'a theory of language is part of a theory of action' (1969:17). In addition to illocutionary acts, Searle envisages grammatical acts of various kinds; in other words, he notionally translates the grammatical system into the performance of various speech acts:

> ... for certain purposes one might wish to break up what I have called utterance acts into phonetic acts, phonemic acts, morphemic acts, etc. And, of course, for most purposes, in the science of linguistics it is not necessary to speak of acts at all. One can just discuss phonemes, morphemes, sentences, etc.
>
> [Searle 1969:25]

The 'And, of course ...' acknowledges, like a hand waving away a matter too slight to hold up discussion, the limitation of the paradigm *'language = action'*. Yet Searle presses ahead with this paradigm in his treatment of meaning. The paradigm embodies, in fact, a half-truth: there are things that can be done with language, but that does not mean that language is all a matter of doing. I shall consider Searle's speech-act theory critically in Chapters 8 and 9.

2.2 Rules and principles

P2: SEMANTICS IS RULE-GOVERNED (GRAMMATICAL); GENERAL
    PRAGMATICS IS PRINCIPLE-CONTROLLED (RHETORICAL).

I have already associated the rules of grammar with Searle's concept of 'constitutive rules', and the principles of pragmatics with his concept of 'regulative rules'. As regards rules in grammar and logic, it is scarcely necessary to illustrate the first part of this distinction further. A general schema for such rules is:

Under condition(s) *X, Y* is derived/derivable from *Z* (where *X, Y,* or *Z* is sometimes null). In English transformational syntax, for example, the rule of *do*-support may be stated as follows:

> If the Tense-marker is not attached to a verb, replace the
> Tense-marker by *do* + Tense-marker.
>
> [*cf* Akmajian and Heny 1975:124]

In propositional logic, the rule of Modus Ponens says:

From A and $A \supset B$, derive B.

Such rules either apply or they do not apply. There is no question of rules being applied *to a certain extent*, of one rule *conflicting* with another, of one rule *overruling* another, etc., according to variable factors of context. The idea that grammar is 'rule-governed' in this way will be examined more carefully later on (see 3.4), since there are well-known difficulties in this view. On the other hand, I shall assume, as is assumed by all who attempt to write grammars, that such a view of grammar is substantially correct.

The division of labour between rules and principles can be illustrated by the passive in English. The rule of changing an active structure into a passive one is constitutive: it defines a set of changes to a transitive clause, such that if those changes are made, the result is another clause, which is grammatically well formed and has the same sense as the structure with which one started (see, however, 3.4):

Martha killed the fly ~ The fly was killed by Martha.

If one fails to apply one part of this rule (for example, the insertion of *by* in front of the agent), the result is an ungrammatical sentence, something that is no longer part of the English language: *The fly was killed Martha*. The maxims governing Textual Rhetoric (see 3.3.3) are, however, regulative. They include the Maxim of End-focus, which recommends that if the rules of the language allow it, the part of a clause which contains new information should be placed at the end:

The fly was killed by MÀRTHA.

In this sense, both grammar and pragmatics conspire to provide an explanation of the passive: one explains how the passive is formed, the other explains the conditions under which it is likely to be preferred to the corresponding active.

Here again there is a difference between the present position and that adopted by Searle (1969:33–42). Searle regards speech acts, including illocutionary acts, as defined by rules:

> ... the hypothesis of this book is that speaking a language is a matter of performing speech acts according to systems of constitutive rules.
>
> [*ibid.*, p 38]

An illocution, for him, 'counts as' a promise/order/request/etc. according to a defined set of rules, classified as propositional content rules, preparatory rules, sincerity rules, and essential rules. Thus a warning is defined (Searle 1969:67) by the following rules:

Propositional content: Future event or state, etc. E.
Preparatory: (1) h [*sic*] has reason to believe E will occur and is not in h's interest.
　　　　　　　(2) It is not obvious to both s and h that E will occur.
Sincerity: s believes E is not in h's best interest.
Essential: Counts as an undertaking to the effect that E is not in h's best interest.

Such rules assume a taxonomic decision: either an utterance counts as a warning, or it does not.[3] For example, there is a clear distinction between a warning (in which the future event, as envisaged by s, is not in the interests of h) and a piece of advice (where the future event, as envisaged by s, is in the interests of h). It is true that such clear-cut interpretations occur in a few cases, for example in performative utterances beginning *I promise you...*, *I warn you...*, *I advise you...*. But on the whole, they represent an unrealistic and unsubtle view of what communication by means of language is like. Any account of illocutionary force which defines it in terms of rules like this will present a limited and regimented view of human communication. By this view, all human communication boils down to performing certain action-categories. It is almost as if rituals such as baptizing a baby, sentencing a criminal, or naming a ship were somehow typical of the way human beings interact with one another.

I would like to quote the following utterance as a counterbalance to that impression, and as in some ways a more representative specimen of human speech behaviour:

> Considering that I am a hostage, I should say that I have been treated fairly.

This highly ambivalent utterance is reported to have been said by an American hostage in Iran in 1980, when he was due for early release. It was said to reporters who asked him how he had been treated. The utterance was presumably intended to supply some information which the reporters could treat as news; at the same time, to tell the truth; to reassure the public in the USA (no doubt including the speaker's family) that he had not been ill-treated; to avoid saying something that might give offence to his captors and so delay his release. The way in which such motives interrelate and conflict in the function of the utterance makes any classification of it in terms of 'declaring', 'reporting', 'acknowledging', etc. as a naively simplified account of what kind of communication was involved. A better model might be something nearer to a linguistic juggling act, in which the performer has to simultaneously keep several balls in the air: to fulfil a number of goals which compete with one another. Of these goals, obeying the CP (giving the required amount of information, telling the truth, speaking relevantly) must be considered only a part. This may be an extreme case, but it manifests an ambivalence and multiplicity of function that is far from unusual as an exemplar of what language can do. The indeterminacy of conversational utterances also shows itself in the NEGOTIABILITY of pragmatic factors; that is, by leaving force unclear, s may leave h the opportunity to

choose between one force and another, and thus leaves part of
the responsibility of the meaning to *h*. For instance,

If I were you, I'd leave town straight away.

can be interpreted according to context as a piece of advice, a
warning, or a threat. Here *h*, knowing something about *s*'s likely
intentions, may interpret it as a threat, and act on it as such; but *s*
will always be able to claim that it was a piece of advice, given
from the friendliest of motives. In this way, the 'rhetoric of conversation' may show itself in *s*'s ability to have his cake and eat it.

2.3 Convention and motivation

P3: THE RULES OF GRAMMAR ARE FUNDAMENTALLY CONVEN-
TIONAL; THE PRINCIPLES OF PRAGMATICS ARE FUNDA-
MENTALLY NON-CONVENTIONAL, *ie* MOTIVATED IN TERMS
OF CONVERSATIONAL GOALS.

Searle's account of illocutionary acts also conflicts with P3. Searle
says that the rules for performing and interpreting illocutionary
acts are conventional. For example, 'it is a matter of convention
... that the utterance of such and such expressions under certain
conditions counts as the making of a promise' (1969:37). Hence if
we ask *why* a sentence such as *I'll pay you back tomorrow*,
spoken by someone who has just borrowed some money, counts
as a promise in Searle's definition, the only answer must be: 'Because the rules say so.' But we *can* give reasons, in terms of motivated discourse, as to why such a proposition, describing some
action in the future by *s*, will be understood as a promise – as a
means of assuring *h*, that is, that the action will be carried out,
and hence, in effect, of putting oneself under an obligation to ensure that outcome. I would argue from the opposite direction
from Searle: that a promise is recognized as a promise not by
means of rules (except in so far as rules are required in determining sense), but by means of a recognition of *s*'s motive;[4] and that
Searle's rules apply only to the extent that they specify conditions
which will normally follow from that recognition.

What is conventional is the semantic fact that a sentence of the
syntactic form *I'll pay you back tomorrow* expresses a proposition
describing a particular future act by the speaker. That is, the
sense is conventional, in that it is deducible from the rules of
grammar (among which I here include lexical definitions); but the
force is arrived at by means of motivated principles such as the
CP. The CP will imply, that is, that unless *s* is breaking the
Maxim of Quality, *s* will make sure that the action will be carried

out; and that unless *s* is breaking the Maxim of Relation, *s*'s statement of the undertaking to pay back the money has some relevance to the present speech situation, in which the money is
being borrowed. Thus if one
(a) knows the sense of the utterance,
(b) knows the conversational principles that apply to it,
(c) knows the context,
(d) is able to employ informal common-sense reasoning to (a),
    (b), and (c),
one will easily arrive at the conclusion that *I'll pay you back
tomorrow* is intended as a promise (see further Ch. 7). In this
way we recognize a 'division of labour' between convention and
motivation in language.

However, the matter is not that simple. I have here taken
'conventional' to mean the same as 'arbitrary' in the Saussurian
sense. Saussure's notion of the arbitrariness of the linguistic sign
(1959 [1916]:67ff) is one of the cornerstones of modern linguistics, and in general, linguists have taken it for granted that
linguistic categories and linguistic rules are arbitrary: that is, they
are in no way predictable from, or deducible from, extralinguistic
realities. While I take this to be true in a fundamental sense of
grammar, I shall also argue that there are two levels of explanation of grammar. The rules of a grammar (that is, of the grammar
of a particular language) are arbitrary; but there is also a 'meta-
grammar': an explanation of the typological or universal characteristics of grammars in general. I hold that at this level we can
reasonably attempt to give explanations of why grammars have
the rules that they have, and that such explanations may appeal
to pragmatic motivation. For instance, it is well known that in
many languages, including English, it is possible (and in fact
usual) to delete the subject of an imperative sentence: (*You*)
come here! This irregularity clearly has a pragmatic motivation: in
the majority of cases we can predict (imperatives having a horta-
tory function) that *you* will be the understood subject, and therefore there is nothing to be lost by its omission. (See the Principle
of Economy, *p* 67.)

To clarify matters, let me distinguish between two kinds of
conventionality. There is the absolute conventionality of the rule,
for example, that in English the word designating the male of the
human species is pronounced /mæn/. This one has to learn as a
bare fact when learning English (either as a native or as a foreign
learner), and no motivation can be found for it. (Historical explanations can, of course, be given as to why the word has come
to have its present pronunciation, but these will also be ultimately

arbitrary, in so far as they derive the word from an earlier arbitrary form.) There is, however, the MOTIVATED CONVENTIONALITY of a rule for which some motivation is evident, but which overdetermines the choice of linguistic behaviour which would be predictable from that motivation. For such cases, two kinds of statement are required: the first states the rule as a matter of convention, and the second states that given that this rule exists, it is a reasonable, on extralinguistic grounds, that it does so.

One case of such motivated conventionality is the following:

[1] Good luck! = 'I wish you good luck'
[2] Bad luck! = 'I regret your bad luck'

The fact that [1] cannot mean 'I regret your good luck' and [2] cannot mean 'I wish you bad luck' follows from the PP, the principle which (as it applies to language) means that people on the whole prefer to express polite rather than impolite beliefs (see *pp* 81–2). But at the same time, it is a matter of convention in English that (for example) *Good luck* functions as an expression of good wishes, rather than as a means of congratulating *h* on *h*'s good luck; and that although *bad luck* and *misfortune* have the same sense, we can commiserate with someone by saying *Bad luck!*, but not by saying *Misfortune!*

Consider another case where grammatical possibilities are limited by pragmatic principles:

[3] Can you post these letters?   Yes, I can.
    Will she post these letters?   Yes, she will.
    Shall I post these letters?   ?*Yes, you shall.

The regular paradigm relating questions to elliptical responses is broken in the case of *shall*. If we interpret *Shall I* as meaning 'Is it your wish that I . . .?', the question is polite, and is regularly used for making an offer. The reply, however, is not polite, because the relevant sense of *you shall* implies the imposition of *s*'s will on *h* (see 5.4). In this case we could give a conventional grammatical explanation for the non-occurrence of *you shall, viz* that *shall* is obsolescent in present-day English, and does not occur (in general) with second-person subjects. But we could also give a pragmatic explanation: that *you shall* is an impolite, if not positively imperious reply to give. It is likely, in fact, that both explanations are partly correct: we can argue that it is on account of the PP that *shall* in modern English syntax has a defective paradigm.

There is therefore a need for two levels of statement in grammar: one conventional and the other non-conventional. The basic statements about grammatical rules are conventional, whereas the metagrammatical explanations are not. In contrast, constraints in pragmatics are primarily motivated, and only secondarily, if at all, conventional. Part of the essence of Grice's CP, for example, is its extralinguistic motivation in terms of social goals. Grice postulates, as a means of explaining conversational implicature, that speakers usually make their contribution to a conversation 'such as is required by the accepted purpose or direction of the talk exchange'. He points out that his maxims apply both to linguistic and non-linguistic behaviour: for example, one can violate the Maxim of Relation not only in what one says, but in what one does:

> I expect a partner's contribution to be appropriate to immediate
> needs at each stage of the transaction; if I am mixing ingredients
> for a cake, I do not expect to be handed a good book, or even an
> oven cloth. . . .
>
> [Grice 1975:47]

Similarly, one can show politeness not only in one's speech, but (say) by opening a door for someone, rather than slamming it in someone's face.

In so far as grammar is motivated, it is motivated at least in part by pragmatic considerations. For example, grammar is to some extent adapted to such needs as performing illocutionary acts while at the same time being polite and cooperative. It would not be surprising to discover, in more ways than have so far been suggested, that grammar is like it is because it is useful.

Pragmatic adaptations of grammar can presumably be studied, in the long term, as a matter of historical change and evolution,[5] or synchronically, by noting exceptions to rules in the present state of the language. Such exceptions may either be PRAGMATIC RESTRICTIONS or PRAGMATIC EXEMPTIONS: that is, some restriction may be made on an existing rule, or some exception may be made to it. An example of the former which, like *shall* above, is from the field of modality is the suffix *-ooṭṭe* in Malayalam. This suffix has the meaning 'permission', but is restricted to optative sentences, and to questions with first-person pronouns.[6] Hence this grammatical form is limited to illocutions of requesting and granting permission. An example of exemption is:

[4] Would you mind if I smoke? (*cf* the more regular *Would you mind if I smoked?*)

which combines the unreal past *would mind* with the present *smoke*. This is an exception to the normal rule that conditional

sentences have concord of mood between the main and the conditional clauses. The pragmatic reason for this exception is
evidently that sentences such as [4] are PRAGMATICALLY SPECIAL-
IZED for use as polite requests. The hypothetical past in such
sentences is in origin a device of polite evasion; but this device
has become so conventionalized in formulae such as *Would you
mind...?* that its hypothetical force has atrophied. Consequently, the non-hypothetical verb *smoke* is irregularly substituted for
the grammatically regular *smoked*. These and other pragmatic influences are characterized as exceptions to rules. But this does
not prevent them from being regarded themselves as rules: new
rules entering the grammar normally begin as exceptions to other
rules. The idea that one rule states a condition on, or exception
to, another more general rule is standard in grammar.

The process whereby pragmatic constraints become conventionalized'[7] in the pragmatically specialized features of grammar
provides an explanation of how, over a long time-scale, grammar
itself becomes adapted to pragmatic constraints. In this, these
features show a resemblance to other partly conventionalized features of language, and of other semiotic systems. One such phenomenon is metaphor. Metaphors vary in their degree of conventionalization, from the totally unconventional 'poetic' metaphor,
to the totally assimilated 'dead' metaphor. Another such feature
is the iconicity associated with onomatopoeic words. The English
word *pipe*, for example, is less onomatopoeic now than it was
when, before the Great Vowel Shift, it was pronounced /piːp(ə)/
(Intonation patterns may be partially conventionalized in a similar way.)

The main reason for mentioning these parallels in the present
context is to bring out the gradience of conventionalization in
pragmatics, a gradience which is particularly noticeable in the
case of utterances used indirectly as requests (see Sadock
1974:97ff). At the non-conventional end of the scale are indirect
illocutions such as:

[5] Are you able to repair this watch?

Although it will be pragmatically interpreted in the right context
as carrying the force of a request ('I want to know if you can
mend this watch, and if so, I want you to do so'), this sentence is
not grammatically specialized for that purpose. Partly conventionalized are requests like

[6] Can you repair this watch?

which are specialized to the extent that they are grammatically associated with items and structures which resemble those of imperatives rather than of questions (*cf* Sadock 1974:73-95); *eg* the medial *please* in [6a], and the *can you* tag-question in [6b]:

[6a] Can you *please* repair this watch?
   [*cf Please repair this watch.*]
[6b] Repair this watch, *can you*?
   [*cf Can you repair this watch?*]

At the most conventional end of the scale, among other structures, are grammatical formulae such as oaths and greetings (*How do you do?*) and the word *please* itself, which has lost what grammatical analysability it once had, and is just treated as a particle of politeness.

Semi-institutionalized speech forms such as [6] have another similarity to metaphors and intonation patterns in that they are sometimes, but not always, translatable into semantically equivalent forms in other languages. For example, [6] can be straightforwardly translated into Portuguese:

[7] (Você) pode consertar este relógio?
   (You) can mend this watch?

But there are also types of construction which cannot be translated from English into Portuguese or vice versa:

[8] Será que você $\left\{ \begin{array}{l} \text{consertaria} \\ \text{poderia consertar} \end{array} \right\}$ este relógio?
   It is that you would/could mend this watch?

This indirect request with the verb *to be* has no corresponding form in English. In the more extreme cases like *please*, meaningful literal translations are unlikely: *please* contrasts semantically with equivalent polite formulae in other languages, such as Portuguese *por favor* ('as a favour'), Arabic *min fadlak* ('out of your graciousness').

This discussion, by emphasizing the overlap between grammar and pragmatics, has demonstrated that one cannot simply say: 'Grammar is conventional, pragmatics is non-conventional.' Nevertheless, such demarcation difficulties are met with in all areas of language: one might cite, for example, the difficulty of deciding whether sequences like *on to* and *cannot* consist of one or two words. These peripheral phenomena are symptoms of the fact that language is an open and evolving system, and do not undermine the essential distinction, in conventionality, between grammar and pragmatics. The difference may be summarized in the formula: grammar is primarily conventional and secondarily

motivated; pragmatics is primarily motivated and secondarily
conventional.

2.4 The relation between sense and force

P4: GENERAL PRAGMATICS RELATES THE SENSE (OR GRAMMATI-
CAL MEANING) OF AN UTTERANCE TO ITS PRAGMATIC FORCE.
THIS RELATIONSHIP MAY BE RELATIVELY DIRECT OR
INDIRECT.

It has already been claimed that semantics and pragmatics describe the meaning of an utterance in different ways. The task of
pragmatics is to explain the relation between these two types of
meaning: the sense (which has often been described as the 'literal' or face-value meaning) and the (illocutionary) force. I assume,
along with many others, that the sense can be described by means
of a SEMANTIC REPRESENTATION[8] in some formal language or
notation. The force will be represented as a set of implicatures.
'Implicature' is here used in a broader sense than Grice's, but I
follow Grice in believing that 'the presence of a conversational
implicature must be capable of being worked out' (1975:50), by
means of the type of informal reasoning referred to in 2.5.2. This
is a corollary of the claim that pragmatics studies behaviour that
is motivated, in terms of conversational goals. I must stress,
however, that in the present account all implicatures are probabilistic. We cannot ultimately be certain of what a speaker means
by an utterance. The observable conditions, the utterance and the
context, are determinants of what s means by the utterance U; it
is the task of h to diagnose the most likely interpretation. Since,
as I have already pointed out, utterances are liable to illocutionary indeterminacy, it is not always possible for h, although a
reasonable diagnostician, to come to a definite conclusion about
what s means.

Interpreting an utterance is ultimately a matter of guesswork,
or (to use a more dignified term) hypothesis formation. I shall
illustrate this with an example of the type which Grice uses to
exemplify the CP:

[9] A: When is Aunt Rose's birthday?
     B: It's sometime in April.

The sense of the reply is simply a proposition to the effect that
Aunt Rose's birthday occurs in April (it could have been expressed in the form of a long disjunction *It's either on the first of April,
or on the second of April, or* ...). But A will derive from it an
additional piece of meaning: *viz*. that B doesn't know the exact

date of the birthday (*ie* B doesn't know whether Aunt Rose's birthday is on the first, the second, the third . . . or the thirtieth of April). How is the extra meaning, or implicature, arrived at? The following are the three main stages:

(i) The *prima-facie* observation is that there is something 'up' with B's reply. B does not give the right amount of information for A's needs. That is, B has apparently violated the CP (specifically, the Maxim of Quantity).

(ii) There is, however, no reason to suppose that B is being deliberately uncooperative. Therefore, A can reasonably assume that B IS observing the CP, and that this apparent breach of the Quantity Maxim is due to A's wish to uphold the CP at another point. Therefore we must look for a reason why the CP should cause B to give less information than A needed.

(iii) This reason can be supplied on the grounds that B was trying to uphold the Maxim of Quality. Suppose that B is observing the CP and that B does not know when Aunt Rose's birthday is, except that it is in April. Then B will not randomly state that her birthday is (say) on 1 April, or on 6 April, or on 19 April, since to do so, although it would uphold the Maxim of Quantity, would be to violate the Maxim of Quality (*ie* to risk telling a lie). Therefore, to be on the safe side, B will merely say that the birthday is in April. In the absence of any other explanation, this explanation will be accepted, as consistent with the CP. Therefore it will be concluded that *B does not know which day in April is Aunt Rose's birthday*.

The three stages of this inference are (i) rejection of the face-value interpretation as inconsistent with the CP; (ii) search for a new interpretation consistent with the CP; (iii) finding a new interpretation, and checking that it is consistent with the CP. The new interpretation includes an implicature *I*, on the grounds that the assumption that *I* is necessary in order to make *s*'s saying *U* consistent with the CP.

This is not a formalized deductive logic, but an informal rational problem-solving strategy. It consists in (a) formulating the most likely available hypothesis, then (b) testing it, and, if it fails, (c) formulating the next most likely available hypothesis, and so on. This kind of strategy is a general strategy employed by human beings for solving interpretative problems. It is found on the one hand in highly abstract and complex scientific theorizing,[9] and on the other hand in homely examples, such as the following. If an electric light fails when the switch is turned on, the first and most likely hypothesis is that the bulb is broken; if the bulb is replaced, and the light still does not go on, the next most likely guess is that the lights have fused, or perhaps that the connection is faulty. The process goes on until a solution (*ie* a hypothesis consistent with the observed facts) is found.

Another point to notice about the Aunt Rose example is that one maxim of the CP is upheld at the expense of another. In this case, as is normally the case, *s* is assumed to have given preference to the Maxim of Quality over the Maxim of Quantity. But there are cases where the preference is reversed. It has been reported to me that in certain places (*eg* in parts of Italy and Brazil) a stranger asking a question (*eg* asking the way to a destination) will characteristically be given a false answer in preference to an uninformative one.

Further, the elaborate spelling-out of a rational process, as in (i)–(iii) above, should not, of course, be taken to imply that such processes necessarily happen laboriously and consciously in the mind of the interpreter. The purpose of such a commentary is, first, to demonstrate that the pragmatic force is motivated by general principles of rational and social behaviour (in the sense of 2.3), and second, to give a rough outline of the postulated interpretative process which may, however, be to a greater or lesser degree automatized. Searle (1979 [1975b]: 56–7) aptly describes the problem of interpreting an indirect illocution such as *Can you pass the salt*? as follows:

> The problem seems to me somewhat like those problems in the epistemological analysis of perception in which one seeks to explain how the perceiver recognizes an object on the basis of imperfect sensory input. The question, How do I know he has made a request when he has only asked me a question about my abilities? may be like the question, How do I know it was a car when all I perceived was a flash going past me on the highway?

Just as one may automatically condense a complex set of visual and auditory impressions and inferences into a single observation 'That was a car', so one may condense a long argument into a single unheeding response '*A* wants me to pass the salt'.

Can you pass the salt is an example (a stock example, as it happens) of an indirect illocution, *ie* in Searle's definition, a case 'in which one illocutionary act is performed indirectly by way of performing another'. I follow Searle (1979 [1975b]) in proposing for such illocutions an explanation modelled on Gricean implicature. Grice's conversational implicatures were devised to explain sentences in which a speaker appears to mean more than he says.

It is a natural extension of this type of explanation (which he applied only to declarative sentences) to apply it to other, non-declarative examples of 'meaning more than one says'. But Searle's speech-act theory leads him, naturally enough, to treat indirect illocutions as defined by the same kinds of rules as apply to other kinds of illocutionary act. My own position on indirect illocutions (to be developed in Ch. 7) differs from Searle's in two respects.

First, I take it that no special illocutionary rules are required for indirect illocutions; indirect illocutionary force is stated simply by means of a set of implicatures. Such implicatures are state-ments attributing mental states (*eg* propositional attitudes such as belief) to *s*. In the case of [9] for instance, the implicatures associ-ated with *B*'s reply *It's sometime in April* (assuming that *B* is observing the CP) include the following:

[10a] *B* believes that Aunt Rose's birthday is in April (via Maxim of Quality).

[10b] *B* is not aware of which day in April is Aunt Rose's birthday (via Maxims of Quantity and Quality).

Although the interpretation of an indirect illocution like *Can you pass the salt* is more complex than this (involving, for example, the PP as well as the CP), the general method of description is the same, and the final implicature (corresponding to Searle's 'in-direct speech act') is that *s* wants *h* to pass the salt (see *p* 120).

Second, I do not draw a distinction between direct and indirect illocutions. All illocutions are 'indirect' in that their force is de-rived by implicature. There is, however, a great deal of variation in their degree of indirectness. The most direct illocutions are simply those to which, in the absence of contrary evidence, we may apply the most likely pragmatic hypothesis, *ie* what may be called the default interpretation. If, for example, the response of *B* in [9] had been *It's on 10 April*, the default interpretation would have applied:

[11a] *B* believes that Aunt Rose's birthday is on 10 April (via Maxim of Quality).

Grice applies the term 'conversational implicature' to cases such as [10b], but I shall extend it also to default interpretations such as [10a] and [11a]. This extension is a consequence of the thesis that sense and force are two distinct kinds of meaning. It is nor-mal, that is, for an utterance to have both a sense and a force, even in cases (such as straightforward statements of information) where an utterance's meaning-in-context seems to follow auto-

matically from its sense.[10] The advantage of this position, which
is the one I shall adopt, is that it capitalizes on two very different
sets of insights about pragmatic meaning – those of Grice's theory
of conversational implicature, and those of Searle's speech-act
theory. In fact, the latter is reinterpreted in terms of a generalized version of the former. For example, Searle's sincerity rules
are treated simply as cases of s obeying the Maxim of Quality
(see 2.5.2).

I have said that pragmatic force is specified by means of statements attributing some mental state to s. A crucial point, however, is that statements such as [10a] and [10b] are not direct
claims about what is going on in s's head. Rather, they are statements about what s means to convey by the utterance in question.
This conclusion depends on the assumption that s is observing the
CP, and perhaps other rhetorical principles. Despite appearances, then, pragmatics is a study in which only the meaning that
is publicly available for interpretation is analysed. In pragmatics,
as elsewhere, the linguist is interested in making publicly confirm-
able observations about language, and in constructing theories to
explain such observations.

Since pragmatics is about meaning in speech situations, we
clearly cannot make any pragmatic claims about what is going on
privately in someone's head. If s, for example, says *It's six
o'clock*, we cannot take it for granted that s believes that it is six
o'clock. For all we know, s may be an inveterate clandestine liar.
But we can say that the implicature that s believes that it is six
o'clock is part of the meaning, or the force, of that utterance. To
be more precise, then, [10a] and [10b] should have been prefaced
as follows:

In saying $\left\{ \begin{array}{l} \textit{It's sometime in April} \\ \textit{It's on 10 April} \end{array} \right\}$ B implicates, among other

things, that . . .

But meaning is two-sided: as Searle (1969:43), paraphrasing
Grice (1957:385) puts it:

> In speaking I attempt to communicate certain things to my hearer by
> getting him to recognize my intention to communicate just those
> things. I achieve the intended effect on the hearer by getting him to
> recognize my intention to achieve that effect.

In other words, 'meaning' as it is used in pragmatics (*ie* in the formula 's means F by U,' where s = speaker, F = force, and U =
utterance) is characterized as a REFLEXIVE INTENTION, *ie* an in-

tention whose fulfilment consists in its recognition by h.[11] As
Bach and Harnish (1979:15) point out, however, this reflexive intention is executed only by virtue of what they call 'the Communicative Presumption', *ie* the mutual belief, shared by s and h,
that when someone says something to somebody else, it is done
with some illocutionary goal in mind. Such a presumption, indeed, may be said to follow, as a limiting case, from the Maxim of
Relation as interpreted in 4.3 below:

'An utterance U is relevant to a speech situation if U can be interpreted as contributing to the conversational goal(s) of s or
h.'

To this may be added yet another presumption about the nature
of pragmatic force: that if s means F by U, then s intends h to recognize the force F *by way of the sense* (*ie: the grammatical meaning*) *of U*.

This does not mean, of course, that miscommunication does
not take place. It means that pragmatics is concerned only with
publicly conveyed meaning, and does not take account either of
miscommunication, or of secret communication. Thus if s says
My aunt has a villa in Vladivostok!, meaning by that that s has
three aces and two kings up his sleeve, this is no concern of
pragmatics, because the meaning conveyed in that case has nothing to do with the sense of the utterance.[12] The factors which
can lead to failure of communication are varied, and not all of
them are in the pragmatic domain: for example, s and h may not
share the same linguistic knowledge; the physical channel between s and h may be impaired; s may not be observing rhetorical
principles; s and h may have different socio-pragmatic values. But
in so far as what s means by U is different from what h understands by U, it is not part of pragmatics to bother about such differences. At the same time, it has to be admitted, as I have
already indicated, that what s means by U may be to some extent
indeterminate, so giving h opportunity, within limits, to negotiate
or decide the force of U (see further 7.1). Thus pragmatics must
be concerned, quite centrally, with indeterminacy.

Having emphasized the reciprocal participation of s and h in
the illocutionary act, I must now point out an essential way in
which their roles are different.

2.5 Pragmatics as problem-solving

P5: GRAMMATICAL CORRESPONDENCES ARE DEFINED BY MAP-

PINGS; PRAGMATIC CORRESPONDENCES ARE DEFINED BY
PROBLEMS AND THEIR SOLUTIONS.

Pragmatics involves PROBLEM-SOLVING both from s's and from h's
point of view. From s's point of view, the problem is one of planning: 'Given that I want the mental state of the hearer to change
or to remain unchanged in such and such ways, how do I produce an utterance which will make that result most likely?' From
h's point of view, the problem is an interpretative one: 'Given
that s has said U, what is the most likely reason for s's saying U?'
The problem-solving procedures are very different in these cases.
The latter case, that of interpretation, may in fact be considered a
'meta-problem-solving' procedure, since the problem h has to
solve is 'What was the communicative problem s was trying to
solve when s said U?'

Unlike the sense–sound mappings and the sound–sense mappings of grammar, these problem-solving procedures cannot be
defined by algorithms. They involve general human intelligence
assessing alternative probabilities on the basis of contextual
evidence.

2.5.1 The speaker's task, viewed in terms of means–ends analysis

Briefly, the problem-solving strategy of s can be viewed as a form
of means–ends analysis.[13] This analysis represents a problem and
its solution in the form of a directed graph, with initial states and
final states (see Fig. 2.1).

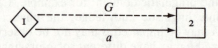

FIGURE 2.1

I = initial state (individual feels cold).
2 = final state (individual feels warm).
G = goal of attaining state 2 (getting warm).
a = action (switching heater on).

This is the very simplest graph possible. The diamond represents
the initial state, and the square the final state. The solid arrow
represents an action taken by some individual in order to fulfil
the goal. The broken arrow represents the goal (possessed by the
individual at state 1) of attaining the final state.

There is a natural extension of this model to include intermediate states (which are both objects of subsidiary goals, and conditions for the fulfilment of the final goal). Further extensions
introduce multiple goals, simultaneous states, negative goals (*ie* the

maintenance of status quo), etc. The simplest case of a means–ends analysis involving language is one like Fig. 2.1, in which *a* represents a speech act. In this way we may interpret the fulfilment of the reflexive intention described in 2.4 above as follows:

I = initial state (*s* means *h* to understand *F* by *U*)
2 = final state (*h* understands *F* by *U*)
G = goal of attaining state 2
a = speech act (act of uttering *U*)

A slightly more complicated linguistic example of means–ends analysis is that in which *s* takes for granted that *h*'s understanding of the message will lead *h* to perform a required action (Fig. 2.2).

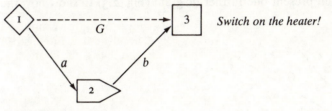

Switch on the heater!

FIGURE 2.2

I = initial state (*s* feels cold)
2 = intermediate state (*h* understands that *s* wants the heater on)
3 = final state (*s* feels warm)
G = goal of attaining state 3 (getting warm)
a = *s*'s action of telling *h* to switch on the heater
b = *h*'s action in switching on the heater

The box of the following shape ▷ is used to represent an intermediate state which is (i) the fulfilment of a subsidiary goal, and (ii) a condition for the attainment of the final goal. It is thus a final state with respect to an immediate goal, and an initial state with respect to an ulterior goal.

Compared with the action represented in Fig. 2.1, that of Fig. 2.2 may be thought to represent an 'indirect' fulfilment of a goal. But by this standard, all purposeful uses of language will be regarded as indirect:[14] that is, whenever we use language as a *means* of bringing about some end, this implies some chain of actions such as is found in Fig. 2.2 – but often the chain is longer and more complex. In fact, such illocutions as that of Fig. 2.2 have been called DIRECT SPEECH ACTS OR DIRECT ILLOCUTIONS by those who have contrasted them with INDIRECT SPEECH ACTS OR

INDIRECT ILLOCUTIONS (see Searle 1979 [1975b]; Sadock 1974). Searle defined indirect speech acts as 'cases in which one illocutionary act is performed indirectly by way of performing another' (1979 [1975b]:60). That is, for Searle, an indirect speech act can be regarded as a means of performing a direct speech act. But in the present means–ends framework, even a 'direct' speech act such as the imperative *Switch on the heater!* is an indirect means of achieving some goal, in that it is directed at a subsidiary goal. Therefore 'indirect illocutions' are simply illocutions which are more indirect than others; and indirectness is a matter of degree. The scale of indirectness can be notionally represented in terms of the means–ends analysis by the length of the means–ends chain connecting the speech act to its goal.

I shall present one further diagram (Fig. 2.3) to show how the

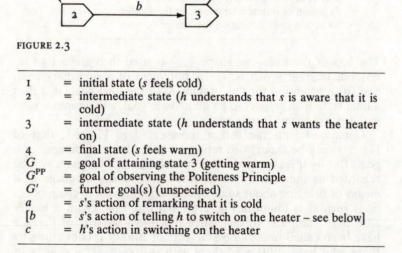

FIGURE 2.3

1	= initial state (*s* feels cold)
2	= intermediate state (*h* understands that *s* is aware that it is cold)
3	= intermediate state (*h* understands that *s* wants the heater on)
4	= final state (*s* feels warm)
G	= goal of attaining state 3 (getting warm)
G^{PP}	= goal of observing the Politeness Principle
G'	= further goal(s) (unspecified)
a	= *s*'s action of remarking that it is cold
[*b*	= *s*'s action of telling *h* to switch on the heater – see below]
c	= *h*'s action in switching on the heater

goal that was achieved in the examples represented in Figs. 2.1 and 2.2 can be achieved by a more indirect illocution. Figure 2.3 represents Searle's view that an indirect speech act (= action *a*) is a means of performing another speech act (action *b*). The diagram suggests, however, that Searle's concept of a direct speech act underlying an indirect speech act is an unnecessary construct, resulting from Searle's way of looking at illocutionary acts as defined by conventional rules, rather than as defined by their function in a means–ends analysis.[15]

There is only one speech act in question here: the uttering of *Cold in here, isn't it*? Searle's analysis, however, requires that this one illocution actually instantiates two illocutions, one being the means to the other. Searle appears to claim that (i) there are two speech acts, (ii) that one is performed by means of the other, and (iii) they take place simultaneously, both being performed in the same utterance. But this analysis makes the concept of a speech act quite mystical and abstract. A better way to interpret a diagram like Fig. 2.3 would be to say that *b* is an action performed not by *s*, but by *h*, and that this action is the act of interpreting the utterance *Cold in here, isn't it*? as having the implicature that *s* wants *h* to switch the heater on. That is, we should replace the statement regarding *b* in brackets under Fig. 2.3 by:

b = *h*'s action in inferring that *s* wants *h* to switch the heater on.

This is not the only interpretation of the sentence *Cold in here, isn't it*?, but it is a probable one, given certain circumstances. Such a remark about the temperature could be, alternatively, a piece of chit-chat, of phatic communion, without ulterior goal except the maintenance of social relations (see 6.2). And we should also note this as a case of potential indeterminacy: it could be that *s* uttered *Cold in here, isn't it*? partly in order to maintain friendly social relations, and partly in the hope that *h* will do something to alleviate the cold: in which case, it is up to *h* to interpret the illocution as having an impositive or coercive force, but only if he so wishes. It is with this in mind that I have represented *s* in Fig. 2.3 as having other potential goals (marked G').

The goal of upholding the PP (G^{PP}) is included in Fig. 2.3 for another purpose. It may be taken as a general principle of goal-directed behaviour that individuals adopt the most direct course of action that is judged to be consistent with the fulfilment of their goals. (This is one way of interpreting the Maxim of Manner.) Hence if an *s*, as in Fig. 2.3, employs an indirect strategy to fulfil a goal, the reason for this is likely to be that *s* wants to achieve some other goal, in addition to G. This is the justification for positing the extra goal G^{PP} of preserving the PP, and thereby maintaining good social relations. The CP, the PP, and other rhetorical principles may, in this analysis, be seen as regulative goals which persist as part of the background against which all other goals must be considered. Or perhaps it is better to think of them as negative goals: the goals of avoiding uncooperative and impolite behaviour. Other goals may conflict or compete with these goals, and most obviously, an impositive goal (one requiring imposition of one's will on someone else) runs counter to the principle of politeness. Thus the making of an 'innocent', non-impositive remark such as *Cold in here, isn't it*? becomes a gambit for reconciling competing goals: for evading a breach of politeness while still aiming at an impositive goal. Providing, in accordance with Gricean conversational implicature, that the force can be 'worked out', s can rely upon h's own compliance with the PP as a reason for h's performance of the desired action.

There is likely to be one dissatisfaction with the above interpretation of linguistic behaviour in terms of a means–ends analysis. It is that such analysis appears to regard all uses of language as having an instrumental function. Surely, it might be argued, we cannot treat all discourse as motivated by the goal of bringing about some result in the mental or physical condition of the addressee? While one cannot, of course, rule out the occurrence of non-communicative uses of language (*eg* purely expressive speech), it is indeed my contention that, broadly interpreted, the means–ends analysis applies to communicative uses of language in general. However, the term 'goal' is slightly restrictive, and the term 'intention' even more so, in suggesting a degree of conscious or deliberate planning of discourse which the model does not necessarily imply. One can, needless to say, uphold the CP or the PP in one's behaviour without being conscious of the existence of such principles; and the same applies even to more specific goals. The concept of 'goal', in this analysis, should be applicable to the phatic use of language (see 6.2), the avoidance of taboo subjects and taboo vocabulary, etc., and other cases where although the pattern of linguistic behaviour may be clear, few people would claim that the user is aware of the goals that motivate this behaviour. In short, the term *goal* is used in the neutral Artifical Intelligence sense of 'a state which regulates the behaviour of the individual' in such a way as to facilitate a given outcome.

2.5.2 The addressee's task, seen in terms of heuristic analysis

The kind of problem-solving task which an addressee faces in interpreting an utterance may be described as HEURISTIC. A heuristic strategy consists in trying to identify the pragmatic force of an utterance by forming hypotheses and checking them against available evidence. If the test fails, a new hypothesis is formed. The whole process may be repeated cyclically until a solution (a hypothesis which is successful, in that it does not conflict with evidence) is arrived at. The whole cycle can be represented, in a rather oversimplified way, as shown in Fig. 2.4. The problem, in this case, is a problem of interpretation. From the sense of what is said, together with background information (about context) and background assumptions (that s is observing the usual principles) h forms a hypothesis about the goal(s) of the utterance. For example, if s says *It's Aunt Mabel's birthday next Monday*, the most likely hypothesis is:

s means [h to be aware [that Aunt Mabel's birthday is next Monday]]

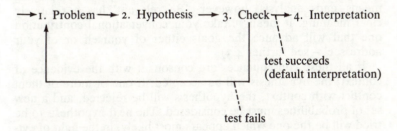

FIGURE 2.4

The whole thing can be simplified if we use P as a symbol for the sense of U (in this case P is a proposition). Then the sense of the utterance can be taken as given for the purpose of the problem-solving process, and can be stated as follows:

A. s says to h [that P]

The hypothesis about the force of P can likewise to generalized as follows:

B. s means [h to be aware [that P]]

This amounts to a claim that U is an information-giving utterance; what Searle and others have called an assertion. This claim or hypothesis can now be checked by observing whether it is consistent (assuming the relevant pragmatic principles) with the evidence of context:

C. *s* believes [that *P*]   (Maxim of Quality)
D. *s* believes [that *h* is not aware [that *P*]](Maxim of Quantity)
E. *s* believes [that it is desirable
    [that *h* be aware [that *P*]]]   (Maxim of Relation)

Once the hypothesis has been formed, certain conditional consequences, such as *C, D*, and *E*, follow from the assumption that (i)
the hypothesis is correct, and (ii) that *s* is observing the CP. *C*
follows, since if *C* were not the case, *s* would be telling a lie, and
breaking the Maxim of Quality. *D* follows, since, if *D* were not
the case, *s* would be saying something which so far as *s* is aware
has no information value for *h*, and in that case *s* would be breaking the Maxim of Quantity (by giving too little information, *ie*
none at all). *E* follows since, if it were not the case that *E*, then *s*
would be saying something irrelevant to the situation, and would
thus be breaking the Maxim of Relation.

(The Maxim of Relation has been criticized on the ground that
its vagueness makes it almost vacuous. In a pragmatics employing
means–ends analysis, however, 'Be relevant' has a relatively
clear meaning: it means 'Make your conversational contribution
one that will advance the goals either of yourself or of your
addressee' – see further 4.3).

If all these consequences are consonant with the evidence of
context, the hypothesis will be accepted. If one or more of them
conflict with context, the hypothesis will be rejected, and a new
set of probabilities must be considered. The next hypothesis to be
tried will be the one which appears most likely, in the light of evidence already noted. The acceptance of the initial and most likely
interpretation will be called the DEFAULT INTERPRETATION. That
is, it is the interpretation that is accepted *in default of* any evidence to the contrary. The statement regarding the goal(s) of *s* (*B*
above) will be called the MINIMUM ILLOCUTIONARY ASSUMPTION,
and the implicatures derived from that (*eg: C, D, E*) will be
called CORROBORATIVE CONDITIONS.

In a general sense (more general than that of Grice) all these
statements (except *A*) may be called implicatures. They are provisional pragmatic implications, which can, however, be cancelled
if they are inconsistent with other evidence. Grice applies the
term *implicature* principally to cases where the default interpretation is rejected, due to an apparent flouting of a maxim; but this,
in the present model, is a special case of a more general inferential pattern.

The earlier example of *Cold in here, isn't it?* illustrates how a
face-value or default interpretation may have to be rejected. Sup-

pose, on the one hand, that this utterance is spoken (as is quite likely) in a context where *h* is fully aware of the coldness of the temperature. Then the implicature *D* above fails, and consequently *E* fails as well, unless some other kind of illocutionary force (*eg* phatic remark about the weather) can be postulated. Suppose, on the other hand, that *Cold in here, isn't it*? is uttered in circumstances where the temperature is very high. In this case, implicature *C* would fail, and some new hypothesis (*eg* that *s* is being ironical) is sought. By this process, a pragmatic interpretation may be arrived at more or less indirectly, according to the number of problem-solving steps needed for *h* to arrive at a satisfactory solution (for further examples, see 4.4). In this heuristic analysis, there is a scale of indirectness corresponding to that already observed in the means–ends analysis of *s*'s planning of the utterance. The more indirect *s*'s illocution, the more indirect is *h*'s inferential path in reconstructing it.

This account of pragmatic interpretation can be misconstrued unless it is understood in a sufficiently abstract way. First, 'problem-solving' suggests a deliberate puzzling-out of meaning; but in the case of pragmatic interpretation, the process may well be highly automatized; there is no implication that decisions are conscious, or are arrived at as a result of explicit cerebration. Second, one should not expect that default interpretations are the same in different contexts. The expectations of addressees will vary according to situation, so that what may be a default interpretation in one context will not be so in another. For instance, the default interpretation of a question in many situations will be 'an information-seeking illocution', carrying the corroborative condition that *s* does not know the answer to the question concerned. But this is presumably not the most likely interpretation in an examination paper or in a legal cross-examination. Thirdly, in the account I have assumed, there is a deductive ordering of implicatures, whereby the hypothesis is formed first of all, and the consequences are derived from it subsequently. In practice, though, it may well be that some of the corroborative conditions are registered before the hypothesis is formulated; in other words, a partially inductive sequence may be followed. The account I have given may be something of an idealization, departing at various points from the actual intellectual processes of the hearer. At this point, however, I shall merely stress the general plausibility of a heuristic procedure in showing how conversational implicatures are (in Grice's terms) 'capable of being worked out', and 'replaceable by an argument'. In this way, a general method of showing how force can be derived from sense without resort to arbitrary convention can be demonstrated.

Another look at the set of statements $A-E$ above will show that they correspond remarkably closely to Searle's speech-act rules. Searle's rules for assertions (1969:65) in fact run as follows:

Propositional content: Any proposition P.
Preparatory: (1) s has evidence (reasons, etc.) for the truth of P.
              (2) It is not obvious to both s and h that h knows (does not need to be reminded of, etc.) P.
Sincerity: s believes P.
Essential: Counts as an undertaking to the effect that P represents an actual state of affairs.

Of these, the propositional content rule corresponds to A ('s says to h that P'). The second preparatory rule corresponds to B ('s means [h to be aware [that P]]'). The sincerity rule and the first preparatory rule correspond to C ('s believes [that P]'). The lack of correspondence is in E (which has no equivalent in Searle's rules), and in Searle's essential rule, which states a 'convention' by which an assertion will be interpreted, but is arguably redundant. Without going into the merits of this or that set of rules, I wish to argue that Searle's speech-act rules, with one category of exception, can all be replaced by implicatures. The exception is the propositional content rule, which in my account corresponds to a statement of the sense of the utterance. The sense alone is conventional; all other 'rules', in my account, are non-conventional implicatures, derived (by means of the heuristic strategy) from the sense and from general conversational principles such as the CP.

2.6 Conclusion

This chapter has explained five out of the eight postulates listed on p. 5. The remaining three postulates will be dealt with in the next chapter, the main topic of which will be a functional account of the relation between grammar and pragmatics.

Notes

1. Ross (1970), in his famous article 'On declarative sentences' putting forward the performative hypothesis, actually points out this difficulty.
2. Similarly, Ross (1970:254) points out the advantage of an alternative 'pragmatic hypothesis', which would have made use of speech situations, but which, since it involved postulating extra-grammatical entities, he regarded as incapable of formulation.

3. To be fair to Searle, he does recognize that there is a great deal of unclarity as to what counts as one kind of illocutionary act, and what counts as another (see Searle 1979 [1975a]: 29: '... the illusion of limitless uses of language is engendered by an enormous unclarity about what constitutes the criteria for delimiting one language game or use of language from another').

4. Searle himself (1969:44–9) criticizes the approach, which he attributes to Grice, of defining meaning in terms of 'intending to perform a perlocutionary act'. But I find unconvincing Searle's claim that some illocutionary acts, such as greetings and promises, are not associated, in terms of their meaning, with perlocutionary effects.

5. I know of no historical studies of the influence of Interpersonal Rhetoric on the evolution of grammar; but regarding Textual Rhetoric, the views put forward by Bever (1976) and Bever and Langendoen (1976) are relevant.

6. This example is from Veloo (1980: 54–5).

7. See Bach and Harnish (1979:195–202) on 'standardized indirection'. Bach and Harnish distinguish standardization, as a short-circuiting of the process of working out illocutionary intent, from conventionality.

8. On semantic representation, see Clark (1976:12–14), Leech (1981 [1974]:96–7).

9. Cf Popper's formula representing the hypothetico-deductive method of science (1972:119, 242–3, 297). For an analogue in artificial intelligence problem-solving algorithms, see Newell (1973:12ff).

10. Exceptionally, the force of an utterance is determined by convention: see 8.2.1 on 'declarations'.

11. For various versions of the 'reflexive intention' definition of meaning, see Grice (1957), Searle (1969: 44–9), and Bach and Harnish (1979:13–15).

12. Cf Searle's criticism of Grice for disregarding the role of convention in determining meaning (Searle 1969:43–4).

13. On means–ends analysis in artificial intelligence, see Winston (1977:130–42); means–ends analysis is applied to pragmatics by Parisi and Castelfranchi (1981).

14. Cf Bloomfield's famous parable of 'normal speech' (1933/35:22–7), the story of Jack, Jill, and the apple. Bloomfield, however, was not concerned with illocutions, but with stimuli and responses within a behaviourist paradigm, ie with perlocutionary effects.

15. The sense of 'indirect' I am using is different from that of Searle, and hence does not in itself imply a conflict with his position on indirect speech acts. Searle's position has the further difficulty that arises in cases such as *Can you pass the Times?*, where it is clearly absurd that a question about *h*'s weightlifting ability is intended, and therefore the only illocutionary force one can attribute to the utterance is that of a request.

Chapter 3

Formalism and functionalism

For use almost can change the stamp of nature.   [*Hamlet*, III. iv]

The Form remains, the Function never dies.

[Wordsworth, *The River Duddon*]

As two approaches to linguistics, formalism and functionalism tend to be associated with very different views of the nature of language.[1]

(a) Formalists (*eg* Chomsky) tend to regard language primarily as a mental phenomenon. Functionalists (*eg* Halliday) tend to regard it primarily as a societal phenomenon.

(b) Formalists tend to explain linguistic universals as deriving from a common genetic linguistic inheritance of the human species. Functionalists tend to explain them as deriving from the universality of the uses to which language is put in human societies.

(c) Formalists are inclined to explain children's acquisition of language in terms of a built-in human capacity to learn language. Functionalists are inclined to explain it in terms of the development of the child's communicative needs and abilities in society.

(d) Above all, formalists study language as an autonomous system, whereas functionalists study it in relation to its social function.

On the face of it, the two approaches are completely opposed to one another. In fact, however, each of them has a considerable amount of truth on its side. To take one point of difference: it would be foolish to deny that language is a psychological phenomenon, and equally foolish to deny that it is a social phenomenon. Any balanced account of language has to give attention to both these aspects: the 'internal' and 'external' aspects of language. More generally, my conclusion will be that the correct approach to language is both formalist and functionalist.

3.1 Formal and functional explanations

The approach I am taking is summarized in P6:

P6: GRAMMATICAL EXPLANATIONS ARE PRIMARILY FORMAL;
    PRAGMATIC EXPLANATIONS ARE PRIMARILY FUNCTIONAL.

This postulate overlaps with P3 (2.3). To the extent that grammatical rules are conventional, the theory or model of grammar which explains them will be formal. In so far as the principles of general pragmatics are motivated or goal-oriented, the theory which explains them will be functional.

Broadly, a formal grammatical theory such as transformational grammar (Chomsky 1965:15–18) defines a language as a set of sentences. These sentences have meanings (senses) and pronunciations, and so in effect the grammar has to define a set of mappings whereby particular senses are matched with particular pronunciations (Chomsky 1965:15–18). The central level of syntax, at which each sentence is represented as a string of words or formatives, is an essential component of this complex mapping. Three levels of representation – semantics, syntactic, and phonological – are therefore assumed, and the justification of distinguishing these levels is that there are many-many mappings between them. In addition to mapping rules, there are rules of well-formedness, specifying what is a well-formed or grammatical representation at each level.

Such a model is intended to represent what native speakers implicitly know to be the case about their language. Native speakers of English, for example, know that *That girl washed himself* is semantically ill-formed (*ie* nonsensical); that *The purse was stole a burglar* is syntactically ill-formed; that /dva/ and /xlep/ are unphonological sequences in English (though not in Polish); that the sentences *It is possible that not all the plates were broken* and *Some of the plates may not have been broken* are capable of expressing the same sense; that *We need more public schools* is ambiguous between the two readings 'We need a larger number of public schools' and 'We need schools which are more public'. A formal theory must account for innumerable facts of these kinds, providing an account of our linguistic knowledge in the form of a set of rules and categories determining the form of linguistic representations at different levels. The requirements made of this theory, as of any theory, are those of consistency, predictive strength, simplicity, and coverage of data. In this formal sense it explains the facts of a speaker's knowledge of his language.

Explanation in pragmatics goes further than this, and yet is in

a sense a weaker form of explanation. It is weaker because
pragmatic principles impose weaker constraints on language behaviour than grammatical rules: they can only be predictive in a
probabilistic sense. On the other hand, it answers the question
'Why?' in a way that goes beyond the goals of formal grammatical theories. It explains that X occurs rather than Y because X is
more in accord with the way language functions as a communicative system. Formal explanation will always leave something un-
explained, and hence, if a functional explanation is available, we
should not hesitate to use it. Let it be added that the predominance of a formalist approach to language study up to the present
time has led to inappropriate attempts to fit pragmatic phenomena into theories of grammar (see 3.5). Hence functionalism
may be brought in to redress a balance which has tipped in favour
of formalism.

3.2 Biological, psychological, and social varieties of
functionalism

What is meant by a functional explanation? It means explaining
why a given phenomenon occurs, by showing what its contribution is to a larger system of which it is itself a sub-system. As far
as language is concerned, a functional theory is one which defines
language as a form of communication, and therefore is concerned
with showing how language works within the larger systems of
human society. Talk of purposes, ends, goals, plans, also presupposes functionalism. When we discuss illocutions or meanings in
terms of intentions (as is common among philosophers – see
Grice 1957, Searle 1969:42–50) or in terms of goals (as I did in
2.5.1), we are indulging in a functional explanation. In discussing
properties of language, it is better to use the term 'function', because it leaves open how far the attainment of goals is due to conscious states of the individual, or for that matter, whether the
goal is an attribute of the individual, the community, or the
species.

Even so, functionalism is a problem, because it appears to require a non-empirical, teleological explanation. There is a major
exception to this: in biology, we are entitled to use functional explanations in a scientific context, on the grounds that through the
theory of natural selection, Darwin 'showed that it is in principle
possible to reduce teleology to causation' (Popper 1972:267). I
shall go further in sketching how such a reduction can be made
also for linguistic functionalism, adapting for this purpose Popper's evolutionary epistemology (1972:106ff), together with his
functional theory of language (1972 [1963]:134–5, 1972:119–22).

Evolutionary theory explains why a species, through elimination of its less successful stock, always ends up more or less well adapted to its environment. Equally, an animal communication system is successful in a biological sense in so far as it promotes the survival of the species which uses it. But this biological functionalism will not get us very far with human language. Although the language-using ability is no doubt to a considerable extent genetically inherited, linguistic behaviour itself is something that is learned by each individual, and is passed on by cultural transmission. Other kinds of functional explanation – psychological and social – are required to account for the successful development of rich and complex linguistic behaviour patterns in the individual, and in society.

Here Popper's epistemological theory of the three worlds is helpful. He argues (1972:106) that the following three worlds are distinct domains of human knowledge:

> first, the world of physical objects or physical states; secondly, the world of states of consciousness, or mental states, or perhaps behavioural dispositions to act; and thirdly, the world of *objective contents of thought*, especially of scientific and poetic thoughts and works of art.

A major concern of Popper's is justifying the existence of 'the third world' of 'objective knowledge', or knowledge 'without a knowing subject'. This involves showing how language itself has been the channel whereby the biological level of evolution became the basis for a more rapid and powerful kind of evolution, the evolution of knowledge: 'the linguistic formulation of theories enables us to criticise and to eliminate them without eliminating the race which carried them' (1972:70). An essential part of this explanation is postulating a progression from lower to higher functions in the evolution of human language. Whereas in more primitive communicative systems the expressive and signalling functions of language (corresponding to the interpersonal func-

D *Argumentative function*   (using language to present and evaluate
↑   arguments and explanations)

C *Descriptive function*   (using language to describe things in the
↑   external world)

B *Signalling function*   (using language to communicate information about internal states to other individuals)
↑

A *Expressive function*   (using language expressing internal states of the individual)

FIGURE 3.1

tion of human language) are uppermost, Popper attributes the accelerated evolution of knowledge to 'the tremendous biological advance of the invention of a descriptive and argumentative language'. The functional stages in the evolution of language from non-linguistic communication may be represented as shown in Fig. 3.1 (although Popper does not himself put the functions in a strict order).

These functions form a hierarchy, in that a higher function must coexist with all functions lower than itself, whereas a lower function does not necessarily imply the presence of higher functions. There is also, however, feedback from higher to the lower functions, in that once a communication system has progressed to the higher functions, these functions can give rise to more sophisticated behaviour at the lower levels. For example, a descriptive language permits one to *describe* one's internal states, and thereby to express them more explicitly than would otherwise be possible. This hierarchy may be postulated, I would add, not only phylogenetically, in the linguistic development of the human race or species, but ontogenetically, in the development of the individual child. In Popper's philosophy of science, the evolution of theories (through the argumentative function of language) is an analogue, on the higher plane of the third world, of the Darwinian principle of natural selection which operates in biological evolution in the world of physical phenomena.

The question that Popper needs to answer is: How do the evolutionary 'jumps' from one level to a higher one take place? He offers the following illustration of how language and other forms of learned, socially useful products of behaviour may arise from unintended causes:

> How does an animal path in the jungle arise? Some animal may break through the undergrowth in order to get to a drinking-place. Other animals find it easiest to use the same track. Thus it may be widened and improved by use. It is not planned – it is an unintended consequence of the need for easy or swift movement. This is how a path is originally made – perhaps even by men – and how language and any other institutions which are useful may arise, and how they may owe their existence and their development to their usefulness. They are not planned or intended, and there was perhaps no need for them before they came into existence. But they may create a new need, or a new set of aims: the aim-structure of animals or men is not 'given', but it develops, with the help of some kind of feed-back mechanism, out of earlier aims, and out of results which were or were not aimed at.

[Popper 1972:117]

The following linguistic parallel may be offered. The expressive behaviour of new-born babies (*eg* crying) produces a reinforcing reaction on the part of the mother. But it is not clear at what point the unintended behaviour patterns of the baby become rudimentary intentions, and thence fully-formed intentions, so advancing the baby's communicative role from the involuntary expressive stage to the deliberate signalling stage.[2]

Popper does not claim that either his three worlds or his four language functions are exhaustive. I therefore do not feel I am contradicting his framework in proposing to extend his three worlds to four. The missing link, in Popper's evolutionary epistemology, is a world of societal facts (or what Searle has called 'institutional facts') intervening between his second (subjective) and his third (objective) worlds. Thus Popper's objective 'third world' becomes, in this redefinition, a 'fourth world' (Table 3.1). The four worlds now ascend by a natural order of emergence to the objective world of facts, and Popper's four functions of language provide the means of transition whereby one world could have emerged out of another. The expressive function of behaviour may evolve in a purely physical world, as a symptom of some biological state: a bird's fluttering its wings, for example, as an indication of alarm. But once this symptom is reinterpreted as an expressive sign of the internal state of the individual, we have access to a world of subjective experience. The event may be the same, but its interpretation as representing the internal state or disposition of the animal opens up a new world of possibilities. The next step on the ladder of communication admits us from a world of psychological to a world of societal phenomena. We treat our pets as communicating expressively when they exhibit signs of hunger, excitement, pain, etc.; but at some undetermined stage the same pets can, by an act of reinterpretation, be supposed to 'signal' to us information about their inner states, and so to act in a goal-oriented, communicative way. Once this step is taken, entry has been made to a world of social objects, states, and events. This is no longer a subjective world, but rather an *inter*subjective one, for, as the triangulation performed by more than one observer can establish the location of some observed object, so a number of individuals from the same social group can mutually confirm the meaning of some phenomenon which is external to all of them. On the basis of such confirmed communicative values there may arise social institutions such as ownership, marriage, rights, obligations: these 'institutional facts' could not exist outside a world in which the 'signalling' function of communication has established a reality beyond the individual. The

TABLE 3.1

	World 1	World 2	World 3	World 4
A. The 'inmates' of these worlds are:	Physical (including biological) objects, states, etc.	Mental (subjective) objects, states, etc.	Societal objects, states, etc.	Objective facts, existing independently of particular objects, minds, or societies
B. Communication functions:	Expressive	'Signalling' or conative	Descriptive	Argumentative (or metalingual)
C. Historical transmission and accumulation of information:	Genetic	Learning	Cultural transmission	Linguistic transmission (by texts)
D. Unit of transmission:	Species, etc.	Individual	Society, tribe, culture, etc.	Linguistic community
E. Adaptation to environment by:	Natural selection	Conditioning	Social and technological advance	Error-elimination through argument (scientied method)

intersubjective world of social fact, in turn, becomes the prerequisite of the descriptive function of language. Concepts of reference, truth, and falsity could not exist outside a social world in which individuals can share and compare their descriptions of reality.

The last world, the objective world of World 4, can in turn be explained as evolving out of the descriptive function of language. The hypostatization of descriptions of the world through the descriptive functioning of language can easily lead to a reinterpretation whereby the appropriateness of 'true' and 'false' is judged not by direct means (*ie* comparing a description with the reality it is meant to describe), but by indirect means (*ie* judging truth value on the basis of reasoning and argument). Once this step has been taken, we are able to postulate the existence of facts which are independent of the observations by individuals, or even by groups of individuals.

This account of the development of language functions can be readily observed in children's language development, but cannot be observed in an evolutionary sense. Our knowledge of the origin and evolution of language is limited in large measure to that very brief and recent period of human development for which we have historical records. Even so, it is perhaps not unreasonable to suppose that the argumentative function of language could not have developed its full potential until the invention of writing. Without the means to record linguistic messages, so that addressers and addressees can be widely separated in time and space, it is difficult to conceive of the existence of 'objective knowledge' in Popper's sense, *ie* knowledge which exists independently of any knower. Popper's examples of such knowledge (*eg* mathematical knowledge, knowledge stored in libraries, scientific knowledge) all presuppose a written medium.

Lines *C*, *D*, and *E* of Table 3.1 show how there are parallels of functional adaptation at the levels of the four worlds, in each of which we can observe a principle of adaptation by some 'organism' to its environment through the transmission of information. In the biological sphere, information is passed from one generation to another genetically and the unit of transmission here is the species. In the psychological sphere, the individual member of the species can transmit information to itself in the sense of learning through positive and negative reinforcement of previous behaviour patterns. The adaptive mechanism is not natural selection, but its psychological analogue, in the life history of the individual, of conditioning: a process whereby unsuccessful behaviour patterns are abandoned and successful ones adopted. In the cultural or societal sphere, the social group (which may be a small group such as a tribe, or a large group such as a civilization) transmits information to new generations through acculturation of its new members. In this way, a whole society may be said to learn from the experience of previous generations. In the field of technology, for example, the present generation can avoid the necessity of having to invent the wheel anew, or of repeating unsuccessful attempts at flight undertaken by pioneer aviators of the nineteenth century. Finally, the same paradigm of progress through error elimination is observed in the area of ideas, as illustrated pre-eminently in the hypothetico-deductive method of science. 'In this world we can make theoretical discoveries in a similar way to that in which we make geographical discoveries in world 1,' says Popper. For example, 'we discover prime numbers, and Euclid's problem of whether the sequences of prime numbers is infinite arises as a consequence' (1972:74). All these achievements are due in large measure to the fact that man, the speaking animal, can pass on the fruits of experience by means of language.

Popper's hierarchy of worlds is important for understanding what we are doing when we study linguistics. Since the fourth world incorporates the other three worlds, science can subsume the study of physical, psychological, and social reality. The question therefore arises: what kind of world are we studying when we study language? There is a hierarchy of linguistic theory-types, corresponding to the four worlds. The most basic type, which treats language as purely physical, *ie* as belonging to World 1, is plainly inadequate; however, we noted earlier (*p* 2) that this view has not been universal: that the post-Bloomfieldian structuralists regarded linguistics at least by aspiration as a physical science. The second theory-type, which treats language as a mental phenomenon, is the type advocated by Chomsky and others of the generative grammar school. A defect of this theory is that it cannot handle social facts about language; and a further defect is that in consequence, it cannot generalize linguistic descriptions beyond the linguistic competence of the individual. This difficulty has been disguised by Chomsky's claim to be dealing with the knowledge of the 'ideal native speaker-hearer' – an abstract and fictional version of the individual.

The third theory-type treats language as a social phenomenon. Examples of such theories are those of Saussure, Firth, and Halliday. But Saussure's concept of a language as a social institution which exists apart from any particular members of the linguistic community is already half-way towards the fourth and final theory-type, which regards language as an inmate of the fourth world – the world of objective knowledge. It is this which gives point to Saussure's observation that language is 'outside the individual who can never create nor modify it by himself' (Saussure 1959 [1916] :14). Just as, in Popper's examples, the knowledge contained in books and logarithm tables may exist outside the subjective knowledge of any living individual, so a language may exist apart from the speech community to which it belongs. The existence of Latin, for instance, does not depend on the survival of a Latin-speaking community. Further, a language may exist even though no one person exists who can speak, read, or understand it. Although at face value this seems absurd, there is nothing odd about saying that the Etruscan language exists, even though the Etruscan language is at present not known by anyone in the world. In fact, it would be rather perverse to take the contrary view, and to claim that when the community of Etruscan-speakers died out, the language thereby ceased to exist; for if scholars decipher Etruscan writings in ten years' time, their achievement will not be in *inventing* the language, but rather in *rediscovering* it. It is in this sense that languages exist in an autonomous world which cannot be reduced to a World 3 of social phenomena, a World 2 of mental phenomena, or a World 1 of physical phenomena. I therefore propose that a linguistic theory, properly regarded, is a World 4 theory about a World 4 phenomenon. This position, although it has not been overtly adopted by Chomsky, is covertly adopted by him when he argues that the adequacy of grammars (*eg* in representing the boundary between grammatical and ungrammatical sentences) can be directly checked against the intuitions of native speakers. It is reasonable to argue, indeed, against more orthodox views of empirical confirmation, that linguistic knowledge is public knowledge, because native speakers, in sharing a language, also share a commonality of implicit linguistic knowledge. Thus although our introspections are private, the data which we obtain through introspection are public and objective, being available for corroboration by the introspections of other people. (This does not mean that reports of intuitions are always clear and free from error.) Chomsky's mentalist position would be indefensible if he really claimed, as he appears to believe, that the *private* and *subjective* judgements of the native speaker are the basis for determining the descriptive adequacy of a grammar.[3] In practice, Chomsky's position has been more realistic. And in fact all those linguists, including Saussure and Chomsky, who have made language, as a system abstracted from particular speakers and hearers, the focus of their studies, have unwittingly taken up a World 4 position.

If we now return to the distinction made in Chapters 1 and 2 between grammar and pragmatics, it can be seen that the grammar is a 'World 4' phenomenon, and that linguistics is unique, among scientific disciplines, in that it aims to provide *World 4 explanations of World 4 phenomena*. (This reflexive characterization of linguistics may go a long way towards explaining the peculiar difficulties of the discipline.) Pragmatics, on the other hand, deals with relations between language as a World 4 phenomenon, and language as a World 3 (social) phenomenon. Grammar, studying language as a thing in itself, provides formal explanations. Pragmatics, studying language in relation to society as a whole in World 3, aims at a functional perspective.

But the hierarchy of worlds is not a matter of one-way dependence. There is the requirement that we interpret higher levels as being realized in lower-level phenomena, and as evolving diachronically under their influence. And there is also the requirement that the lower levels be interpreted in the light of how language interacts with more general societal and mental domains. Hence, in spite of the general validity of the postulate P6, we recognize not only that functional explanations play a role in grammar, but that formal explanations play a role in pragmatics.

3.3 The ideational, interpersonal, and textual functions of language

From Popper's four language functions, I move on to those of Halliday, to which they bear a strong resemblance. However, whereas Halliday treats all his functions as being intrinsic to grammar, I interpret them differently:

P7: GRAMMAR IS IDEATIONAL; PRAGMATICS IS INTERPERSONAL AND TEXTUAL.

Halliday's three functions (see Halliday 1970, 1973) are:

(a) *The ideational function*: language functioning as a means of conveying and interpreting experience of the world. (This function is subdivided into two sub-functions, the *Experiential* and the *Logical* sub-functions.)
(b) *The interpersonal function*: language functioning as an expression of one's attitudes and an influence upon the attitudes and behaviour of the hearer.
(c) *The textual function*: language functioning as a means of constructing a text, *ie* a spoken or written instantiation of language.

Functions (a) and (b) subsume Popper's four functions in the following way. The ideational function is an amalgam of two sub-functions which Halliday calls 'experiential' and 'logical', and which correspond to Popper's descriptive and argumentative functions. The interpersonal function corresponds to Popper's expressive and signalling functions, which are based on similar functions (*Ausdrück* and *Appell*) distinguished by Karl Bühler (1934). Halliday has explained that he finds it unnecessary to maintain this distinction which Bühler, Popper, and also Jakobson (1960) have drawn between functions oriented towards the speaker's and the hearer's ends of the communicative process: he sees the expressive and signalling functions are being merged in a single interpersonal function. For the purposes of pragmatics, I agree with him: in 2.4 I have already suggested that there is no point in distinguishing between *s*'s meaning and *h*'s meaning. The third function of Halliday, the textual function, is of a very different status from the others. Halliday gives it the special status of an 'enabling function', and says that it is instrumental to the other two (1970:143, 165). I shall argue that although the textual organization of language plays an important part in an overall functional account of language, it is misleading to call the textual function a 'function' at all: there is something back-to-front about saying that language has the function of producing instantiations of itself. It is not language that has the function of transmitting itself through texts, but texts that have the function of transmitting language.

My main disagreement with Halliday, however, is over his wish to integrate all three functions within the grammar. I maintain, in contrast, that the ideational function belongs to grammar (which conveys ideas to the hearer through a sense–sound mapping), and that the interpersonal function and the textual 'function' belong to pragmatics. From the speaker's point of view the Interpersonal Rhetoric and the Textual Rhetoric may be characterized respectively as 'input constraints' and 'output constraints' on the grammar (Fig. 3.2). From the hearer's point of view, these constraints are reversed, so that the Textual Rhetoric constrains the input, and the Interpersonal Rhetoric constrains the output of the decoding process. Although Halliday insists that the three functions are of equivalent status, he does drop one or two hints as to the special importance of the ideational function. While he deprecates, for example, the popular view that language is a vehicle of ideas, he concedes that 'the ideational function.... is a major component of meaning in the language system which is basic to more or less all uses of language' (1973:38–9). My own opinion, in contrast to this, is that the popular view of language is essentially correct: that it is the ideational function (subsuming,

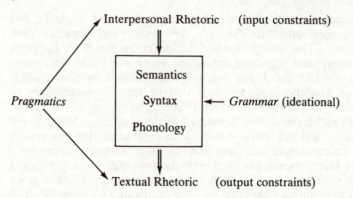

FIGURE 3.2

as we have noted, Popper's descriptive and argumentative functions) which makes human language what it is: an extraordinarily
powerful instrument of thought and communication. Without the
ideational component, the grammar, we could well be in the
same communicative league as gibbons and chimpanzees.

I have criticized Halliday elsewhere (Leech 1980:22–5) for
what I regard as a tendency to 'overgrammaticization': that is, a
tendency to seek a grammatical explanation (in terms of rules and
categories) of the interpersonal and textual aspects of language.
It is notable that recently, however, Halliday (1980:66–70) has
presented an altogether more flexible concept of grammar, in
which the interpersonal and textual functions are associated with
non-discrete types of structure, which he calls 'prosodic' and
'periodic'. It is also notable that he has drawn attention to a factor shared by the interpersonal and textual functions – namely,
the fact that they each have a speaker-oriented and a hearer-
oriented aspect. In these respects, Halliday seems to be moving
closer to a conception of language in which the ideational component is grammatical in an orthodox sense (dealing in constituent structures, rules, and systems), as distinct from the interpersonal and textual components, which are more pragmatic in
conception.

3.3.1 A process model of language
To show how the interpersonal and the textual pragmatics fit into
an overall functional view of language, I shall build on Fig. 3.2 so
as to represent both the speaker's and the hearer's ends of the
communicative process.[4] In the following diagram, which
shows linguistic communication in terms of means–ends analysis

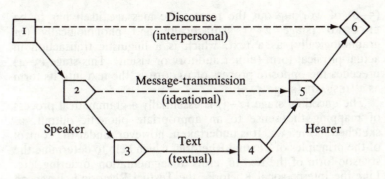

FIGURE 3.3

(see 2.5.1), the three functions of Halliday form a hierarchy of instrumentality. In Fig. 3.3, a linguistic act of communication (an utterance) is described as constituting a transaction on three different planes: as (a) an interpersonal transaction, or DISCOURSE; as (b) an ideational transaction or MESSAGE-TRANSMISSION; and as (c) a textual transaction or TEXT.[5] But these are ordered such that the discourse includes the message, and the message includes the text. Hence the whole utterance may be described as:

$\boxed{\text{DISCOURSE}}$ by means of $\boxed{\text{MESSAGE}}$ by means of $\boxed{\text{TEXT}}$

The discourse is the whole transaction, regarded as an attempt to convey a particular illocutionary force to the hearer. The goal which s has in state 1 is fulfilled as the force of the discourse is understood by h. This successful outcome is signified by the final state 6. (The term 'discourse' is used in preference to 'illocution' or 'illocutionary act' which would also be an appropriate term for the whole transaction. But 'discourse' suggests that the field of activity in fact contains a sequence of illocutions. I do not, that is, wish to limit the value of Fig. 3.3 by suggesting that it only applies to single utterances. On the other hand, I do not wish to embark upon the particular problems of analysing continuing discourse – a task which is best left to discourse analysts (see further pp 231–2).

In order to achieve the goal indicated by 6 in the diagram, s must choose a sense (or ideational content) which conveys the intended force. This stage (1–2 on Fig. 3.3) is the one at which the interpersonal rhetoric, including the CP and the PP, imposes 'input constraints' upon the message. Assuming that the message is correctly transferred to h, h must go through the parallel stage

(5-6) of working out the force. The message itself has to be
ENCODED (stage 2-3) syntactically and phonologically (or
graphologically) as a text, which is a linguistic transaction in
actual physical form (either auditory or visual). This stage (3-4)
precedes the opposite process of DECODING the text into its form
as a MESSAGE (stage 4-5).

The encoding stage (2-3) is essentially a grammatical process
of mapping the sense to an appropriate phonetic output, as
sketched in Fig. 3.2. It is undertaken, however, under the control
of the principles of Textual Rhetoric, which help to determine the
stylistic form of the text in terms of segmentation, ordering, etc.
Like the Interpersonal Rhetoric, the Textual Rhetoric is based on
speaker–hearer cooperation, a textually 'well-behaved' utterance
being one which anticipates and facilitates h's task in decoding, or
making sense of, the text. The constraints of Textual Rhetoric
also operate to stage 4-5, which stands for h's phonological, syntactic, and semantic decoding of the text. From h's point of view,
they take the form of expectations which, so long as they are fulfilled, ease the decoding process. For example, h may feel entitled to expect that s will observe normal word-order constraints,
and will avoid ambiguities. In conversation, these expectations
are often disappointed: s faces the problem of simultaneously
planning and executing the utterance, and this is the unintended
cause of many factors of 'normal non-fluency', such as false
starts, syntactic blends, and other grammatical or textual infel-
icities. To produce a well-behaved text is to coordinate a number of
complex skills, and it is not surprising if failure in the performance of these skills often leads to a rhetorically 'unhappy' utterance. For this reason, it is in written language (where planning
and final execution can be separated in time) that the operation
of the Textual Rhetoric can be observed more directly.

It will be noticed that Fig. 3.3, in representing a functional
model of language, also provides a PROCESSING model, in which
the stages of linguistic production and interpretation are spelled
out in a means–ends chain. There is no harm in construing the
model as such, so long as we remember that there is no necessary
inference from 'means → goal' to 'before → after'. As an attempt
to represent linguistic processing in real time, Figs 3.2 and 3.3
would fail in fairly obvious ways. Thus Fig. 3.2 would suggest that
we process a discourse semantically in its entirety before we
embark upon its syntactic encoding, and that we process it syntactically in its entirety before we embark upon phonological processing. But psycholinguistic evidence shows that in both the
encoding and decoding of utterances, the different levels of linguis-

tic processing, frequently (perhaps typically) are simultaneously in operation.[6] Similarly, Fig. 3.3 would suggest that we plan the
utterance as a discourse before we tackle its encoding as a text.
But again, it is common experience that we often start talking
without being sure of what it is, in entirety, that we want to say,
and that we often change and modify our illocutionary goals in the
course of speaking. Nevertheless, I propose that the model of
Fig. 3.3 has most of the design features we would need to build
into a real-time model of language-processing. To make such a
model more adequate, we should have to recognize that a text is
in itself a phenomenon which unfolds in time, and that all the
components of Fig. 3.3 can themselves undergo temporal progression. Fig. 3.4 (in which sequence in time is indicated by
the variables a, b, c, ...) therefore gives a better approximation
to a real-time language-processing model:

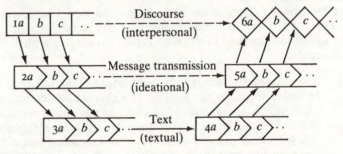

FIGURE 3.4

The model I have adopted is 'functional' in an everyday sense:
it shows how the various elements of grammar and rhetoric contribute to the *functioning* of language in the service of goal-
directed behaviour. Thus, although I have retained Halliday's
three functional labels, I have construed *function* in a goal-
oriented sense which is not evident from Halliday's use of the
term. Halliday's reference to the 'textual function' of language as
an 'enabling function' can be made sense of in this framework, as
the text functions as a *means* of transmitting the message, just as
the message functions as a *means* of transmitting the illocutionary
force to the addressee. However, rather than to say with Halliday
that a language has a textual function, it would make better sense
to say that a text has a linguistic function – a function in the communication of linguistic messages.
    In this model, the interpersonal function appears to be super-
ordinate to the other two. We should, however, distinguish two

ways in which one function can be subordinate to another. It can be inferior to the other function in the chain of events in a means – ends framework (in this sense the ideational function is inferior to the interpersonal). But it can also be subordinate in the sense of being less organizationally developed, or less important in its contribution to the total meaning. In this latter sense, the interpersonal function is often – perhaps usually – subordinate to the ideational function. Its contribution to the whole may be great (*eg* in the case of indirect illocutions), but it may also be negligible, as in the case of straightforward informational uses of language. The most 'desituationalized' uses of language – those in which interpersonal pragmatics has least role to play – are those (*eg* encyclopaedia articles) in which the World 4 communication of 'objective knowledge' is paramount.

3.3.2 An illustration
The following is a simple example of how the model represented by Fig. 3.3 (or for that matter Fig. 3.4) works out in practice. The situation I propose to examine is that of ordering a meal in a restaurant.

1 The customer(s) wants to be served with Steak Diane.
2 In order to attain the goal in 1, *s* chooses a message, an ideation of this illocution: *ie s* formulates the proposition 'I'd like Steak Diane'. Note that *s* could have formulated this speech act in many other ways: for example, more economically but brusquely ('Steak Diane'), more politely ('I would like the Steak Diane, please'), more dictatorially ('Waiter, bring me some Steak Diane'). The choice between these is determined in part by the extent to which the situation demands politeness: *eg* choosing a dish at a restaurant is in this respect different from choosing a dish at a private dinner party.
3 In order to convey the message, *s* encodes it as a text, and the phonation of the sentence *I'd like Steak DIÀNE* (with a falling nucleus on *Diane*) results. (Note that *s* could have chosen other texts to express the same proposition: *eg: Steak DiANE I'd like.* This utterance would be less in accord with Textual Rhetoric, however, as it would violate the end-focus maxim.)
4 The text is heard by *h*.
5 Then *h* decodes it into a message, which (if the transmission is successful) has the same sense as the original message at 2.
6 Finally, *h* interprets the force of the message, which (if

transmission of the discourse is successful) is recognized as
s's giving an order for Steak Diane to h. The order is relatively indirect, in that s simply states his preference,
leaving it to h to work out what is intended. But this force
is determined by well-established implicature.

The Interpersonal Rhetoric enters into this example in the stages
1–2 and 5–6, in that s clearly relies on h's deriving an implicature
's wants to be served with Steak Diane', and that this derivation
depends on h's assumption that s is observing the CP and (possibly also) the PP. The role of the Textual Rhetoric is not so
obvious. But to illustrate textual choices let us imagine that the
waiter has returned with the dishes for both s and s's fellow-diners.
At this point s might say either (a) *Mine is the Steak Diane*, or (b)
The Steak Diane is mine. Although they have the same sense,
there two utterances would be appropriate to different contexts:
(a) would be appropriate where the waiter was trying to remember which dish s had ordered (as contrasted with what others had
ordered); (b) would be appropriate where the waiter was carrying
the Steak Diane, and trying to remember to whom that dish
should be given. More generally (a) would be appropriate where
Mine (the fact of identifying s as the recipient) was given information, and *the Steak Diane* was new information; whereas (b)
would be appropriate where the given–new relations were reversed. One may assume here that the end-focus maxim would
be observed, and that each utterance would be pronounced with
the nucleus as indicated here:

(a) Mine is the Steak DIÀNE.   (b) The Steak Diane is MÌNE.

Suppose, however, that the nucleus were placed on the subject
(with a subsidiary rise on the complement):

(a′) MÌNE is the Steak Diane.   (b′) The Steak DIÀNE is mine.[7]

In these cases the intonation would indicate a reversal of the
given–new relations as indicated in (a) and (b). The end-focus
maxim would be violated, but in these cases probably not to an
extent to cause any difficulties for the hearer. The most we could
say is that the decoding task would be to some extent more complex in the cases of (a′) and (b′), as compared with (a) and (b).
This is an example of how the Textual Rhetoric fits into the total
communicative process.

3.3.3 The textual pragmatics
The textual pragmatics has so far been chiefly illustrated only by
one maxim: the Maxim of End-focus. I shall now propose a

scheme for the Textual Rhetoric which resembles that already proposed for the Interpersonal Rhetoric: there is a set of four principles, and each principle can be subdivided into maxims. The four principles are those outlined in Slobin (1975):

1. 'Be humanly processible in ongoing time';
2. 'Be clear';
3. 'Be quick and easy';
4. 'Be expressive'.

Slobin's reasons for postulating these principles are somewhat different from the present one. He argues that these precepts are observed by languages themselves, rather than by the users of languages. Thus under conditions of change, languages will always tend to change in directions which preserve these principles. This is so whether we examine diachronic language development (eg the drift towards analyticity of Indo-European languages), or the child's acquisition of language, or borrowing between languages in contact, or the evolution of creoles from pidgins.

I have no reason to quarrel with the evidence Slobin presents for arguing that these principles are actually at work in languages themselves: such arguments are consonant with the case for regarding grammars (as I have suggested) as being under the functional influence of pragmatics. However, my present interest is in observing these principles in the exercise of stylistic preference in language use. I shall label Slobin's principles as follows:

1. The processibility principle
This principle recommends that the text should be presented in a manner which makes it easy for the hearer to decode in time. A text (in contrast to a message) is essentially linear and time-bound: thus in encoding we are often presented with choices as to (a) how to segment the message into units; (b) how to assign degrees of prominence or subordination to different parts of the message; and (c) how to order the parts of the message. These three types of decisions are interrelated. For example, the End-focus Maxim applies to tone-units and therefore its operation is dependent on logically prior choices regarding the segmentation of the utterance into tone-units; the segmentation decision implies a decision about focus (which part of the tone-unit will be signalled as prominent by means of the nuclear tone); and the End-focus Maxim implies that this decision, in turn, entails a decision about order. I assume that the End-focus Maxim is functional in that it facilitates phonological decoding of the message. The way in which it does this is not entirely clear,[8] but the fact

that this principle is a universal or near-universal of language (Clark and Clark 1977:548) in itself provides a reason for believing its functionality.

The Processibility Principle applies not only to phonological, but also to syntactic and semantic aspects of the text. For example, regarding syntactic ordering, we may postulate for English a Maxim of End-weight, which (broadly) induces a syntactic structure in which 'light' constituents precede 'heavy' ones. Hence the characteristic English sentence has a predominance of right-branching over left-branching, and many movement transformations (*eg* the rule of extraposition) serve the Maxim of End-weight by helping to ensure that complex constituents are placed at the end of a clause or sentence.

That Simon will resign is on the cards.
It is on the cards *that Simon will resign*.

Again, the exact formulation of and motivation for this maxim are not clear, but that it exists in some form or other for English and other SVO (subject-verb-object) languages is hardly to be doubted.[9] Notice that the two maxims, that of End-focus and that of End-weight, although they operate on different levels of coding (phonological and syntactic), tend to be mutually supporting: a complex constituent also tends to be a constituent which contains a major focus of new information; and there are therefore likely to be two reasons for wishing to place it at the end of the sentence. Parallel to the End-weight Maxim there appears to be, on the semantic level, an End-scope Maxim. This says that logical operators such as a negative operator or a quantifier precede, rather than follow, the elements (including other logical operators) which are within their scope. This maxim would explain the preferred readings of [1] and [2]:

[1] Everyone in the room knows at least two languages.
[2] At least two languages are known by everyone in the room.[10]

Preferred reading of [1]:

$(\forall x \,(\text{PERSON } x \,\&\, \text{INROOM } x) \rightarrow (\exists y^{\geq 2} \,(\text{LANGUAGE } y \,\&\, \text{KNOW } x, y)))$

Preferred reading of [2]:

$(\exists y^{\geq 2} \,(\text{LANGUAGE } y \,\&\, (\forall x \,((\text{PERSON } x \,\&\, \text{INROOM } x) \rightarrow (\text{KNOW } x, y)))))$.

Although there has been considerable controversy over the interpretations of sentences such as these, an explanation which broadly fits the facts is that both readings are possible with both [1] and
[2], but that in [1] the reading in which the existential quantifier is
within the scope of the universal quantifier is greatly preferred,
whereas in [2] there is an equally strong preference for the reading in which the scope-relations are reversed. This preference
may be regarded as a pragmatic preference, and it follows from a
maxim corresponding to the End-weight Maxim. Just as the
End-weight Maxim gives preference to greater depth of bracketing to the right on the syntactic level, so the End-scope Maxim
gives preference to greater depth of bracketing towards the right
on the level of semantic representation. It can be surmised that
the End-weight and the End-scope Maxims are motivated by
similar restrictions on human memory capacity in the left-to-right
parsing of tree-structures.

2. *The clarity principle*

The Clarity Principle again applies to different levels of coding,
but in general it may be broken down into two maxims, (a) a
Transparency Maxim, and (b) an Ambiguity Maxim:

(a) Retain a direct and transparent relationship between seman-
    tic and phonological structure (*ie* between message and
    text).[11]
(b) Avoid ambiguity.

(On the overlap between these and Grice's Maxim of Manner,
see 4.5.)

To illustrate (a) on the syntactic level: for clarity's sake, it is a
good idea for semantically adjacent items also to be syntactically
adjacent.[12] It is for this reason that discontinuous structures in
syntax tend to cause problems of understanding:

[3] *The morning* came at last *when we were due to leave.*

The separation of the modifying clause *when we were due to leave*
from its head *morning* obscures the relationship between argument and predicate. The requirement to avoid ambiguity is closely connected with transparency, but it can be important in its own
right. For example, ambiguity occurs notoriously with pronoun
anaphora:

[4] If the baby won't drink cold milk, *it* should be boiled.

and we may extend the avoidance of ambiguity to include avoidance of 'garden path' ambiguities, *ie* syntactic ambiguities which are temporary, and are resolved by a later part of the same sentence:[13]

[5] *Before we started eating the table* was absolutely loaded with delicacies.

It could be argued that such cases do not ultimately lead to a loss of clarity (*eg* the reading that someone was eating the table, in [5], is soon ruled out by subsequent context). But the same point can be made about all ambiguity: the danger from ambiguity is not so much that it will end by misleading *h*, as that it will confuse and delay *h*'s interpretation of the sentence. In this respect, the Clarity Principle might be regarded as subordinate to the Processibility Principle.

3. The economy principle

The Economy Principle ('Be quick and easy') can be regarded as a valuable precept not only for *h* but for *s*. If one can shorten the text while keeping the message unimpaired, this reduces the amount of time and effort involved both in encoding and in decoding. As this description implies, the Economy Principle is continually at war with the Clarity Principle. On the phonological level, for example, economy favours elisions, assimilations, and other abbreviating and simplifying processes. But obviously to maximize the 'principle of least effort' in this way would be to make the text unintelligible. In practice, a balance has to be struck between saving time and effort, and maintaining intelligibility. This balance will clearly depend in part on contextual factors, such as the physical distance between *s* and *h*, and the social predictability of the message.

Similarly, on the syntactic level, the Economy Principle has a contributory Maxim of Reduction which might be simply enunciated as 'Reduce where possible'. But reduction should evidently not be recommended where it leads to ambiguity. The processes which are subsumed under the heading of 'reduction' here are (a) pronominalization, (b) substitution by other pro-forms, *eg*: *do*, *so*, and (c) ellipsis (or deletion). For example, sentence [4] above is an example of injudicious pronominalization: in order to avoid ambiguity in this case, *s* would have to sacrifice economy by repeating the noun *milk*:

[6] If the baby won't drink cold milk, *the milk* should be boiled.

The same considerations apply to other forms of reduction, for example to pro-form substitution and ellipsis:

[7a] James enjoys golf more than James enjoys tennis.
[7b] James enjoys golf more than he does tennis.
[7c] James enjoys golf more than tennis.

Of [7a]–[7c], the longest sentence [7a] is the 'unhappiest' variant and the shortest one [7c] is the 'happiest'. Thus far the Principle of Economy dictates the preferences. But if the most reduced form, as in [8c] below, introduces ambiguity, then a less reduced but unambiguous sentence, *eg* [8b], will probably be preferred:

[8a] James likes Mary more than Doris likes Mary.
[8b] James likes Mary more than Doris does.
[8c] James likes Mary more than Doris.

The pragmatic point about reduction is that it abbreviates the text, and often simplifies its structure, while maintaining the recoverability of the message. It is when, for some reason, the message's recoverability is impaired that reduction comes into conflict with the Clarity Principle.

4. The expressivity principle

The fourth principle is more diffuse and difficult to define. It is easier to say why we need it, than what it consists in. If the three principles of Processibility, Clarity, and Economy were the only pragmatic factors constraining the form of texts, language would be limited to efficient, but pedestrian transactions. With the Expressivity Principle we are concerned with effectiveness in a broad sense which includes expressive and aesthetic aspects of communication, rather than simply with efficiency. For example, an Iconicity Maxim (which invites the user, all other things being equal, to make the text imitate aspects of the message) should be included in it.[14] For the present, we may note the influence of the Expressivity Principle in inhibiting reduction:

[9]   John Brown was guilty of the crime, and John Brown would have to pay for it.
[10] They put in the best they had and we put in the best we had and we beat them and beat them bad.
      [Jody Powell: reported in the *Gainesville Sun*, 15 Oct. 1979].[15]
[11] She saw there an object. That object was the gallows. She was afraid of the gallows.
                                    [Joseph Conrad, *The Secret Agent*, Ch. 12]

In each of these examples, it would be possible to abbreviate the text without causing ambiguity. The fact that the Economy Principle does not operate, although it is not inhibited by ambiguity, suggests that some other principle is in play. We can reasonably argue that these are cases of EXPRESSIVE REPETITION, where the emphasis of repetition has some rhetorical value such as surprising, impressing, or rousing the interest of the addressee. Thus the repetition of *John Brown* in [9] seems to carry the implicature: 'John Brown and no one other than John Brown would have to pay for it.'

What has been said about the Textual Rhetoric suggests strong parallels with the Interpersonal Rhetoric. Thus textual maxims, like the maxims of the CP and the PP,

  (i) apply differently to different contexts;
 (ii) apply to variable degrees;
(iii) may compete with one another;
 (iv) may be exploited for the purpose of implicature;
  (v) are regulative rather than constitutive;
 (vi) are interpreted as goal-oriented, and as serving goals which are common between *s* and *h*.

Of these similarities, (iii) and (iv), which are central to Grice's treatment of the CP, may need further explication. With regard to (iii), we have already noted that whereas some maxims may tend to work towards a common end (*eg* the End-focus and the End-weight Maxims), others (such as, in general, the Clarity Principle and the Economy Principle) tend to compete or conflict with one another. A further example of such competition arises between the End-weight Maxim and the Transparency Maxim, in the case of a discontinuous constituent such as the modifying clause in [3]:

[3] The morning came at last *when we were due to leave*.

The discontinuity is an infringement of the Transparency Maxim, in the interests of the Maxim of End-weight. Note that [3] is slightly less felicitous than [3a]:

[3a] The morning came *when we were due to leave*.

and this appears to be due to the greater claim of the Maxim of End-weight in [3a]. That is, if the relative clause in [3a] were not postponed to the end of the clause, the result would be a very strong violation of the Maxim of End-weight (a complex subject followed by a very simple predicate):

[3b] The morning *when we were due to leave* came.

Hence the postponement of the relative clause has stronger motivation in [3a] than in [3]. The felicity of an utterance, here as elsewhere, is a matter of balancing the competing claims of different maxims.

The exploitation of maxim violation for the purpose of implicature has already been illustrated above in connection with expressive repetition. A further example is the implicature which arises from a violation of end-focus in cases like these:

[12] Is she BÁDly hurt?
[13] Is ŚHE badly hurt?
[14] ÍS she badly hurt?

In [12], for instance, s implicates that s is already aware of the fact that 'she' is hurt. In [13], s implicates that s is already aware that *someone* is badly hurt. In [14], s implicates that s is aware that someone has claimed or believed her to be badly hurt.

3.4 The ideational function: discreteness and determinacy

I have tried to show that the 'textual function' of language (in Halliday's terms), like the 'interpersonal function', can most appropriately be handled by pragmatic rather than by grammatical description. This depends, however, on how happy one can be with the grammar/pragmatics distinction for which I argued in Chapter 2. It is time to reconsider this question with reference to the last of the eight postulates I listed on *p 5*:

P8: IN GENERAL, GRAMMAR IS DESCRIBABLE IN TERMS OF DIS-
    CRETE AND DETERMINATE CATEGORIES; PRAGMATICS IS DE-
    SCRIBABLE IN TERMS OF CONTINUOUS AND INDETERMINATE
    VALUES.

This postulate, even though it is hedged by qualifications, amounts to a claim that grammar is a much more orderly affair than pragmatics. On the whole, I believe this to be true; but it cannot just be taken for granted. The difficulty is that in recent years, the assumptions of discreteness and determinacy which have characterized grammatical descriptions (particularly those of transformational grammarians) in the past have been challenged, particularly in semantics. Labov's well-known study of the meaning of *cup* (1973), and Ross's well-known study of 'squishes' in syntax (1973), have been among the more influential papers drawing attention to scalar phenomena in grammar. Similar studies of gradience, emphasizing the fuzziness of grammatical categories, are those of Bolinger (1961), Quirk (1965), and others.[16] Recent developments bringing into question the discreteness of grammatical descriptions have also taken place in sociolinguistics, where variable rules and implicative scales have been used to account for sociolectal variation in quantitative and scalar terms.

It would be overhasty, however, to reject the postulate of grammatical discreteness on the basis of such evidence. Firstly, I am not convinced that studies such as those mentioned actually count as evidence against a *categorical* view of grammar;[17] and secondly, I believe that even in the face of a considerable amount of evidence demonstrating the fuzziness of grammatical categories, it would still be reasonable to assume that in grammar the primary processes are discrete (categorical), whereas the secondary processes are continuous (non-categorical).

Scalar values might encroach upon grammar in any of the following three ways. First, there may be cases of syntagmatic continuity between two segments (*eg* the transitions between vowels and consonants in continuous speech). Secondly, there may be cases of paradigmatic fuzziness between two classes (this is again illustrated by segmental phonology: in, for example, the articulatory distinction between [p] and [b], which is gradual rather than absolute).[18] Thirdly, a rule which makes reference to one or more categories may operate indeterminately, to produce sentences which are grammatical only to a certain degree. If all three of these kinds of continuousness were present at the same time there would no doubt be grave unclarity about the working of grammar. But it is likely that the grammatical system can tolerate a considerable amount of fuzziness without failing to operate as an essentially discrete system. A partial analogy might be drawn with a digital computer in which certain tolerances are built in to allow for fluctuations of voltage. So long as the fluctuations were within certain limits, there will be no serious indeterminacy in the system, and there will be no possibility of mistaking the machine for an analogue computer.[19]

The psychological notion of a CATEGORY, as investigated by Rosch and her associates, is crucial to the understanding of the categorical nature of grammar.[20] Rosch's categories are defined by reference to prototypes, or 'good examples' of the category in question (for example, a prototype fish has a cigar-like shape, fins, scales, a tail, etc.; trout and haddock are close to the prototypic fish, whereas eels, octopus, and barnacles are not). Another way to regard a category is as a fuzzy set of defining features: the category 'vehicle', for instance, may be defined by such features as (i) mobility; (ii) having wheels; (iii) locomotion; (iv) movement along the ground; (v) carrying passengers; (vi) propelled by an engine, etc. But certain of these features (*eg* (i)) will be more important than others (*eg* (vi)). The most prototypic of vehicles (perhaps, in this modern age, a car) will have most or all of the more important defining features. On the other hand, disagreements can arise as to whether a specimen remote from the prototype belongs to a category or not. For example, is a child's scooter or a helicopter a vehicle?

The idea of a prototypic category is apparently applicable to perceptual and cognitive processes in general; it is also applicable to linguistic or logical concepts such as agency, causation, ability. No doubt the same concept can be applied to syntactic and phonological categories: some verbs are more 'verby' than others, some consonants are more 'consonantal' than others, etc. But it is important to observe that categories imply two stages of experiential processing: on the one hand, we must recognize the individual features which assign an entity to the category; and on the other hand, we must recognize the category as a whole, as a *Gestalt*. On the former level there may be a considerable amount of indeterminacy: it may be unclear whether a given specimen belongs to a given category (in Labov's experiment, there was considerable peripheral uncertainty about what objects could be called cups). But on the latter level, there is no doubt that two categories are distinct: that there is, for example, a distinction between consonants and vowels, even though the actual boundaries between the two categories may in certain instances be unclear.

What I am suggesting here is something that has been generally taken for granted on the phonic level: the continuousness and overlap of phonetic parameters has not prevented phonologists from postulating, and working with, discrete segments and contrasts. The emic–etic distinction, or the form–substance distinction, has been assumed to have this basis. On the semantic level, there has been less agreement. But the same principle holds good; the language handles experience in terms of categories, and the actual criteria for recognizing membership of these categories belong to the psychological theory of reference, rather than to the linguistic theory of sense.[21] On the syntactic level, too, we are dealing with categories: for example, word classes such as verb and adjective, and clause elements such as subject and object invite this kind of treatment. It is probably true that there is less categorical indeterminacy in syntax than in the 'outer' levels of coding, semantics and phonology. This would fit in with a reasonable theory of the ideational function of language, in which grammar is regarded as a categorical system mediating between two domains of largely non-discrete data: the referential data of our models of experienced reality, and the phonetic data of speech.

My general conclusion, therefore, is that so long as 'categorical' is defined in a sense consonant with Rosch's prototypic categories, we may rephrase P8 much more simply as follows: GRAMMAR IS ESSENTIALLY CATEGORICAL; PRAGMATICS IS ESSENTIALLY NON-CATEGORICAL. Note that this statement does not commit me to denying some indeterminacy in the operation of grammatical rules; we can still maintain the idea that grammatical rules operate in an all-or-none fashion, and yet hold that the categories which define conditions for the rules are fuzzy to a certain degree. Such an in-between position will be consistent with these two observations: (a) that gradients between grammatical categories do occur; and (b) that linguists have managed in the past, and will probably continue to manage, to obtain good approximations to the nature of language without abandoning assumptions of syntagmatic and paradigmatic discreteness.

3.5 Examples of 'overgrammaticization'

Since I have argued, on this basis, the distinctness of the ideational component of language (the grammar) from the interpersonal and textual components (which belong to pragmatics), I will conclude by underlining the advantage which this distinction brings to the treatment of grammar. The tendency in the past (particularly in transformational grammar) has been to 'overgrammaticize', *ie* to treat grammatically aspects of linguistic behaviour which are more suitable for pragmatic explanation. I have already referred to this tendency in the treatment of the interpersonal function (*eg* in the grammatical treatment of illocutionary force by means of the performative hypothesis). It remains to point out some examples of 'overgrammaticizing' of the textual function.

A standard transformational treatment of discontinuous noun phrases involves a condition whereby a postmodifying clause may be extraposed, but a postmodifying phrase may not.[22] This results in a discrimination between [15], which is supposed to be grammatical, and [16], which is supposed to be ill-formed:

[15] A jug got broken *which was from India*.
[16] *A jug got broken *from India*.

Such a distinction is based on doubtful acceptability judgements, and the restriction on the rule is unnecessary if we assume that the difference between [15] and [16] is a matter of degree of pragmatic acceptability, rather than of grammaticality. Thus [16] is predictably less 'happy' than [15] because the Maxim of End-weight provides a stronger motivation for the extraposition in the case of [15] than in the case of [16]. Here is a good example where grammar imposes a discrete distinction on data for which a pragmatic solution, in terms of the relative strength of one maxim over another, is more appropriate.

A further example involving the Maxim of End-weight is:

[17a] Don't leave out William.
[17b] Don't leave William out.
[18a] Don't leave out the boy who scored two goals in the match last Saturday.
[18b] Don't leave the boy who scored two goals in the match last Saturday out.
[19a] Don't leave out yourself.
[19b] Don't leave yourself out.
[20a] Don't leave out him.
[20b] Don't leave him out.

[17a] and [17b] are routine illustrations of the need for a Particle-Postponement rule which moves a particle such as *out* to the end of the sentence. A standard transformational grammar formulation of this rule (see Chomsky 1957:112; Akmajian and Heny 1975:178) is to make it obligatory in just those cases where the object noun phrase is a pronoun. According to this formulation, therefore, [20a] is ungrammatical. However, it is obvious from examples such as [18a] and [18b] that there can be strong rhetorical reasons for preferring one ordering to the other. The application of the postponement rule flagrantly violates the End-weight Maxim in [18b], and the result is an extremely 'unhappy' sentence. Conversely, both the End-weight and the End-focus Maxims will predict that where the object is a personal pronoun, as in [20a] and [20b], there will be no motivation at all for postponing it, and indeed there will be clear reasons for not doing so. In other words, the virtual unacceptability [20a], like that of [18b], is predictable from pragmatic considerations, and there is no need to exclude it as ungrammatical. To make the argument more forceful, however, we may note that an example like [19a], in which the object is a reflexive pronoun, is somewhere on the scale of acceptability between [17a] and [20a]. Moreover, the grammatical restriction is too strong: [20a] is not unacceptable if, for some contextual reason, there is a contrastive nucleus on *HIM*:

[21] He's the best player we've got: you can leave out any of the others, but for Heaven's sake *don't leave out HǏM*.

In this exceptional case, the End-focus Maxim provides a motivation for the postponement, in defiance of the End-weight Maxim.

A final example of 'grammaticizing' textual pragmatics involves an obligatory transformation which reduces a noun phrase:

[22a] John Smith$_i$ admires *John Smith$_i$* more than any other politician.

[22b] John Smith admires *himself* more than any other politician.

Again, a standard transformational analysis would be to treat the reflexivization of [22b] as obligatory, at least if the subject and object NPs are co-referential. Consequently, [22a] would either be ungrammatical, or would be grammatical only on condition that the two John Smiths are different people. But this is clearly incorrect: [22a] is not only apparently grammatical, but its more likely interpretation is one in which the two *John Smiths* refer to one and the same person. A pragmatic explanation, of the kind proposed on *pp* 68–9, is preferable: we note that *s* has failed to reduce (even though there is no threat of ambiguity in the substitution of a reflexive pronoun), and therefore we interpret this as 'expressive repetition', in this case for the purposes of irony. The same explanation may be offered for cases where, according to transformational grammars, the rule of Equi Noun Phrase Deletion operates obligatorily (see Akmajian and Heny 1975:298 –300), thus ruling out [23a] as ungrammatical:

[23a] John Smith$_i$ would like John Smith$_i$ to become the next Prime Minister.

[23b] John Smith would like to become the next Prime Minister.

Once again, then, there is advantage in an appropriate division of labour between grammar and pragmatics. And the distinction between the discrete values of grammar and the continuous values of pragmatics is strengthened in so far as examples of gradable acceptability, such as those just discussed, can be convincingly shown to have a pragmatic origin.

A rather different kind of overgrammaticization is found in the functional grammar of Halliday. Regarding the interpersonal function, he handles illocutionary force in terms of discrete options within semantic networks, and regarding the textual function, he handles intonational factors such as the segmentation of the text in tone-units and the placing of the tonic, in terms of grammatical systems of discrete choice.[23] For Halliday, such textual choices are often described in terms of 'marked' and 'unmarked' options. For example, what I have described as 'end-focus' has been described by Halliday as 'unmarked information focus', such that the choice between, say,

[24] Is she badly HÚRT?

and the variants without end-focus, given as [12]–[14] on *p* 70
would be described as a grammatical choice between unmarked
and marked options. Similarly, the choice between *I love peaches*
and *Peaches I love* he describes as one of 'unmarked theme' versus 'marked theme', the theme being the element (in unmarked
declarative cases, the subject) which is placed first in the clause.
A significant point is that Halliday's definition of 'unmarkedness'
points to a pragmatic interpretation of this concept: he describes
it as the choice that is made under neutral conditions, 'unless
there are reasons to the contrary'. In pragmatic terms, the unmarked term is the one which is chosen by default, where there
are no factors (such as competing maxims) to override it. In this
way, Halliday's textual choices within the grammar readily lend
themselves to reinterpretation in terms of a Textual Rhetoric.

3.6 Conclusion

In Chapters 2 and 3 my purpose has been to enumerate some
essential differences between grammar and pragmatics, and to
develop these differences through discussion and exemplification.
I have argued for a formalist account of grammar, and for a functionalist account of pragmatics. At the same time, I have argued
for necessary interrelations between these two ways of explaining
language. The formalist–functionalist view of language I have
been putting forward can be summarized as follows:

'Language consists of grammar and pragmatics. Grammar is an
abstract formal system for producing and interpreting messages.
General pragmatics is a set of strategies and principles for achieving success in communication by the use of the grammar. Grammar is functionally adapted to the extent that it possesses
properties which facilitate the operation of pragmatic principles.'

Notes

1. See Dik's discussion of 'two paradigms for the study of language'
   (1978:4–5). For a sample of formalist and functionalist views of the
   basis of linguistics, see Chomsky (1976) and Halliday (1973, 1978).
2. Trevarthan (1977) reports research on the emergence of purposeful
   communicative behaviour in infants.
3. For Chomsky's views on introspection and his rejection of objectivity, see Chomsky (1964:61, 79–81). For his views on descriptive
   adequacy, see Chomsky (1964:62–3).

4. The treatment of language in terms of communicative process is something which pragmatics has in common with psycholinguistic (see Clark and Clark 1977:35–292) and some textlinguistic (see de Beaugrande and Dressler 1981:31–47) approaches to language.

5. The use of 'text' and 'discourse' as distinct levels in the analysis of the connected use of language is familiar in the work of Widdowson (1975:6) and others.

6. On multi-level processing in language comprehension, see Clark and Clark (1977:49); on similar processing in language production, see Clark and Clark (1977:292).

7. These examples show a subsidiary rising tone on the last word: for this pattern of distribution of information, see Firbas (1980).

8. End-focus is consonant with the principle of Functional Sentence Perspective, that communicative dynamism, or weight, increases towards the end of a given textual segment. The concept of FSP has been developed among Czech linguistics, and especially by Firbas (see *eg* Firbas 1980).

9. End-weight as a principle which facilitates syntactic processing is discussed, in somewhat different terms, by Yngve (1961), Bever (1970, 1976), and Frazier (1979:20). For an explanation within a neurolinguistic framework, see Luria (1976:158–9).

10. These examples are from Chomsky (1957:100–1). Chomsky argues that [1] and [2] have different meanings, whereas Katz and Postal (1964:72–3) and Leech (1969:52) maintain that both sentences are ambiguous in the same way. Carden (1973), through informant testing, finds a basis of support for both views. I believe that the 'rhetorical' explanation proposed here is the one which best fits what would otherwise be a rather puzzling set of observations.

11. *Cf* the 'Transparency Principle' put forward by Lightfoot (1979:121–40) as a means of explaining constraints on historical changes in syntax.

12. *Cf* the principles of Natural Serialization and Natural Constituent Structure (the latter attributed to R. Bartsch) in Vennemann (1973:40–1). Like Lightfoot's 'Transparency Principle', these are introduced to explain properties of grammars; but they have an obvious rhetorical motivation.

13. On 'garden paths', see Clark and Clark (1977:80–2).

14. On the importance of iconicity in syntax, see Bolinger (1980: Ch. 3), and (with reference to literary style) Leech and Short (1981:233–42).

15. Quoted in de Beaugrande and Dressler (1981:168).

16. Quirk's term for the phenomenon of gradience is 'serial relationship'. Like Ross, he studies this phenomenon by means of a two-dimensional array in which instances are plotted against criteria.

17. There is considerable disagreement about the status of variable rules: according to one view, the variability is not part of grammatical 'competence', and the rules themselves are categorical (for a survey, see Romaine 1981). Similarly, it is arguable that categorical

rules do not exclude gradience. Contrast Labov's use of the term 'categorical' (1973) with that associated with prototypic categories on the lines of Rosch (see note 20 below).

18. *Cf* the experiments of Miller and Nicely (1955), and the discussion of these and other speech-perception experiments in Clark and Clark (1977:191–220). Essential to speech perception is the ability of the hearer to make categorical decisions on the basis of continuously variable auditory cues.

19. Leech and Coates (1980) argue, on the basis of semantic analysis of modal auxiliaries, that gradience and indeterminacy can be a relatively minor problem in the recognition of categories, because of the establishment of a 'quantitative stereotype'.

20. The extensive research carried out by Rosch and her associates on the 'prototype' basis of conceptual and perceptual categories may be sampled in Rosch and Mervis (1975) and Rosch (1977). For linguistic applications of this research, see Lakoff (1977), Leech (1981 [1974]:84–6).

21. This is argued in Leech (1981 [1974]:84–6).

22. See, for example, the formulation of the 'Extraposition from NP' transformation in Burt (1971:72).

23. This criticism of Halliday is elaborated in Leech (1980:22–6).

Chapter 4

The interpersonal role of the Cooperative Principle

It is undesirable to believe a proposition when there is no ground whatever for supposing it true.

[Russell, *Sceptical Essays*, p. 1]

Jack: Gwendolen, it is a terrible thing for a man to find out suddenly that all his life he has been speaking nothing but the truth. Can you forgive me?

[Wilde, *The Importance of Being Earnest*, Act III]

In the remaining chapters, I shall investigate the interpersonal rhetoric in greater depth than has so far been possible. In this way, I shall be seeking answers to some major problems at the 'pragmatic end of semantics', by seeking to apply the model outlined in Chapters 2 and 3 to the description of English. I shall be considering, in particular, how to deal with politeness phenomena, illocutionary force, performatives, indirect illocutions, and the meanings of speech-act verbs. In this, I shall be treading some familiar ground, but the approach I shall use will be to some extent unfamiliar. For example, I shall be trying to show exactly how the CP and the PP interact in the interpretation of indirectness. If I can show that both these principles are required to account for pragmatic interpretations, I shall be on the way to explaining the need for a 'rhetoric', in the sense of a set of principles which are observed in the planning and interpretation of messages.

4.1 The Cooperative Principle (CP) and the Politeness Principle (PP)

So much has been written in general support of Grice's concept of the CP that I may take this principle to some extent for granted. But it is necessary to give some explanation here of (a) why the CP is needed, and (b) why it is not sufficient, as an explanation of the relation between sense and force. It will also be necessary to consider the function, in the present model, of each of its constituent maxims (see 4.2.5). This will be the task of the present chapter.

In brief, the answers to questions (a) and (b) in the previous paragraph are as follows. We need the CP to help to account (as already explained) for the relation between sense and force; and this kind of explanation is particularly welcome where it solves puzzles which arise in a truth-based approach to semantics. However, the CP in itself cannot explain (i) *why* people are often so indirect in conveying what they mean; and (ii) what is the relation between sense and force when non-declarative types of sentence are being considered. Grice himself, and others who have invoked the CP, have understandably reflected the logician's traditional concern with truth, and hence with propositional meaning; whereas I shall be more interested in a broader, socially and psychologically oriented application of pragmatic principles. This is where politeness becomes important.

There have also been objections to Grice's CP on the grounds that it does not stand up to the evidence of real language use. For example, it has been argued that conversational constraints such as those of the CP do not work because the majority of declarative sentences do not have an information-bearing function (Larkin and O'Malley 1973). It has also been argued that the maxims of the CP are not universal to language, because there are linguistic communities to which not all of them apply (Keenan 1974). My first observation on these criticisms is that they are not necessarily so damning as they look. To reject the CP on purely quantitative grounds would be to mistake maxims for statistical norms – which they are not. And no claim has been made that the CP applies in an identical manner to all societies. Indeed, one of the main purposes of socio-pragmatics, as I envisage it, is to find out how different societies operate maxims in different ways, for example by giving politeness a higher rating than cooperation in certain situations, or by giving precedence to one maxim of the PP rather than another (see 6.1.3). However, it must be admitted that the CP is in a weak position if apparent exceptions to it cannot be satisfactorily explained. It is for this reason that the PP can be seen not just as another principle to be added to the CP, but as a necessary complement, which rescues the CP from serious trouble.

Two examples where the PP rescues the CP are the following:

[1]   *A*: We'll all miss Bill and Agatha, won't we?
       B: Well, we'll all miss BĬLL.
[2]   *P*: Someone's eaten the icing off the cake.
       C: It wasn't MĚ.

In [1], *B* apparently fails to observe the Maxim of Quantity:

when A asks B to confirm A's opinion, B merely confirms part of it, and pointedly ignores the rest. From this we derive an implicature: 'S is of the opinion that we will not all miss Agatha.' But on what grounds is this implicature arrived at? Not solely on the basis of the CP, for B could have added '. . . but not Agatha' without being untruthful, irrelevant, or unclear. Our conclusion is that B *could* have been more informative, but only at the cost of being more impolite to a third party: that B therefore suppressed the desired information in order to uphold the PP.

In [2], typically an exchange between parent P and child C, there is an apparent irrelevance in C's reply: C seems to react as if he needs to exonerate himself from the evil deed in question. C's denial is virtually predictable in such a situation, as if C were being directly accused of the crime. My explanation of this apparent breach of the Maxim of Relation is as follows. Suppose P is not sure who is the culprit, but suspects that it is C. Then a small step of politeness of P's part would be to withold a direct accusation, and instead to make a less informative, but undoubtedly true assertion, substituting an impersonal pronoun *someone* for the second-person pronoun *you*. Thus P's remark in [2] is interpreted as an indirect accusation: when C hears this assertion, C responds to it as having implicated that C may well be guilty, denying an offence which has not been overtly imputed. What this suggests, then, is that the apparent irrelevance of C's reply is due to an implicature of P's utterance. C responds to that implicature, the indirectness of which is motivated by politeness, rather than to what is actually said.

It is notable that the replies in both [1] and [2] would almost certainly have a fall–rise tone, which is an intonation often associated with indirect implicature. A more important point, however, is this: both examples illustrate how an apparent breach of the CP is shown, at a deeper level of interpretation involving the PP, to be no such thing: in this way, the CP is redeemed from difficulty by the PP.

In its negative form, the PP might be formulated in a general way: 'Minimize (other things being equal) the expression of impolite beliefs', and there is a corresponding positive version ('Maximize (other things being equal) the expression of polite beliefs') which is somewhat less important.[1] In [1] and [2], the suppressed impolite beliefs are 'We won't miss Agatha' and 'You have eaten the icing off the cake'. Polite and impolite beliefs are respectively beliefs which are favourable and unfavourable to the hearer or to a third party, where 'favourable' and 'unfavourable' are measured on some relevant scale of values (see 6.1). It should be stressed, again, that the real beliefs of *s* are not in question, but what *s* PURPORTS to believe.

Here we should consider the general social function of these two principles, and the 'trade-off' relation between them. The CP enables one participant in a conversation to communicate on the assumption that the other participant is being cooperative. In this the CP has the function of regulating what we say so that it contributes to some assumed illocutionary or discoursal goal(s). It could be argued, however, that the PP has a higher regulative role than this: to maintain the social equilibrium and the friendly relations which enable us to assume that our interlocutors are being cooperative in the first place. To put matters at their most basic: unless you are polite to your neighbour, the channel of communication between you will break down, and you will no longer be able to borrow his mower.

There are some situations where politeness can take a back seat. This is so, for example, where *s* and *h* are engaged in a collaborative activity in which exchange of information is equally important to both of them. But there are other situations where the PP can overrule the CP to the extent that even the Maxim of Quality (which tends to outweigh other cooperative maxims) is sacrificed. That is, in certain circumstances, people feel justified in telling 'white lies'. For example, *s* may feel that the only way of declining an invitation politely is to pretend to have an alternative engagement. But we should distinguish 'white lies' such as this, which are meant to deceive the hearer, and cases which are only APPARENT breaches of the CP. There is a difference between politeness 'off the record' (*cf* Brown and Levinson 1978:134*ff*) and politeness 'on the record' (for example when *s* says *You couldn't help me move these tables could you*?, and it is quite evident that *h* COULD move them).

Notice that examples like [1] and [2], which belong to the second type, can easily tip over into an ironic interpretation. Irony is in fact a second-order principle, which builds upon, or exploits, the principle of politeness.[2] The Irony Principle (IP) may be stated in a general form as follows:

'If you must cause offence, at least do so in a way which doesn't overtly conflict with the PP, but allows the hearer to arrive at the offensive point of your remark indirectly, by way of implicature.'

Irony typically takes the form of being too obviously polite for the occasion. This can happen if *s* overvalues the PP by blatantly breaking a maxim of the CP in order to uphold the PP. For example, in [1] there was an obvious breach of the Quantity Maxim, and in [3] there is an obvious breach of the Quality Maxim:

[3] *A*: Geoff has just borrowed your car.
   B: Well, I like THÀT!

The implicature derived from the Irony Principle works roughly as follows in this case:

'What *B* says is polite to Geoff and is clearly not true. Therefore what *B* really means is impolite to Geoff and true.'

We can put it in Grice's own terms as follows. In being polite one is often faced with a CLASH between the CP and the PP so that one has to choose how far to 'trade off' one against the other; but in being ironic, one EXPLOITS the PP in order to uphold, at a remoter level, the CP. A person who is being ironic appears to be deceiving or misleading *h*, but in fact is indulging in an 'honest' form of apparent deception, at the expense of politeness:

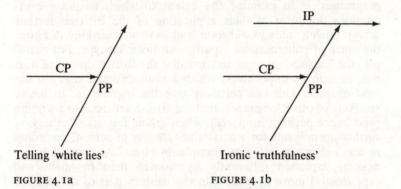

Telling 'white lies'   Ironic 'truthfulness'

FIGURE 4.1a   FIGURE 4.1b

This discussion has perhaps indicated some dangers in the use of the term 'politeness'. There is an unfortunate association of the term with superficially 'nice', but ultimately insincere, forms of human behaviour, and it is therefore tempting to write off politeness (at least in some cultural environments) as being a trivial and dispensable factor which is no more than a 'garnish' on the serious use of language. In pointing out the importance of the PP for the explaining of other principles (the CP and the IP) I have tried to show otherwise. What tends to confuse the issue, I think, is a failure to distinguish between ABSOLUTE POLITENESS and RELATIVE POLITENESS.[3] In general, in these chapters I shall be dealing with absolute politeness, as a scale, or rather a set of scales (see 5.7, 6.1), having a negative and a positive pole. Some illocutions (*eg* orders) are inherently impolite, and others (*eg* offers) are inherently polite. Negative politeness therefore consists in minimizing the impoliteness of impolite illocutions, and positive politeness consists in maximizing the politeness of polite illocutions (which includes taking opportunities for performing polite illocutions in situations where no speech may be otherwise called for). I shall be dealing with the strategies for producing and interpreting polite illocutions, and placing them on a scale of absolute politeness.

At the same time, I am aware that people typically use 'polite' in a relative sense: that is, relative to some norm of behaviour which, for a particular setting, they regard as typical. The norm may be that of a particular culture or language community. For example, I have been seriously told that 'Poles/Russians/etc. are never polite', and it is commonly said that 'the Chinese and the Japanese are very polite in comparison with Europeans', and so on. These stereotypic comments are often based on partial evidence, and one of the tasks of what I earlier called 'socio-pragmatics' is to examine the extent to which language communities do differ in their application of the PP (see further 6.1.3). Such a study would soon lead us to another kind of norm: the norm of politeness for a particular illocution-type. For example, the English language, in particular the British variant of it, is rich in indirect impositives, which I shall examine later, in the next chapter. This can certainly give the impression, to native speakers of other languages, that the British are excessively polite (and hence perhaps insincere), when asking favours of others. A further norm is one for a particular category of person, according to sex, age-group, etc. For example, in Japan, the scale of polite-ness is exploited differently by women than by men, and (apparently) more by people in the western part of the country than by people in the eastern part of the country.[4] It is on the basis of such group norms that we judge individual people as being 'polite' or 'impolite' in particular speech situations ('John was very rude to his mother', etc.). Relative politeness is there-fore variable on many dimensions, according to the standard or set of standards under scrutiny. General pragmatics may reason-ably confine its attention to politeness in the absolute sense.

Returning to the CP, let us consider the grounds on which its various maxims have been proposed and justified, and how they will fit into the present model.

4.2 Maxims of Quantity and Quality

The first two maxims can be considered together, since (as I indi-cated earlier) they frequently work in competition with one another: the amount of information s gives is limited by s's wish to avoid telling an untruth. For this reason, Harnish has even proposed a combined maxim as follows:

Maxim of Quantity–Quality: Make the strongest relevant claim
                                                justifiable by your evidence.

[Harnish 1976:362]

And he quotes (*ibid.*) a more detailed version of the same maxim
formulated by O'Hair (1969:45): 'Unless there are outweighing
good reasons to the contrary, one should not make a weaker
statement rather than a stronger one if the audience is interested
in the extra information that could be conveyed by the latter.'

'Strength' here refers to the amount of information communi-
cated. The strictest way to interpret it, in terms of two propositions P and Q, is to say: 'If P entails Q and Q does not entail P,
then P is stronger than Q.' On this basis, we can explain why certain implicatures arise in the interpretation of logical operators
such as the quantifiers, *not, and,* and *or*. Consider first the quantifiers 'all' $\forall$ and 'some' $\exists$:

[4] Jill ate *some* of the biscuits.

leads one to conclude the falsity of:

[4a] Jill ate *all* the biscuits.

But this is not a logical inference (assuming a standard interpretation of *some* and *all* as representing the existential and universal
quantifiers), but is due to implicature *ie*: h concludes that s, in
asserting [4], implicates that NOT [4a]. This is evident from the
fact that the inference can be cancelled by the addition of contradictory information:[5]

[4b] Jill ate *some* of the biscuits – in fact she ate *all* of them.

The way to understand this is as follows. First, let 'all' and 'some'
be an ordered pair on a scale of 'operator strength', construing
this to mean 'A proposition P containing "all" is stronger than an
otherwise equivalent proposition Q containing "some"'. (Strictly,
this applies only when 'all' and 'some' are outside the scope of
other operators). Then note, as a general rule, that THE WEAKER
PROPOSITION IMPLICATES THAT S BELIEVES THE NEGATIVE OF THE
STRONGER PROPOSITION. In the present case, [4] implicates that 's
believes that Jill did not eat all the biscuits'. The explanation of
this implicature is as follows:

(a) s has uttered a weaker proposition Q where s could just as
       easily and relevantly have uttered a stronger proposition P.
(b) By the Maxim of Quantity–Quality, this, in the absence of

contrary information, means that the evidence s has does not justify the assertion of P, but does justify the assertion of Q.
(c) This leads to the implicature that s believes P to be false, *ie*: s believes that *not-P*.

(There is, however, a need to distinguish this POSITIVE version from NEUTRAL version of the implicature at (c). The neutral version is: 'S does not believe that P is true, nor does s believe that P is false.' This would be the conclusion if s simply did not have enough evidence to decide, as in:

[4c] Jill ate SÒME of the biscuits (but I don't know whether she ate all of them).

Whether the positive or the neutral implicature is assumed depends on the situation. One context will suggest that s has witheld the information because of lack of knowledge, and another that s has witheld it because of a definite belief to the contrary.)

Now note that a converse relation of 'strong-to-weak' obtains between the negations of [4] and [4a]:

[5] Jill did not eat any of the biscuits. (negation of [4])
[5a] Jill did not eat all of the biscuits. (negation of [4a])

In this case, the former proposition is stronger than the latter, *ie* [5] is stronger than [5a] rather than [5a] being stronger than [5]. In fact, it is a general rule that if P is stronger than Q, then *not-Q* is stronger than *not-P*. Hence when s utters *not-P*, the implicature (in its positive version) is that s believes the negative of *not-Q*; or to simplify, that s believes that Q. Thus the implicature of [5a] 'Jill did *not* eat *all* of the biscuits' is that 's believes that [4], *ie* that Jill ate *some* of the biscuits'.

What is true of this particular example can be generalized as follows:

[6] (POSITIVE VERSION) If P is stronger than Q, then
    (i) s implicates by Q that s believes that *not-P*, and
    (ii) s implicates by *not-P* that s believes that Q.
[7] (NEUTRAL VERSION) If P is stronger than Q, then
    (i) s implicates by Q that s is not aware whether P or *not-P*
    (ii) s implicates by *not-P* that s is not aware whether Q or *not-Q*.

Implicatures therefore hold between the 'weaker' propositions, and are reciprocal, in the manner indicated by the arrow in Fig. 4.2 for 'all' and 'some'.

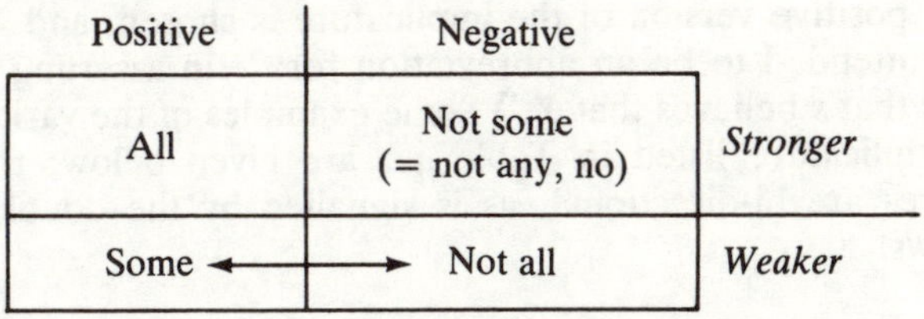

Positive	Negative	
All	Not some (= not any, no)	*Stronger*
Some ←——→	Not all	*Weaker*

FIGURE 4.2

(For simplicity, I have again extended the use of 'strong' and 'weak' from the propositions themselves to the operators in terms of which the propositions differ.) The generalizations [6] and [7] can then be illustrated by a set of logical pairs as shown in Table 4.1 (*cf* Gazdar 1979:49–50). The list could be extended.[6] In the case of 'become' and 'remain' it is necessary that the event described by 'become' should take place at a time (t^0) anterior to the time of the state described by 'remain' (t^+).

TABLE 4.1

	POSITIVE P is stronger than Q		NEGATIVE not-Q is stronger than not-P	
	P	Q	not-Q	not-P
A.	All	Some	Not any	Not all
B.	More than n	(As much/ many as) n	Not (as much/ many as) n	Not more than n
C.	Have to, must	Be able to, can	Not be able to, cannot	Not have to
D.	Be certain that	Think that	Not think that	Not be certain that
E.	Remain [at t^+]	Become [at t^0]	Not become [at t^0]	Not remain [at t^+]
F.	X and Y	X or Y	not-(X or Y)	not-(X & Y)
G.	Succeed in	Try to	Not try to	Not succeed in

Using P for the stronger and Q for the weaker term (*eg* 'have to' = P and 'can' = Q) we can derive implicatures of the following kinds:

$$\text{not } P \xrightarrow{\quad I \quad} Q \quad (eg \text{ 'not have to'} \xrightarrow{\quad I \quad} \text{'can'})$$
$$Q \xrightarrow{\quad I \quad} \text{not-}P \quad (eg \text{ 'can'} \xrightarrow{\quad I \quad} \text{'not have to'})$$

(The positive version of the implicature is chosen, and $X \xrightarrow{\text{I}}$ Y is intended to be an abbreviation for: 's in asserting X implicates that s believes that Y.') Some examples of the various kinds of implicature listed in Table 4.1 are given below; the implicatures are bi-directional, as is signalled by the double-headed arrows:

B1   'Nora has (as many as) three children.' $\xleftrightarrow{\text{I}}$
       'Nora has no more than three children.'
C1   'Employees do not have to retire at 65.' $\xleftrightarrow{\text{I}}$
       'Employees CAN retire at 65.'
D1   'I think Grandpa is asleep.' $\xleftrightarrow{\text{I}}$
       'I am not certain that Grandpa is asleep.'[7]
E1   'Betty did not remain ill.' $\xleftrightarrow{\text{I}}$
       'Betty got well.'
F1   'Sue works at the office on Thursday or on Friday.' $\xleftrightarrow{\text{I}}$
       'Sue does not work at the office on both Thursday and Friday.'
G1   'Frank tried to open the door.' $\xleftrightarrow{\text{I}}$
       'Frank did not succeed in opening the door.'

By way of the 'Quantity–Quality Maxim', then, a large number of informal inferences can be accounted for. This not only shows the explanatory value of the CP, but also strengthens the grammar, by helping to show that standard logical analysis can work quite well on natural language, in spite of appearances to the contrary. Alleged indeterminacies and illogicalities have afflicted attempts to interpret natural language in terms of formal logic. But there is a strong hope that, by means of the CP, they can be attributed not to logic, but to pragmatics.

At the same time, a pragmatic account of conversational inferences such as those exemplified in B1–G1 above leads to simplification of standard logics. Thus the distinction which has been drawn between inclusive and exclusive disjunction is an embarrassment from the point of view of natural language semantics, in that it involves ascribing to one connective (or) two distinct logical interpretations, which are nevertheless so close that one includes the other. (That is, all sentences which are true on an exclusive-or interpretation are also true on an inclusive-or interpretation.) But in a 'complementarist' account which interrelates logic and pragmatics, or needs to be given only one meaning, that of inclusive disjunction; then the exclusive interpretation is derived from the inclusive one by implicature, as in F1 above.[8]

The 'Quantity–Quality Maxim' therefore provides further illustrations of a type of explanation which is by now familiar: a pragmatic explanation of something which, in grammatical terms, appears problematic or anomalous. This suggests that the division of labour between semantics and pragmatics results in more satisfactory solutions for both disciplines.

As a further example, consider the asymmetry of:

[8] *I ran fast and could catch the bus.
[9] I ran fast but couldn't catch the bus.

[from Palmer 1980:92]

[8a] I ran fast and was able to catch the bus.
[9a] I ran fast but wasn't able to catch the bus.

The unacceptability (ungrammaticality?) of *could* in [8] is the problem. We may accept, with Palmer (1977, 1980), that *could* contrasts with *was able to* in terms of actuality. That is, *can/could* represents the state of being capable of doing something, but without the actuality of the action, which is additionally indicated by *be able to*. In this way *was able to* and *could* form a strong/weak pair of the type exemplified in Table 4.1 above. Whereas *could* signals just the state of potentiality, *was able to* signifies both the potentiality and the performance. By the argument that applies in Table 4.1, speakers will prefer to use the stronger alternative (*was able to*) where evidence justifies it, so that *could* is used to implicate *s*'s lack of belief in the performance, as in [9]. Hence the oddity of [8] in contrast to [8a]. That this is a pragmatic matter is supported by the observation that in a different context, the sentence with *could* is acceptable:[9]

[10] I could just/almost reach the branch.

[from Palmer 1980:95]

In such sentences as this, it is precisely the state of potentiality, as opposed to the actual act of performance, that is given prominence. This is only a partial explanation (which does not account for the acceptability of the 'weaker' negative *wasn't able to*) but the outline of the argument is clear: *could* is associated with non-performance because the CP urges that if a stronger statement can be truthfully made, then make it we will. The same reasoning does not apply to the present tense form, *can*, because the actual performance arising from a potentiality in the present is much less likely to be known, lying as it does in the future.

Here is a further example of asymmetrical acceptability, from the syntactic domain:

[11a] My sister is married, and her husband works for NASA.
[11b] ?*My sister's husband works for NASA, and she is married.

The oddity of [11b] in contrast to [11a] is a puzzle for someone working entirely within a sentence-grammar framework. Since both sentences have the same sense, and since they both appear to be syntactically well formed, there is no sensible way of accounting for this asymmetry by grammatical rule. But as soon as we look at the pragmatics of [11b], we notice that its second clause violates the Maxim of Quantity: in fact, its second clause is entirely redundant, in that it provides no information other that what has already been presupposed in [11a]. This illustrates how the Maxim of Quantity must sometimes be interpreted in a way which applies to one part of a sentence, but not to another: what is informative at the beginning of a sentence is not necessarily so half-way through it.

4.2.1 Implicatures connected with definiteness

A pair of words which might have been added to the 'strong–weak' pairs in Table 4.1 is *the* and *a(n)*: as with the other pairs, if the definite article is substituted for the indefinite article in some proposition, the result is a proposition which entails the original one. For instance (assuming we know what is meant by *the secretary*):

'Sally is the secretary' entails 'Sally is a secretary'.

Similarly:

'Sally is not a secretary' entails 'Sally is not the secretary'.

But the articles differ from the other pairs we considered, because the basic contrast between them is of a pragmatic nature. The element of definiteness expressed by *the* (and also, incidentally, by many other words such as personal pronouns and demonstratives) conveys s's understanding that there is some referent that is to be identified uniquely in the contextual knowledge shared by s and h. Thus when someone uses the phrase *the X*, we infer from this that

[12] There is some X that can be uniquely identified as the same X by s and h.

Since this is essential to the meaning of *the*, rather than derived from that meaning by means of conversational principles, [12] should be called a CONVENTIONAL implicature (see p 11) rather than a CONVERSATIONAL one. 'Uniquely' means that we should be able to select the one X concerned from all other X's, (or, if X is plural, that we should be able to select the one *set of X's* concerned from all other sets of X's). Since the decision to use *the* rather than $a(n)$ is a matter of appropriateness to situation, the reference of *the X* is likely to vary from one situation to another.

On the other hand, the indefinite article, as its name suggests, may be more negatively defined by the absence of this feature of 'definiteness' in the meaning of *the*. *A table*, for example, will be employed in conditions where the shared contextual knowledge mentioned in [12] does not obtain, and where there is therefore no situational basis for the use of *the*. It is for this reason that the use of $a(n)$ (and for that matter, of other indefinite determiners such as *some, few*, and *several*) is associated with denotata previously unmentioned. *I won a prize today* implicates that h cannot be expected to know *which* prize is intended. This, indeed, is the negative implicature corresponding to [12] above, and it can be arrived at via the Maxim of Quantity, by reasoning as follows: since s avoided using the more specific and informative expression *the prize*, s does not believe that h has enough knowledge to identify uniquely the prize concerned. But the CP has more work than this to do in the interpretation of the articles. Consider the following example, which is given by Clark and Clark (1977:122), following the model of Grice (1975:56):

Steven: Wilfrid is meeting a woman for dinner tonight.
Susan: Does his wife know about it?
Steven: Of còurse she does. The woman he is meeting ìs his wife.

Susan will normally be justified, following the CP, in assuming that the woman mentioned by Steven is not Wilfrid's wife. This is because, again, *a woman* tends to implicate that s does not have enough knowledge to infer which woman is meant. Since anyone who knows Wilfrid can be expected to know that he has a wife, Steven has broken the Maxim of Quantity in using a relatively uninformative expression (*a woman*) in preference to a much more informative one (*his wife*). He has, in fact, blatantly (and mischievously?) broken the Maxim of Quantity without breaking the Maxim of Quality: this is a good example of a proposition which is true from the logical point of view, but is yet very misleading in a pragmatic way.

Conversational implicatures can also result indirectly from the use of *the*. Although *the X* will normally be used in a context where h is aware of *which X* is meant, there are some cases where, by a kind of *fait accompli*, s causes h to adopt an assumption of unique reference which h probably did not hold before s's utterance. We meet this in sentences like:

[13] Would you like to see *the postcard I got from Helen last week*?

from which *h* may infer, if *h* did not know it before, that there is a unique postcard such that *s* received it from Helen last week. We can say that [13] entails

[14] *s* got a postcard from Helen last week

but also that [13] implicates (because of the uniqueness implicature associated with *the*) that

[15] There exists only one such postcard.

A similar uniqueness by 'fiat' is established in public notices such as *Mind the step* and *Beware of the dog* (see Hawkins 1978:112, 121).

To go one step further, we may observe that the kind of implicature which Clark and Haviland (1974, 1977) call a 'bridging assumption' may also be explained by the CP. For example, the sentence *We went into the garden and sat by the fish-pond* requires, for its normal interpretation, the bridging assumption that 'the garden contained a fish-pond'. First, however, look at an example of anaphoric reference without such assumptions:

[16] *A*: In the end, we got through *the back door*.
[17] *B*: Was *the door* locked?

In [17] we draw the expected conclusion, consonant with the Maxim of Quantity, that *the door* in [17] refers to the same object as *the back door* in [16]. This implicature comes from the simple fact that *the door* must be referring to some door which is uniquely determined in the context, and that in this case there is only one door which is in question, *viz* the back door. But to make sense of [18] and [19], *h* has to use a slightly longer train of inference:

[18] *A*: In the end, we got through *the back door*.
[19] *B*: Did you have to break *the lock*?

We conclude that the lock mentioned in [19] is the lock of the back door, but this implicature is arrived at not just through shared knowledge that the back door is the only door in question, but also from a piece of general knowledge, *viz* that doors often have locks, from which in turn the likely inference is drawn that this particular back door had a lock. This is the bridging assumption from which we are able to reach the conclusion that in [19], *B* refers to the lock of the back door. This implicature, derived by means of the bridging assumption, saves *B* from a violation of the CP.

As yet a further example of an implicature derived from the use of the articles, consider the double occurrence of *a diamond ring* in:

Mary: I've lost *a diamond ring*.

Bill: Well, Julie was wearing $\left\{\begin{array}{l} a\ diamond\ ring \\ one \end{array}\right\}$ this morning.

By using the indefinite article (or equally the substitute form *one*), Bill refuses to commit himself to whether the ring he saw was the same one that Mary lost. By pointedly avoiding an implication of co-reference, he avoids incriminating Julie. Hence

(a) the Maxim of Quantity is superficially violated by refusal to co-refer;
(b) this violation can be interpreted as reticence to avoid impolite accusation;
(c) but in fact, this reticence is countermanded by the fact that Bill's remark will be irrelevant unless he is suspicious of Julie.

Thus the Maxim of Quantity, the Politeness Principle, and the Maxim of Relation help us to an interpretation of Bill's remark as something like an indirect accusation.

Before moving on to a closer look at the Maxim of Relation itself, I wish to point out that these examples show a close inter-relationship between REFERENTIAL pragmatics (*p* 11) and INTERPERSONAL pragmatics. The determination of what objects are referred to by definite and indefinite expressions is in part determined, as we have seen, by the CP and even by the PP.

4.3 Maxim of Relation

The Maxim of Relation 'Be relevant' has received various interpretations, some of which treat it as 'a special kind of informativeness'. Smith and Wilson (1979:177) give an informal definition of relevance as follows:

> A remark *P* is relevant to another remark *Q* if *P* and *Q*, together with background knowledge, yield new information not derivable from either *P* or *Q*, together with background knowledge, alone.

Such a definition means that the connection between *A*'s and *B*'s remarks can be shown to be one of relevance not only in simple cases of replies such as [20]:

[20] *A*: Where's my box of chocolates?
     B: It's in your room.

but in more oblique cases such as [21]

[21] *A*: Where's my box of chocolates?
     B: The children were in your room this morning.
[Smith and Wilson 1979:175)

B's remark in [21] can be made relevant to *A*'s question on the
grounds that, supposing *B* does not know the answer to the question, *B*'s reply will nevertheless help *A* to discover the answer, by
implicating that the children may have eaten the chocolates, or at
least that they may know where they are. Once again, the
assumption that *s* and *h* are observing the CP (together with
background knowledge) enables the implicature to be worked
out. A superficial failure in informativeness leads to a conclusion
that *B*'s reply is relevant in contributing to the Maxim of Quantity at a more indirect level.

However, rather than see the Maxim of Relation as subser-
vient, in this way, to the Maxim of Quantity, I would like to interpret the relevance of one utterance to another (as in [20] and
[21]) as part of a broader conception of relevance: the relevance
of an utterance to its speech situation. In this broader sense, relevance may be defined as follows:

> 'An utterance *U* is relevant to a speech situation if *U* can be in-
> terpreted as contributing to the conversational goal(s) of *s* or
> *h*.'

Conversational goals may include both social goals (*eg* observing
politeness) and personal goals (such as finding one's box of
chocolates). The personal, illocutionary goal of *A* in [20] is to find
out where the chocolates are. In *B*'s reply, *B* adopts *A*'s goal, and
supplies the information required. But this goal is fulfilled by way
of another, social goal which is adopted by *B*: the maintaining of
the CP. In fact, in cooperative and socially motivated conversation, it is normal for one participant to adopt to some extent
the assumed goal or goals of the other.

There are, however, examples where this is not true. Consider
this additional example given by Smith and Wilson (1979:174):

[22] *A*: Where's my box of chocolates?
     B: I've got a train to catch.

We should not call this a very cooperative reply, since it does not
advance *A*'s quest for the chocolates. But *B*'s remark does

become relevant if it is understood as an explanation of why *B* cannot answer *A*'s question. In this function, its contribution to conversational goals is rather negative: it enables *B* to conclude the conversation without (too much) impoliteness. It does not contribute, in this case, to *A*'s goal, but to *B*'s.

Returning to the standard question-and-reply sequence of [20], the contribution of *B* to *A*'s illocutionary goal may be represented, in terms of means–ends analysis, as shown in Fig. 4.3.

Note: The area x, y, z indicates *B*'s contribution to *A*'s goal. The double-shafted arrows ($\Longrightarrow$) symbolize the motivating relation between a goal and an action.

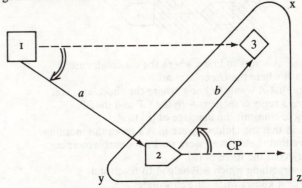

1 Initial state: *A* wants to know where the chocolates are.
  [*a*] *A* asks *B* where the chocolates are.
2 *B* is aware that *A* wants to know where the chocolates are.
  [*b*] *B* tells *A* where the chocolates are.
3 Final state: *A* knows where the chocolates are.

FIGURE 4.3   Question and answer 20

This is the simplest and most direct case of a means–ends analysis of dialogue. Taking the goal-oriented concept of relevance further, however, it is interesting to examine a means–ends analysis of a more oblique reply such as that of [21] (Fig. 4.4). (Both Figs. 4.3 and 4.4 are much simplified, as is almost inevitable in any means–ends analysis involving complicated processes such as the use of language.) In this case the goal symbolized by [*e*] is not achieved: *A* still has to find out what has happened to the chocolates, and this is indicated by the dotted arrow connecting 5 and 6 on Fig. 4.4. Also, the greater complexity of this example is indicated in Fig. 4.4. by the intervention of the Interpersonal Rhetoric at stages *b* and *d*, in the pragmatic planning and

Note: B's contribution to the conversation is represented by the shaded area.

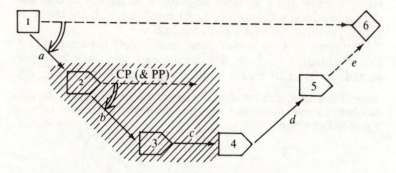

1 Initial state: A wants to know where the chocolates are.
   [a] A asks B where the chocolates are.
2 B is aware that A wants to know where the chocolates are.
   [b] B plans a reply consistent with the CP and the PP.
3 B is ready to transmit the message of [b] to A.
   [c] B tells A that the children were in A's room this morning.
4 A is aware that the children were in A's room this morning.
   [d] A works out the force of [b].
5 A knows something which will help A to reach state 2.
6 Final state: A knows where the chocolates are.

FIGURE 4.4   Question and oblique answer 21

interpretation of the utterance. Admittedly these stages are present even in the simplest of utterances (see 3.3.1), but they are particularly important in cases of obliquity such as [21]. B's reply in *b* (as in *b* of Fig. 4.3) is shown to be motivated by the CP, *ie:* B's reply is intended to be relevant to A's conversational goal. In this case, however, there is an argument for saying that the PP also plays a role. The reason is this. B chooses to make an indirect reply in preference to a more direct one such as *The children may have taken them.* The most likely motive for this indirectness is polite reticence in referring to a possibly sinful act by the children. Instead of accusing the children, B makes a seemingly innocent statement about the whereabouts of the children, leaving A to come to the impolite conclusion. Even this, however, may not be the whole story. B's apparent politeness with reference to the children may be just a piece of archness, and an ironic interpretation may be intended. B may be making the reply deliberately obtuse, but without intending to prevent A coming to an unflattering conclusion.

4.4 The Hinting Strategy and anticipatory illocutions

This example has shown how the interpretation of 'indirect illoc-utions' depends heavily on the Maxim of Relation. This depen-dence manifests itself in what I have elsewhere called a HINTING STRATEGY (Leech 1980 [1977a]:112–14). In polite requests, for example, it is common to ask a question about *h*'s willingness or ability to perform an action *X* as a 'hint' that you want *h* to do *X*:[10] *Will you answer the phone? Could you answer the phone?* etc. The strategy consists in uttering an illocution whose goal is interpreted as a subsidiary goal for the performance of another illocution. Thus the exchange:

[23] *A*: Can you answer the phone?
     B: O.K.

can be thought of as short-circuiting a more elaborate dialogue such as:

[24] *A*: Can you answer the phone?
     B: Yes.
     A: In that case, please answer it.
     B: O.K.

That is, the fulfilment of the information-seeking illocution *Can you...?* is a piece of information which, strictly, *A* has to possess if *A* is to know if the conditions are appropriate for the perform-ance of the desired action by the addressee. The Hinting Strategy, however, ensures that the first illocution in [24] does service for a second, unspoken one. This strategy exploits the Maxim of Relation in that in the context envisaged for [23], a question about *h*'s ability to do *X* will only conceivably be rel-evant as a means of *h*'s eventual performance of *X*.

It is often helpful, in this way, to think of a conversational ex-change as a compressed dialogue. The Hinting Strategy merely illustrates the more conventionalized end of a 'scale of relevance' in terms of which an utterance can be interpreted as an ANTICI-PATORY ILLOCUTION which prepares the way for subsequent illoc-ution. In practice, of course, *s* often assumes the answer to the question to be 'Yes'. But even a *can*-question like *Can you sing more loudly*? may function both as an information-seeking ques-tion and (more indirectly) as a conditional request. Its force may be approximately: '*s* wants to know if *h* can sing any louder, and the reason for this is that *s* wants *h* to sing louder'. It does not therefore cease to be a genuine question because it has an ul-terior purpose to which the question is only an initial step.[11]

One may also allow the term 'anticipatory' to apply to conditional illocutions such as those performed by A in the following:

[25] A: Have you got any matches?
      B: Yes. *Here you are.* (*Gives matches.*)
[26] A: Do you sell paper clips?
      B: Yes. *Would you like large or small?*
[27] A: Have you seen my address book?
      B: Yes, *I think it's in the drawer.*
[28] A: What have you done with the newspaper?
      B: I haven't done anything with it. *It's there in the porch.*
[29] A: Do you happen to know when the next bus leaves?
      B: Yes: *5.20.*
[30] A: Would you like some more coffee?
      B: *Thanks*.
[31] A: Did you eat all those muffins?
      B: Yes, *I was so hungry.*

In all these cases A's question is more directly a means of eliciting information, but more remotely a means to some other purpose. The ulterior illocutionary goal is recognized by the fact that B (in the italicized sections) responds cooperatively with the aim of helping A to fulfil this goal. In [26], for example, B answers the question, but also takes it for granted, in asking 'Would you like large or small?', that A would like to buy some. In [30] A asks a question (with the force of an offer of coffee), and B replies as if the coffee has already been given. In [31], A asks a question with implications of reproach, and B replies as if to excuse himself from the imputed blame. The relative importance of the two illocutionary goals – the preparatory and the ulterior one – varies from case to case.

Perhaps the best illustration of the gap between the anticipatory and the ulterior goal is the bizarre result of mistaking the one for the other:

[32] A: Do you drink?
      B: Of course. All humans drink.

There is another type of implicature failure where the ulterior goal is misinterpreted. This is a fruitful source of stock jokes:

[33] A: Would you like to dance?
      B: Sure. Do you know anyone else who'd like to?
[34] *Lecturer*: You should have been here at nine.
      Student: Why? What happened?
[35] *Customer*:There's a fly in my soup!
      Waiter: Don't make a fuss, sir – they'll all want one.

[36] *Lecturer*: Who wasn't in class today?
　　 Student: George Washington and Moby Dick.

The failure of *B* in all these exchanges is, of course, a failure to understand the relevance of *A*'s remark, *ie* a misunderstanding of how *A*'s remark is meant to contribute to some conversational goal.

It is by now clear that relevance, like informativeness and truthfulness, is not a yes-or-no quality, but a matter of degree. In some cases, like the reply *It's in your room* in [20], the relevance is very strong and very clear. At the other extreme, there are cases where the relevance is unclear and indirect, like the reply *I've got a train to catch* in [22]. Relevance is negatively associated with directness (see 5.7), and correlates with the length of the means-ends chain that has to be constructed to represent the illocutionary force of the remark. The Hinting Strategy in [30] was easy to follow:

[30] *A*: Would you like some more coffee?
　　 B: Thanks.

But one can imagine an even more indirect exchange in which the relevance of the reply is no longer clear:

[37] *A*: Do you like coffee?   [38] *A*: Are you thirsty?
　　 B: Thanks.   　　 *B*: Thanks.

Both these questions could be construed as preliminaries to an offer of a drink. But they are too indirect to act readily as indirect offers. Nevertheless, we can imagine contexts in which the force of such questions would be made clear by non-verbal means (*eg* if *A* were brandishing a coffee pot at the same time), and where exchanges like [37] and [38] could reasonably occur. Here, as elsewhere, it is important to observe that pragmatic descriptions involve scales and indeterminacies. To take account of this, the definition of relevance I proposed earlier should be rephrased in a relative way as follows:

> 'An utterance *U* is relevant to a speech situation *to the extent that U* can be interpreted as contributing to the conversational goal(s) of *s* or *h*.'

4.5 Maxim of Manner

The Maxim of Manner ('Be perspicuous') appears to be the Cinderella of Grice's four categories: others have followed Grice in mentioning it last, and it rarely figures in explanations of conversational implicature. Grice himself sees this maxim as in some sense less important than (*eg*) the Maxim of Quality, and as differing from the others in 'relating not ... to what is said but, rather, to HOW what is said is to be said' (1975:46). This might be taken as a clue that the Maxim of Manner belongs not to the CP – and therefore not to the Interpersonal Rhetoric at all – but to the rhetoric of text. In fact, in the outline of the Textual Rhetoric given in 3.3.3, I introduced the Clarity Principle as one of its constituent principles. And the difference between 'being perspicuous' and 'being clear' is, to say the least, not perspicuous.

None the less, I believe that Grice was right to recognize the Maxim of Manner as one of the elements of his CP, and that the charge to 'be clear' is placed on language users as part of the Interpersonal Rhetoric, as well as of the Textual Rhetoric. There are two kinds of clarity. One kind consists in making unambiguous use of the syntax and phonology of the language in order to construct a clear TEXT. Another type of clarity consists in framing a clear MESSAGE, *ie* a message which is perspicuous or intelligible in the sense of conveying the intended illocutionary goal to the addressee. What this implies is that exchanges such as [32]–[36] should be rather rare – as indeed, they probably are, outside joke books. Perspicuity in this sense is obviously hand in glove with relevance; both the Maxim of Manner and the Maxim of Relation will favour the most direct communication of one's illocutionary point, and both, for that reason, will militate against the obliquity of the Hinting Strategy. It is presumably for this reason that addressees will normally assume the most direct interpretation as the 'default interpretation', and will seek indirect interpretations only when direct interpretations are blocked.

If the Maxim of Manner's only function were to support the Maxim of Relation in this way, there would be grounds for doubting its inclusion as part of the CP. However, I believe that negative sentences provide evidence for the independent role of this maxim.

4.5.1 The obliquity and uninformativeness of negation

There are two reasons for proposing that negative sentences are pragmatically less favoured than positive ones. The first reason is that negatives, all things being equal, are less informative than their positive counterparts:

[39] Abraham Lincoln was not shot by Ivan Mazeppa.
[40] Abraham Lincoln was shot by John Wilkes Booth.

The world's population of negative facts is far greater than its population of positive facts: for example, the number of people who did not shoot Lincoln is many million times greater than the number of people who did shoot Lincoln, and it is for this reason that [39] is much less informative than [40], although both statements are true. The sub-maxim of NEGATIVE UNINFORMATIVE-NESS, as we may call it, when combined with the Maxim of Quantity, implies that a negative sentence will be avoided if a positive one can be used in its place. Moreover, it will imply that when negative sentences ARE used, it will be for a special purpose. In fact, the CP will predict that negative sentences tend to be used precisely in situations when they are not less informative for a given purpose than positive ones: and this will be when s wants to deny some proposition which has been put forward or entertained by someone in the context (probably the addressee). Negative uninformativeness therefore provides an explanation of why negative propositions are, in pragmatic terms, denials of positive propositions which are in some sense 'present in the context'.

This generalization is not, however, convincingly applied in all cases. If we consider a negative sentence like *Our cat is not male*, this is just as informative as the contrasting positive statement *Our cat is male*. Moreover, in this case there is a positive sentence which is for all practical purposes synonymous with the negative one: *Our cat is female*. But the negative sentence still strikes one as being 'marked', and as requiring special interpretation as a denial of what someone else has asserted. Since the Maxim of Quantity cannot explain this case, the Maxim of Manner may be suggested as an alternative means of explanation. The explanation runs as follows: a negative sentence (as psycholinguistic research has shown – see Clark and Clark 1977:107–10) takes longer to process, and is presumably more difficult to process, than a positive sentence. Therefore, by choosing a negative sentence in preference to a positive one, s causes the utterance to be more oblique and obscure than it need be. Therefore s violates the Maxim of Manner. He must be doing this for some reason – and the most obvious reason for using the negative sentence is to deny its positive counterpart.

There are also some exceptions to the generalization that negative sentences are more 'marked' than positive ones, and carry implications of denial. The exceptions tend to be negative expressions of emotion or attitude: *I don't like Kenneth; He doesn't believe in marriage; We don't agree*; etc. The negative is often preferred to the syntactically positive equivalent (*I dislike Kenneth*, etc.) as a form of understatement. Negation here is apparently a hedging or mitigating device, the motivation for which may be politeness or simply euphemistic reticence in the expression of opinion and attitudes (see 6.1.2). Such cases are independently explicable, and do not detract from the general point about negation being pragmatically interpreted as denial.

This discussion of negation, therefore, supports the case for a Maxim of Manner as an independent part of the CP, in spite of the overlap of its function with the Maxim of Relation and the textual Principle of Clarity.

Notes

1. Earlier treatments of politeness within a linguistic framework are Lakoff (1973), Brown and Levinson (1978), and Leech (1980 [1977a]). The 'positive' and 'negative' aspects of politeness derive from Brown and Levinson's distinction between positive and negative *face* (1978:64), and their consequent distinction between positive and negative politeness (1978: *passim*)

2. Grice (1975) treats irony as a special kind of implicature or implicative strategy, rather than as a principle in its own right. There is no necessary conflict between this and my own treatment of irony as a second-order principle. Such a principle may, in fact, be regarded as a highly institutionalized strategy whereby speakers square their language behaviour with more basic principles such as the CP and the PP.

3. By *relative politeness* I mean politeness relative to context or situation. In an absolute sense, [1] *Just be quiet* is less polite than [2] *Would you please be quiet for a moment*? But there are occasions where [1] could be too polite, and other occasions where [2] would not be polite enough. There are even some occasions where [2] would strike one as less polite than [1]; where, for example, [1] was interpreted as a form of banter, and where [2] was used ironically. It is only in a relative sense that we can talk of *overpoliteness* and *underpoliteness*.

4. See Miller (1967:283–90) on politeness phenomena in Japanese.

5. On the cancellability of implicature, see Gazdar (1979:131–2). His notion of *satisfiable incrementation* ('All the news that fits') accounts for the cancellation of implicature where a conflict arises between the Maxims of Quantity and Quality.

6. 'Strong' and 'weak' are interpreted here as terms of a semantic opposition of *inverseness* (Leech 1969:56, 200). For treatments of logical operators on the lines illustrated here, see Horn (1976) and Gazdar (1979).

7. Strictly, the two statements of D1 are abbreviations for: '*s* believes that *s* thinks that Grandpa is asleep', and '*s* believes that *s* is not certain that Grandpa is asleep'. There is a principle of Transitivity of Reflexive Belief (see further *p* 190) which allows these to be simplified to: '*s* thinks that Grandpa is asleep' and '*s* is not certain that

Grandpa is asleep', on the grounds that *s* cannot coherently claim to believe himself to be in belief-state *B*, unless he is indeed in belief-state *B*. At its most general, the principle states that any proposition '*s* believes that *s* PROP (*P*)', where PROP is a belief predicate, allows one to infer the simpler proposition '*s* PROP (*P*)'. This applies not only to positive belief-states, but also to negative ones, such as uncertainty.

8. The traditional logical distinction between inclusive and exclusive *or*, like that between inclusive and exclusive negation, has been recently under attack from more than one quarter. See Barrett and Stenner (1971) and Kempson (1977: 126–8).

9. As Palmer points out (1980:92–3), *could* is also acceptable in a positive habitual sense: . . . *my father could usually lay hands on what he wanted*.

10. Earlier explanations of indirect illocutions are those of Gordon and Lakoff (1971), Sadock (1974), and Searle (1979 [1975b]). See Leech (1980 [1977a]: 87–9, 112–14) for a discussion of these, and their relation to the Hinting Strategy.

11. Searle (1979 [1975b] makes this point, and thereby improves on the account given by Gordon and Lakoff (1971), who regard an indirect illocution as contextually ambiguous between 'direct' and 'indirect' interpretations, rather than as conveying the 'indirect' interpretation *via* the 'direct' one. In the present account illocutionary force is represented by statements about *s*'s volitional attitude. The dual illocutionary force of *Can you sing more loudly*? is reflected in the fact that its illocutionary force description contains two volitional attitude statements, one of them being implicated via the other.

Chapter 5

The Tact Maxim

'Tis a maxim tremendous but trite

[Lewis Carroll, *The Hunting of the Snark*]

Far from being a superficial matter of 'being civil', politeness is an important missing link between the CP and the problem of how to relate sense to force. I have already emphasized the role of politeness in pragmatics in preceding chapters, but in this and the next chapter I shall examine how it works in more detail. Whereas in Chapter 4 I concentrated on the productive strategies of means–ends analysis, I shall now concentrate more on the heuristic strategies of interpretation, looking at politeness from the addressee's rather than from the speaker's end.

5.1 Varieties of illocutionary function

Different kinds and degrees of politeness are called for in different situations. At the most general level, illocutionary functions may be classified into the following four types, according to how they relate to the social goal of establishing and maintaining comity.

(a) COMPETITIVE: The illocutionary goal competes with the social goal; *eg* ordering, asking, demanding, begging.
(b) CONVIVIAL: The illocutionary goal coincides with the social goal; *eg* offering, inviting, greeting, thanking, congratulating.
(c) COLLABORATIVE: The illocutionary goal is indifferent to the social goal; *eg* asserting, reporting, announcing, instructing.
(d) CONFLICTIVE: The illocutionary goal conflicts with the social goal; *eg* threatening, accusing, cursing, reprimanding.

Of these, the first two types are the ones which chiefly involve politeness. Where the illocutionary function is COMPETITIVE (a), the politeness is of a negative character, and its purpose is to reduce the discord implicit in the competition between what *s* wants to achieve, and what is 'good manners'. Competitive goals are those which are essentially DISCOURTEOUS, such as getting someone to lend you money.[1] (For the sake of clarity, I shall make a terminological distinction in applying 'courtesy' and 'discourtesy' to goals, and 'politeness' to the linguistic or other behaviour in which someone engages in as means to those goals.) The PP is therefore required to mitigate the intrinsic discourtesy of the goal. The second type, that of CONVIVIAL functions (b), is, on the contrary, intrinsically COURTEOUS: politeness here takes a more positive form of seeking opportunities for comity. Positive politeness means observing the PP in that, for example, if you have an opportunity to congratulate *h* on his 100th birthday, you should do so. In the third category are COLLABORATIVE illocutionary functions (c), for which politeness is largely irrelevant. Most written discourse comes into this category. And in the fourth category of CONFLICTIVE functions, politeness is out of the question, because conflictive illocutions are, by their very nature, designed to cause offence. To threaten or curse someone in a polite manner is virtually a contradiction in terms: the only way to make sense of the idea is to suppose that the speaker does so ironically (see 6.3). Presumably in the course of socialization children learn to replace conflictive communication by other types (especially by the competitive type), and this is one good reason why conflictive illocutions tend, thankfully, to be rather marginal to human linguistic behaviour in normal circumstances.

Hence, in considering polite and impolite linguistic behaviour, we may confine our attention mainly to competitive and convivial illocutions, with their corresponding categories of negative and positive politeness.

5.2 Searle's categories of illocutionary acts

The above classification is based on functions, whereas Searle's classification of illocutionary acts (1979[1975a]) is based on varied criteria.[2] Before proceeding, however, we will find it useful to relate the two classifications, and show how politeness affects Searle's categories. Roughly speaking, Searle's categories are defined as follows (for further discussion, see 9.2.4):

1. ASSERTIVES commit *s* to the truth of the expressed proposition: *eg* stating, suggesting, boasting, complaining, claiming, reporting. Such illocutions tend to be neutral as regards politeness, *ie* they belong to the *collaborative* category (c) above.

But there are some exceptions: for example, boasting is generally considered to be impolite. Semantically, assertives are propositional.

2. DIRECTIVES are intended to produce some effect through action by the hearer: ordering, commanding, requesting, advising, and recommending are examples. They frequently belong to the *competitive* category (a), and therefore comprise a category of illocutions in which negative politeness is important. On the other hand, some directives (such as invitations) are intrinsically polite. To avoid confusion in using the term 'directive' in relation to 'direct and indirect illocutions', I have preferred to use the term IMPOSITIVE for competitive illocutions in this class.

3. COMMISSIVES commit *s* (to a greater or lesser degree) to some future action; *eg* promising, vowing, offering. These tend to be *convivial* rather than competitive, being performed in the interests of someone other than the speaker.

4. EXPRESSIVES have the function of expressing, or making known, the speaker's psychological attitude towards a state of affairs which the illocution presupposes; *eg* thanking, congratulating, pardoning, blaming, praising, condoling, etc. Like the commissives, they tend to be *convivial*, and therefore intrinsically polite. The reverse is true, however, of such expressives as 'blaming' and 'accusing'.

5. DECLARATIONS are illocutions whose 'successful performance ... brings about the correspondence between the propositional content and reality'; *eg* resigning, dismissing, christening, naming, excommunicating, appointing, sentencing, etc. In this, these actions are, as Searle says (18–19) 'a very special category of speech acts': they are performed, normally speaking, by someone who is especially authorized to do so within some institutional framework. (Classical examples are judges sentencing offenders, ministers of religion christening babies, dignitaries naming ships, etc.) As institutional rather than personal acts, they can scarcely be said to involve politeness. For example, although sentencing a person is an unpleasant thing to do, the judge has complete authority in doing so, and can scarcely be said to sentence someone 'impolitely'. Moreover, politeness is not relevant to declarations because they do not have an addressee in the sense that applies to personal discourse: the person who makes a declaration uses language as an outward sign that some institutional (social, religious, legal, etc.) action is performed. It would thus be totally out of place, and would undermine the force of the declaration, if (say) the

priest baptizing were to hedge his words with politeness; changing 'I baptize you...' into 'Could I baptize you...?', etc. The same applies, to a lesser extent, to more private declarations, such as resigning in a game of chess, or bidding in a game of bridge.

Although there are some cases not covered by the generalizations above, it is worth making the point that, as far as Searle's categories go, negative politeness belongs pre-eminently to the DIRECTIVE class, while positive politeness is found pre-eminently in the COMMISSIVE and EXPRESSIVE classes.

5.3 Tact: one kind of politeness

Let us now relate illocutionary acts more precisely to the kinds of politeness with which they are associated.

I have said that politeness is essential asymmetrical: what is polite with respect to h or to some third party will be impolite with respect to s, and vice versa. The justification for the maxims of politeness is precisely that they explain such asymmetries, and their consequences in terms of indirectness. I shall first of all explain this with reference to what is perhaps the most important kind of politeness in English-speaking society: that which is covered by the operation of the TACT MAXIM.

The Tact Maxim applies to Searle's *directive* and *commissive* categories of illocutions, which refer, in their propositional content X, to some action to be performed, respectively, by the hearer or the speaker. This action may be called A, and may be evaluated in terms of what s assumes to be its cost or benefit to s or h.[3] On this basis, X ('you will peel those potatoes', etc.) may be placed on a COST-BENEFIT SCALE, as in the following examples:

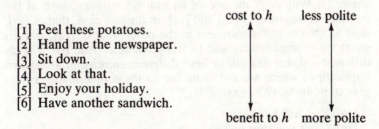

[1] Peel these potatoes.
[2] Hand me the newspaper.
[3] Sit down.
[4] Look at that.
[5] Enjoy your holiday.
[6] Have another sandwich.

At some rather indeterminate point on this scale (depending on the context) the relevant value becomes 'benefit to h' rather than 'cost to h'; but clearly, if we keep the imperative mood constant, there is a general increase in politeness (other factors being equal) between [1] and [6].

Another way of obtaining a scale of politeness is to keep the same propositional content X (*eg*: X = 'You will peel these potatoes') and to increase the degree of politeness by using a more and more indirect kind of illocution. Indirect illocutions tend to be more polite (a) because they increase the degree of optionality, and (b) because the more indirect an illocution is, the more diminished and tentative its force tends to be.

indirectness   less polite

[7] Answer the phone.
[8] I want you to answer the phone.
[9] Will you answer the phone?
[10] Can you answer the phone?
[11] Would you mind answering the phone?
[12] Could you possibly answer the phone?
etc.

more polite

One of the things pragmatics should explain is: Why do some indirect illocutions function as impositives, while others do not? For example, [13] is an offer, rather than an impositive – it implies that sitting down is to h's benefit:

[13] Won't you sit down?
[14] Can't you sit down?
[15] Wouldn't you mind sitting down?

On the other hand, [14] typically has an impositive force, whereas [15] does not seem to be usable in either a commissive or an impositive function. Other things which need explaining here are these: (i) Why does the use of an indirect strategy, such as the addition of negation in [13] and [14], in the one case, that of [13], lead to greater politeness, and in the other, that of [14], with its overtone of impatience, lead to less politeness? And (ii) Why do different indirect illocutions have different emotive or attitudinal implications which are not reducible to the simple matter of degree of politeness? For example,

[16] You will be silent.
[17] Can't you shut up?
[18] I'd keep my mouth shut (if I were you).

are all, in the right context, impositives, whose goal is the silence of *h*; but the way they are formulated suggests a very different strategy on the part of the *s* in each case. Both [16], which suggests the severity of a military instruction, and [17], which suggests extreme irritation with *h*'s behaviour, are impolite; whereas [18] is more like a friendly piece of advice for *h*'s benefit. Thus it is quite insufficient to note, in [7]–[12] and [16]–[18], the correlation between indirectness and politeness: we must be able to say not only *how* polite a given illocution is, but *why* a particular device of indirectness contributes to a particular illocutionary goal. For example in [7]–[12], the degree of indirectness correlates with the degree to which *h* is allowed the option of not performing the intended action, answering the phone. Indeed, the point of the strategy of indirectness, here, is to bias the impositive more and more towards the negative choice, so that it becomes progressively easier for *h* to say no. In this way, negative politeness (*ie* serving the avoidance of the cost to *h*) is increased.

It may seem strange here to describe politeness, as I did earlier, as 'minimizing impolite beliefs'. But on reflection, it is reasonable. The propositional content of all these sentences is discourteous to *h* in so far as it attributes some effort, trouble, or cost to *h*. By using the imperative in [1] and [7], *s* expresses the belief that *h* will perform the action. (The use of the imperative does not allow that *h* has any choice in the matter, whereas the question form of [9], for example, expresses doubt as to whether *h* will do *A*.) But as the element of doubt or negative bias is introduced and increased in examples [9]–[12], so the expression of the belief that *h* will perform the action is weakened.

There are two sides to the Tact Maxim, a negative side 'Minimize the cost to *h*', and a positive side, 'Maximize the benefit to *h*'. The second is less important, but is a natural corollary of the first. It means, for example, that in proposing some action beneficial to *h*, *s* should bias the illocution towards a positive outcome, by restricting *h*'s opportunity of saying 'No'. Thus an imperative, which in effect does not allow *h* to say 'No' is (in an informal context) a positively polite way of making an offer: *Help yourself; Have another sandwich*; etc. The positive bias can even be increased by the persuasive emphasis of: *Do have another sandwich!; You MUST have another sandwich!* In this case, the more indirect forms of [9]–[12] are if anything less polite than the most direct form: *Would you mind having another sandwich?* would suggest that *h* would do *s* a positive favour by accepting – and therefore perhaps that the sandwiches were stale, inedible, or poisoned! The reason for this reversal of polite strategies in impositives and commissives is fairly obvious, and has to do with the asymmetry of politeness: what must be expressed strongly by one participant as a 'polite belief' must be played down equally by the other participant as an 'impolite belief'. So increasing the positive politeness of an offer means anticipating and counteracting the negative politeness of the recipient.

This helps to clarify why the negative form of the question, *Won't you help yourself*, etc., is polite in an offer. The negative question is (as I shall propose later, 7.3.2), a question about a negative proposition, which itself (see 4.5) implies the denial of a positive proposition. The sense can be spelt out literally as follows: 'I hope and expect you to help yourself, but now it appears that you will not help yourself; is this really so?'[4] In effect, it pays *h* the compliment of holding a polite belief, and at the same time politely (from *s*'s point of view) expresses disbelief in that belief, and so invites *h*, in spite of ostensible reluctance, to accept the offer. In this way the question is biased towards a positive outcome. For the opposite reason *Would you mind helping yourself* is polite as an impositive. The sense of *mind* in this construction indicates a negative expectation of the action *A*, in that *Would you mind* is semantically equivalent to *Would you dislike . . .* or *Would you object to . . .* In this respect it has a built-in negative bias, and contrasts with *Would you like . . .* , which is more naturally interpreted as introducing an offer. It is logically speaking a negative answer to this question which expresses *h*'s compliance: (*No, I wouldn't mind . . .*) but even this is a non-committal response, merely carrying the sense 'I would not object', which confirms that *h* is not unwilling rather than that *h* is willing to do *A*. The introduction of a further negative into this strategy makes no sense; hence the unacceptability of *Wouldn't you mind . . . ?*

5.4 Pragmatic paradoxes of politeness

One may argue that in 'ideally polite' circles, the determination of the two participants in the discourse to be as polite as each other leads to an infinite regress in the 'logic' of conversational behaviour. Suppose *a* and *b* are two participants, and that *A* is a courteous action which *a* wishes to perform for *b*; for example, *a* may be making the following offer:

[19] Let me carry those cases for you.

Suppose, in addition, that both *a* and *b* are obeying the Tact Maxim to its fullest extent. Then the following might represent in outline the first two stages of the infinite regress:

(i) *An offer is made by a:*
   (1) *a* is observing the PP   (given)
   (2) *A* is favourable to *b*   (given)
   THEREFORE:
   (3) *a* (politely) implicates '*a* wants *A* to occur'
                                          (from 1 and 2, and PP)
(ii) *b declines the offer made by a:*
   (4) *b* is observing the PP   (given)
   (5) *A* is unfavourable to *a*   (given)
   THEREFORE:
   (6) *b* (politely) implicates '*b* does not want *A* to occur'
                                          (from 4, 5, and PP)

The two implicatures of (3) and (6) amount to what we may call a
PRAGMATIC PARADOX: an attribution of incompatible attitudes to
the participants in a dialogue. However, on the assumption that *a*
can interpret the force of *b*'s remark (see 2.4), it is possible for *a*
to infer from (6) that it is *because b* wants to obey the PP that *b*
implicates that *b* does not want *A* to occur. In other words, it is
possible for *a* to infer that (6) is simply implicated for the sake of
politeness, and therefore that *b* DOES want *A* to occur. Therefore
it is polite for *a* to renew the offer more strongly. But by the same
token, *b* cannot assume from *a*'s offer that the implicature of (3)
is true, for it may be implicated only for politeness' sake. So it is
polite for *b* to decline once more. This tug-of-war of mutual
deference will continue until one of the participants yields to the
greater politeness of the other.

    In (i) and (ii) above, lines (1–6) may be thought of as repre-
senting parts of a means–ends analysis. But from an interpretative point of view, they may also form part of a heuristic analysis,
in which case the derivation works from the opposite direction.
For instance, from the implicature of (3), *h* may infer (1), that *s* is
being polite. More precisely, however, the politeness implicature
may be a 'meta-implicature' which itself contains a reference to
another implicature. Thus from an offer like [9] *Let me carry
those cases for you*, a relatively direct implicature will be:

[20] *s* wants to carry *h*'s cases.

But since, by background knowledge, it is assumed already
that carrying of cases is unfavourable to *s*, this will lead to the
implicature:

[21] *s* is being polite

and may lead more indirectly to the meta-implicature:

[22] It is only because *s* is being polite that *s* implicates that '*s* wants to carry *h*'s cases'.

A further inference from [22] is that *s* may therefore be violating the Maxim of Quality, *ie* that the most direct implicature '*s* wants to carry *h*'s cases' may be false. The question we face here is one of the sincerity or seriousness of polite behaviour. It is possible to infer [21] without taking the further step to [22], with its implication that *s* may not be sincere. That is, it is possible for a polite utterance to be interpreted as genuinely polite, or simply as 'polite on the record'.[5] The latter interpretation will obviously be favoured if all the evidence indicates that [20] is false. Therefore, if [20] is false, *h* is able to discount [20] as a reason for accepting *s*'s offer as a matter of politeness, and the way is open for a polite refusal, as indicated in (ii) above. This refusal in turn may be rejected by *s* as non-serious, and the game of conversational ping-pong may proceed again.

We may observe in the pragmatic paradoxes of politeness a comedy of inaction: it is as if two people are eternally prevented from passing through a doorway because each is too polite to go before the other. Similar paradoxes of behaviour are ritualized in certain cultures in which an offer has to be repeated and declined *n* times before it is accepted. It is just as well that in practice, no one is ideally polite.

The question is: Why does politeness manifest itself in this behavioural or pragmatic paradox? The answer to this appears itself somewhat paradoxical: that the paradoxes of politeness function as an antidote to a more dangerous kind of paradox. This more dangerous paradox is a violation of the logic of goal-oriented action; that is, a state in which two individuals, *a* and *b*, have incompatible goals. It is epitomized in a situation, the opposite of that just visualized, in which each of the two persons wishing to go through the doorway attempts to go before the other, with the result that they collide in the doorway! Such paradoxes clearly lead to direct conflict, and are socially, not to say physically, perilous. They may be placed on a scale of decreasing gravity as follows:[6]

1. ACTUAL CONFLICT (strongest)

$a \begin{Bmatrix} \text{makes} \\ \text{tries to make} \end{Bmatrix} b \text{ do } A, \text{ but } b \begin{Bmatrix} \text{tries to} \\ \text{does} \end{Bmatrix} \text{not do } A.$

2. DISOBEDIENCE

a tells/orders *b* to do *A*, but *b* does not do *A*.

3. WILL FLOUTING

a communicates to *b* that *a* wants *b* to do *A*, but *b* does not do *A*.

4. WILL INCOMPATIBILITY (weakest)

   a communicates to *b* that *a* wants *b* to do *A*, but *b* communicates to *a* that *b* does not want to do *A*.

Corresponding to these types of dangerous situation, there are four more types in which the positions of positive and negative actions are reversed:

1a. ACTUAL CONFLICT (strongest)

$$a \begin{Bmatrix} \text{stops} \\ \text{tries to stop} \end{Bmatrix} b \text{ doing } A, \text{ but } b \begin{Bmatrix} \text{tries to do} \\ \text{does} \end{Bmatrix} A.$$

2a. DISOBEDIENCE

   a forbids *b* to do *A*, but *b* does *A*.

3a. WILL FLOUTING

   a communicates to *b* that *a* wants *b* not to do *A*, but *b* does *A*.

4a. WILL INCOMPATIBILITY (weakest)

   a communicates to *b* that *a* wants *b* not to do *A*, but *b* communicates to *a* that *b* wants to do *A*.

We can compare these conflict situations by imagining a simple drama in which Ann (= *a*) has the goal of getting Bill (= *b*) to give her £50. In the gravest case (1), Ann takes the money by force, and Bill tries to prevent her; or else Ann tries to take the money, and Bill prevents her. (If we leave out 'tries to', these statements do indeed become logical paradoxes or contradictions: *eg* 'Ann took the money, but Bill prevented her from doing so'.) In the least grave case (4), Ann expresses her wish that Bill should give her the money, and Bill expresses his wish not to do so. The outcome here is not direct conflict, but a volitional discord which (as we all know) is often a stepping-stone to a more serious breach of comity.

Against this background, the function of the Tact Maxim is a negative one: it is a means of avoiding conflict. All the conflict situations detailed above involve an incompatibility of the general form:

$$a \text{ VOL } [X], \qquad b \text{ VOL } [not\text{-}X]$$

where *VOL* is a volitional predicate such as *want, intend*. (This is true manifestly of the weakest case 4 and 4a, and also, by implication, of the others.) The Tact Maxim, in its most absolute form, prevents such incompatibilities from arising, since 'Minimize the cost to *h*' carries the implication 'Do not (express the wish to) do what *h* does not want'. If both parties observe this maxim, there will be no more conflict; but on the other hand, the avoidance strategy is, as we have seen, a recipe for inactivity.

This description, however, polarizes a situation which is really a matter of degree. The Tact Maxim is observed *to a certain extent*, and this means that on the one hand, conflict is not always avoided, and on the other hand, that inaction does not always result. In impositives, the action of the Tact Maxim is rather to cause us to suppress, to play down, to hedge, beliefs which are costly to *h*. And we have seen that the chief means of doing this is to weaken the belief by biasing the illocution towards a negative outcome. Also relevant is this general law governing indirectness: that the more indirect an implicature, the weaker its force.

5.5 Semantic representation of declaratives, interrogatives, and imperatives

Bearing the above two points in mind, we will proceed, in 5.6, to examine some of the strategies for making polite and impolite impositives. It is already obvious, from such straightforward sentences as *Sit down!*, *You will sit down*, and *Will you sit down?*, that grammatically, impositives may take the form of any of the three major sentence types. Accordingly, before going further, it is advisable to consider how declarative, interrogative, and imperative sentences are represented on the semantic level.

The terms DECLARATIVE, INTERROGATIVE, and IMPERATIVE are typically used for syntactic categories, and I shall follow this usage, in treating them as basic sentence-types. They are conventionally distinguished from corresponding semantic or speech-act categories, referred to by such terms as 'assertion', 'question', and 'command'. If one accepts the complementarist position of this book, however, one has to make a further differentiation between categories on the semantic and pragmatic levels. The English language is, unfortunately, rather unfavourable to the complementarist view in not providing us with a satisfactory terminology for all three levels. It has consequently been easy to assimilate semantic vocabulary to pragmatic vocabulary, or vice versa – for example, to treat a 'question' as both a semantic (logical) and a pragmatic entity.[7] I shall distinguish terms on the three levels as follows:[8]

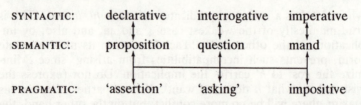

SYNTACTIC:	declarative	interrogative	imperative
SEMANTIC:	proposition	question	mand
PRAGMATIC:	'assertion'	'asking'	impositive

Thus the sense of a declarative sentence, of an interrogative sentence, and of an imperative sentence is respectively a proposition, a question, and a mand. The link between the semantic and pragmatic categories, however, is less clear-cut, as we would expect. It has been seen, for example, that a proposition or a question can have the force of an impositive, and (more generally) that strategies of indirectness ensure that every semantic type can be matched with a variety of pragmatic types. The quotation marks I have put round 'assertion', and 'asking', in fact reflect the uncertainty I feel as to whether these are useful terms, given the non-categorical nature of illocutionary force (see *p* 23). To be at all useful, they should be defined in ways which make them less general than the corresponding grammatical terms. Perhaps these are reasonable first approximations:

ASSERTION: an utterance whose illocutionary goal is to cause *h* to be aware that [*Y*] (where [*Y*] is some proposition).
ASKING: an utterance whose illocutionary goal is to get *h* to cause *s* to be aware that [*Y*] (where [*Y*] is some proposition).

These definitions propose that assertions and askings are to do with the passing of information between *s* and *h*. This means that, for example, an examination question or a rhetorical question would not have the force of an asking.

Another terminological deficiency is the lack of a recognized term for the general class of logical entities of which propositions, questions, and mands are subcategories. There is common ideational content that may be shared by propositions, questions, and mands, and which has been variously described as a 'propositional content', 'predication', or 'sentence radical'.[9] For instance, *You will sit down, Will you sit down*, and (*You*) *sit down!* all share a common propositional content *X*, describing a sitting down of *h* in the future. They differ in terms of logical form, but I shall want to use a single term, PROPOSITIONAL, to apply to all three types of sentence sense. I shall indicate propositionals by the use of square brackets. A proposition is the most fully specified type of propositional, and may be represented by a predication *X, Y, . . .* within the scope of a positive or negative operator: [*neg* (*X*)] or [*pos* (*X*)]. A *yes–no* question can then be represented as a 'propositional function', *ie* a propositional in which the question mark is a free variable ranging over *pos* and *neg*.[10] For example:

[23] Mary opened the door.   [*pos* (*X*)]
[24] Mary didn't open the door.   [*neg* (*X*)]
[25] Did Mary open the door?   [*?* (*X*)]

The free variable is in effect a gap in the sense of a proposition, and so a *yes–no* question is characterizable as a defective proposition, from which one specification is missing, *viz* the polarity sign *pos* or *neg*. This departs from standard logic in introducing a 'positive' as well as a 'negative' operator, but such an addition is reasonable, and is like prefixing a '+' sign to a numerical expression to mark it as positive, rather than negative. In terms familiar to linguists, the arithmetical negative sign is (like the negative operator in propositions) the marked term, which is obligatorily signalled, whereas the positive is normally omitted. The most palpable advantage of this analysis is that it permits a unitary logical treatment of questions, since *wh*-questions can be similarly characterized as propositional functions. The free variable is in this case the unspecified argument represented by the *wh*-word *who, what, when*, etc.; *eg* the variable x in the question:

[26] Where does Tom work?   [*pos* (Tom works at place x)]

A logically well-formed answer to such a question is any proposition which specifies a value for the variable x; *eg* for [26], '(Tom works) in London', '(Tom works) at the post office', etc. Similarly, a logically well-formed answer to a *yes–no* question is a proposition which fills in the missing polarity *pos* or *neg*.[11]

If questions are underspecified in comparison with propositions, mands are even more underspecified, since in contrast to propositions and questions they have no contrasts of tense or modality. They do, however, have the contrast between positive and negative, and so may take the form [*pos* (X)], [*neg* (X)], just like propositions. Mands constitute a more general category than what we normally understand by a 'command': they reflect a common element of meaning shared by three moods, those of the imperative, infinitive, and present subjunctive, in the traditional description of the grammar of English and of many other languages. All may be described as NON-INDICATIVE in that they do not describe some actual state of affairs, but rather invoke or conjure up some state of affairs which is envisaged as unfulfilled. It is not coincidence that these non-indicative constructions, in English, are all represented by the base form of the verb, without inflexion:[12]

[27] *Go home*.   (2nd person imperative)
[28] Let's *all go home*.   (1st person imperative)
[29] *Everyone go home*.   (3rd person imperative)
[30] They wanted *to go home*.   (infinitive)
[31] I vote that *every one of us go home*. (present subjunctive)

Indicative and non-indicative propositions will be signalled by the symbols *I* and *N* respectively.

Apart from the imperative, most non-indicative forms occur in subordinate clauses, where they are governed semantically by particular predicates (most obviously by predicates underlying verbs such as *want, hope, decide*, etc. – see 9.2.3). This leads to the observation that propositionals, whether propositions, questions, or mands, may be included in other propositionals:

[32] I think that you are mistaken. $I[...I[pos(X)]]$
[33] Do you know whether they won? $I[...I[?(X)]]$
[34] They told me not to complain. $I[...N[neg(X)]]$

Notice that non-indicative questions also occur, but are somewhat restricted:

[35] I am not sure *whether to apply for the job.* $I[...N[?(X)]]$

Compare similar examples of non-indicative *wh*-questions:

[36] She told me *what to do.*
[37] *Why not leave straight away?*

There are also, in English, archaic or formulaic subjunctive main clauses such as *God be praised*. These, like first- and third-person imperatives, may be described as mands; but overwhelmingly the most common type of mand realized by a main clause is the second-person imperative, whose pragmatically specialized function (see *p* 28) is recognized in the fact that its subject *you* is optional, and generally omitted.

We have already seen that the imperative cannot be associated with any particular illocution such as an order, nor even with a general illocutionary type such as impositives. Any pragmatic generalization about the use of imperatives has to be broad enough to cover such utterances as: *Have a good time* (good wishes); *Help yourself* (offer); *Make yourself at home* (invitation); *Be whole* (faith-healing); *Go to hell* (curse); *Say that again, and I'll hit you* (threat); as well as the standard impositive command *Stand still*, etc. The common ground that these share is this: they all, in some respect or other, present the propositional content as a candidate for fulfilment by *h*. There are important issues which cannot be pursued here, particularly the question of how far the relation of questions and mands to the illocutions they typically perform (*viz* askings and impositives) is conventional, rather than determined by Interpersonal Rhetoric. Kempson (1975:147) opts for a conventional mapping of one on to the other set of categories, whereas I prefer (in 7.3.3.1–4 below) to go the whole pragmatic hog, and attempt an explanation entirely in terms of Interpersonal Rhetoric. For the present, it is enough to add to the indicative/non-indicative distinction one further logical contrast relevant to impositives: the distinction between REAL and UNREAL (or counterfactual or hypothetical) propositions.

The unreal mood, particularly as manifested in the past-tense modals *would, could*, and *might* is, like the non-indicative mood of the imperative, pragmatically specialized to particular functions. Logically, unreal propositionals may be assigned to the indicative category, for unreal conditional propositions can be true or false.[13] Thus the following are respectively necessarily false and necessarily true.

[38] If I were taller than my sister, she would be taller than me.
[39] If I were taller than my sister, she would be shorter than me.

But no truth value can be assigned to an unreal proposition if it lacks a condition:

[40] Many people would love a house like that.
[41] You could open these letters.

To interpret such sentences logically, we have to add some implicit protasis '. . . if you wanted to', etc. It is therefore reasonable to say, as many have assumed, that whenever an unreal proposition occurs without a protasis, it is logically underspecified, and needs to be supplemented by an implicit condition. Both non-indicative and unreal propositionals have the following properties: they occur more generally in embedded positions, where their occurrence is determined by the selectional restrictions of predicates such as *want, if*, etc.[14]; and when they do occur in non-embedded positions, they are pragmatically restricted to certain illocutionary functions. These two properties are in fact aspects of the same general characteristic, which is that these types of propositional (as the traditional grammatical name 'subjunctive' implies) are not logically independent. When they occur independently, it is therefore with the implication that they are in some respect deficient, as compared with real propositions. This analysis to some extent justifies a view, which accords with the conventional preoccupation of logic with propositions and truth values, that propositions are the minimal logically complete units of language. Nevertheless, other propositionals share with propositions the element of propositional content, and it is possible on this basis to compare them pragmatically with one another.

5.6 The interpretation of impositives

In showing how the interpretation of impositives is graded according to tact, I shall begin with the imperative, as the most direct form of imposition. An imperative impositive is tactless in that it risks disobedience, which is a fairly grave type of conflict situation:

[42] s: Take me home.
   IMPLICATURE: s intends [h to take s home].

It is not clear to me whether this implicature is conventional or conversational, *ie* is it just a matter of convention that mands with second-person subjects express s's intention to get h to do something, or is it that this interpretation is the most reasonable 'default interpretation', given that s has uttered a mand describing some future action by h? I shall not pursue this further. One stage more tactful than [42] is [43]:

[43] s: I want you to take me home.
   IMPLICATURE: s wants [h to be aware that [s wants [h to take s home]]].

In [43] s is observing the Tact Maxim in uttering a proposition, rather than a direct mand. This is because an assertion does not require any action as its most direct response, and so h is left with a choice of whether to carry out s's wishes or to ignore them. But if h is also observing the Tact Maxim, then h will carry out s's wishes, Thus, in so far as s 'banks on' h's observing the Tact Maxim, [43] assumes the force of an impositive.

This means that [43] violates the Tact Maxim at one remove. For if h is observing the Tact Maxim, then h has no choice but to do what s wants. Thus by uttering [43], s forces h EITHER to take s home, OR to break the Tact Maxim. In either case, a violation takes place, since by constraining h to do what s wants, on pain of breaking the Tact Maxim, s is himself breaking the Tact Maxim by imposing his will on h. So to the Tact Maxim we add the following 'meta-maxim':

DO NOT PUT h IN A POSITION WHERE EITHER s OR h HAS TO BREAK THE TACT MAXIM.

It could be said that in [43] s exploits the Tact Maxim for personal advantage. But the following request forms are somewhat more polite:

[44] $\left\{ \begin{array}{l} \text{Will you} \\ \text{Are you willing to} \end{array} \right\}$ take me home?[15]

[45] $\left\{\begin{array}{l}\text{Can you}\\ \text{Are you able to}\end{array}\right\}$ take me home?

The question form of [44] is felt to be more tactful, because a *yes–no* question overtly gives *h* freedom of response, *ie* freedom to say yes or no. Moreover, by asking *h* about *h*'s wishes, *s* is overtly putting himself in the deferential role. Even so, by means of implicature, this question can be seen to have the force of a request:

IMPLICATURE via the CP:

(a) *s* wants [*h* to take *s* home]. (Hinting Strategy, Maxim of Relation)

IMPLICATURE via the PP and (a):

(b) By avoiding a direct imperative, *s* observes the Tact Maxim.
(c) In that [44] is intended as an impositive, *s assumes that h is observing the Tact Maxim.*
(d) In assuming that *h* will interpret [44] as an impositive, *s assumes that h assumes that s is observing the Tact Maxim.* (Otherwise, there would be no motive for *s* to adopt the Hinting Strategy.)

Going one stage further, we notice that the question about *h*'s ability [45] is more tactful, as an impositive, than [44]. This is because [44], construed via its *implicated* meaning as an impositive, resembles [42] and [43] in allowing *h* no freedom to refuse. If *h* answers *No, I won't* to [44], *h* is valuing his own wishes above what he understands to be those of *s*, which is impolite. Therefore, one further implicature is made if one adopts the even more oblique anticipatory illocution of [45]:

(e) In assuming that [44] is an impolite impositive, in that *h* under condition (d) has no choice but to take *s* home, *s assumes that h assumes that s assumes that h is observing the Tact Maxim.*

The question about *h*'s ability to do *A* avoids this impoliteness at third remove, because it gives *h* an 'out': *h* is able to decline to do *A* on grounds of being unable to do so. No one can be blamed for a failure to do something if the failure is due to inability. For example, *h* might say: *I am willing to do A, but I can't,* and might justify himself by saying:

'Unless I am able to do *A*, I cannot be responsible for failing to bring it about.'

The adoption of the unreal forms of [44] and [45] is, of course, yet a further stage in the avoidance of commitment:

[46] *Would* you take me home?
[47] *Could* you take me home?

By replacing *will* and *can* by *would* and *could,* s gives h another excuse for not complying with the request: the past-tense modals signify a hypothetical action by h, and so in reply, h can in theory give a positive reply to the question without committing himself to anything in the real world. To make the implication of an impositive even more remote, tentative or negatively biased items can be added:

[48] Could you *possibly* take me home?
[49] Would you *mind* taking me home?

But one point to notice about the hypothetical forms is that lacking an overt protasis (see 5.5) they cannot (unlike questions with *can*, for example), except in rather unusual contexts, be understood as serious questions. They are therefore pragmatically highly specialized towards the function of indicating 'on the record' politeness. Other transparent politeness markers are, of course, courtesy adverbs such as *please* and *kindly*.

If we turn to declarative sentences, here too there is a scale of tact similar to that noted in the case of questions, with *can* being more indirect than *will*, and the hypothetical form being more indirect than the real form:

[50] You will take me home. (ALSO: You must take me home.)
[51] You can take me home.
[52] You could/might take me home.

The parallel between propositions and questions cannot, however, be extended to *would*: unlike *Would you take me home?*, *You would take me home* does not have an impositive force at all. This lack of correspondence has the following explanation. The statement *You will . . .* in [50] is if anything more impolite than the direct imperative: it cannot therefore be combined with the politely 'hedging' effect of the hypothetical form *would*.

To make the point more explicitly: propositions such as [50]–[52] are noticeably less tactful than their matching question forms in [44]–[47]. They state or implicate the addressee's ability to act, and therefore deny him the opportunity to decline what is offered by the interrogative. But in addition, the *You will* form of [50] is interpreted most directly as a prediction (a kind of assertion about a future happening), and therefore expresses *s*'s confident belief that the future event *A* will take place:

'*s* wants *h* to be aware that *h* will take *s* home.'

The possibility of disobedience associated with a command is effectively ruled out by the use of a proposition beginning *You will*. As though by utterly unassailable authority, *s* claims to guarantee the future compliance of *h*. It is because [50] in this way strengthens the impositive rather than tones it down that *You will* cannot be made more' tentative through the change to *would*. *You will* says 'I am absolutely sure you will obey', but the unreal *would* says 'I am uncertain as to whether you will obey'. In this way, their pragmatic forces are incompatible with one another.

In contrast, the statement beginning *You can* is an appropriate means of softening the effect of an impositive. It can best be regarded as a tentative version of *You must*: by pointing out the ability of *h* to do the task, *s* in effect (by the Hinting Strategy) proposes that *h* do it. It mitigates the force of *You will...* because, as we have seen (p. 87, Table 4.1), *You can. . .*carries the implicature 'You do not have to', and so offers *h*, on the face of it, a pretext for ignoring the hint. Since it is formulated as a proposition rather than as a question, however, [51] does not overtly offer *h* the choice of saying 'No', and is in this respect less tactful than the corresponding question. Its politeness derives, in contrast, from its ambivalence: its sense allows it just as easily to be a recommendation or a piece of advice (an illocution for the benefit of *h*) as to be an impositive. Since *You can . . .* is itself a softened variant of *must*, there is no reason why it should not be hedged further by adoption of the hypothetical form *You could . . .* .

The Interpersonal Rhetoric can explain another lack of parallelism between propositions and questions. A negative question with *can* may have an impositive force, as we noted earlier, whereas there is no comparable force of a negative proposition:

[17] Can't you shut up?   [17a] You can't shut up.

As a negative proposition such as [17a] expresses the impossibility of *h*'s doing *A*, it obviously cannot be used as a means of getting *A* performed. (If anything, it would have the opposite effect of dissuading *h* from doing *A*.) But the negative question [17] can indeed have the force of getting *h* to be quiet. In this respect it has a very different effect from that of the negative question [13] *Won't you sit down*, despite the similarity of their positive counterparts. As we have seen, [13] makes an offer *more* polite, while [17] makes an impositive *less* polite. The explanation is simple enough if we analyse a negative question, as before (*see p* 110), as a question about a negative proposition. The sense of [17] can be roughly spelled out, on this basis, as follows (see 7.3.2):

> 'I have assumed that you cannot shut up. I now doubt whether this is true. I ask you to resolve my doubt.'

We might reconstruct an ironic train of thought behind this question as follows:

A. 'You have been making too much noise.' (impolite observation)
B. 'The only way to reconcile this with politeness is to assume that you cannot help making too much noise.' (polite assumption)
C. 'Therefore I make the polite assumption that you cannot shut up.'
D. 'However, everyone knows that people are able to be quiet when they want to.'
E. 'Therefore my polite assumption at (C) must be false.'
F. 'Therefore there is a conflict between what I believe and what it is polite for me to believe. I ask you to confirm my belief.'

The result of this ironic *negation* is thus to bias the interpretation towards a *positive* reply, and hence towards compliance. Therefore this question is less polite than the more neutral question *Can you...?* Oppositely, *Won't you sit down* biases the answer in favour of the polite assumption 'You will sit down' in the case of an offer, and is therefore more polite than the corresponding neutral question *Will you sit down?*

5.7 Pragmatic scales

The preceding sections have identified three scales with a bearing on the degree of tact appropriate to a given speech situation. These are:

1. The COST–BENEFIT SCALE (*p* 107) on which is estimated the cost or benefit of the proposed action *A* to *s* or to *h*.
2. The OPTIONALITY SCALE on which illocutions are ordered according to the amount of choice which *s* allows to *h* (*p* 109).
3. The INDIRECTNESS SCALE on which, from *s*'s point of view, illocutions are ordered with respect to the length of the path (in terms of means–ends analysis) connecting the illocutionary act to its illocutionary goal.

The indirectness scale can also be formulated from *h*'s point of view, in terms of the length of the inferential path by which the force is derived from the sense. Therefore strictly speaking, there are two scales of indirectness: one for the speaker, and one for the hearer. Since, however, h's inferential strategy is a step-by-step reconstruction of what h understands to be s's illocutionary strategy, we can assume a close correspondence between them. There is generally no need, in discussing indirectness, to distinguish between s's and h's points of view.

The cost–benefit scale is also, strictly speaking, made up of two distinct scales: cost/benefit to s and cost/benefit to h. In general, these two measures vary inversely; but it is possible for them to vary independently. For example, s may propose a course of action which is, in s's estimation, at a cost to himself, and beneficial to h. This is appropriately described as an offer (see Table 9.2, p 217); eg:

[53] Would you like to use my electric drill? ($\uparrow h$, $\downarrow s$)

On the other hand, s may propose a course of action which s regards as beneficial to h, but which is not costly in any way to s:

[54] I'd use an electric drill if I were you. ($\uparrow h$)

This would be more appropriately described as a piece of advice. (The arrows indicate 'beneficial to' ($\uparrow$) and 'at a cost to' ($\downarrow$).

We might add, though, that there is a strong association between these two scales, because impositives and commissives typically propose an action which involves a *trans*action between s and h: that is, where s gets something done for h or vice versa. In such typical cases, it is unnecessary to distinguish between the speaker's and the hearer's cost–benefit scales, since a positive position on one will inevitably imply a negative position on the other, *ie* whatever is $\uparrow s$ is $\downarrow h$, and whatever is $\downarrow s$ is $\uparrow h$.

This brings to mind a useful analogy between many illocutions (or, more directly, the actions which are the subject of those illocutions) and commercial transactions.[16] In an impositive such as *Would you mind cleaning the windows?* there is implied a transfer of 'goods', or more often of 'services', from h to s; while in a commissive such as *Would you like me to clean the windows?* there is implied a transfer in the opposite direction. Some expressives may similarly carry implications of a transfer of goods or services in the past: if you *thank* someone, you presuppose a previous transfer of goods or services from h to s. The commercial metaphor does not have to be restricted, moreover, to 'bilateral' illocutions such as these. Consider the expressive illocutions which we call APOLOGIES and PARDONS. Apologies express regret for some offence committed by s against h – and there is no implication that s has benefited from the offence. Nevertheless, an apology implies a transaction, in that it is a bid to change the balance-sheet of the relation between s and h. If the apology is successful, it will result in h's pardoning or excusing the offence. Significantly, if we commit an offence against someone, we talk of *owing* that person an apology, thereby treating the apology as in some sense an expiation of the offence. The metaphor whereby deeds make us 'debtors' or 'creditors' of one another applies not only to good deeds (favours), but also to bad deeds (offences), so that apologizing, like thanking, can be regarded as an acknowledgement of an imbalance in the relation between s and h, and to some extent, as an attempt to restore the equilibrium.

The mercantile metaphor, in fact, is more than a superficial similitude. It might be argued that the mercantile world, on the contrary, is a special case of a social world in which the standing of one person k relative to another person l can be measured in terms of what k owes l or l owes k. Such an account of human relationships is needed quite generally; without it we should not be able to explain the sense of a speech-act verb such as *pardon*, which does not involve any exchange of goods or services, but nevertheless implies the cancellation of a debt. Without such an account, moreover, there would be difficulty in explaining the meanings of such speech-act verbs as *beg, petition, beseech*, all of which resemble *request*, but have the additional implication that s is in some way acknowledging the debt that would result from h's performance of the designated action:

[55] Jim begged me to lend him my bicycle.
[56] Jim asked me to lend him my bicycle.
[57] Jim demanded that I lend him my bicycle.

On the other hand, *demand* in [57] implies that s does not acknowledge that any debt will result from h's action. In this respect, *beg* in [55] *demand* in [57] represent opposites, while *ask* in [56] is neutral between them. The same point could be made, but with a change of vocabulary, if we said that Jim in [55] regards the loan of the bicycle as placing him under an *obligation*, while in [57] he regards it as a matter of *right*.[17]

The cost–benefit scale therefore brings with it an implicit balance-sheet of s's and h's relative standing, and there also seems to be a tacit assumption that a maintenance of equilibrium is desirable.[18] The goal of some speech acts, such as thanks and apologies, can then be seen as the restoration of equilibrium, or at least the reduction of disequilibrium, between s and h.

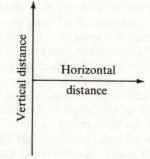

FIGURE 5.1   Social distance

In addition to the three scales already mentioned – the cost–benefit scale, the optionality scale, and the indirectness scale – there are two further scales which are highly relevant to politeness. These are the scales which, in Brown and Gilman's well-known account (1960), determine the choice between familiar and respectful pronouns of address in many European languages (for example, the choice between *tu* and *vous* in French). They can be visualized as a two-dimensional graph as shown in Fig. 5.1. The vertical axis measures the degree of distance in terms of the 'power' or AUTHORITY of one participant over another. This is an asymmetric measure, so that someone in authority may use a familiar form of address to someone who, in return, uses the respectful form. The horizontal axis, on the other hand, measures what Brown and Gilman call the 'solidarity' factor, or what I shall prefer to regard, from the opposite point of view, as SOCIAL DISTANCE.[19] The overall degree of respectfulness, for a given speech situation, depends largely on relatively permanent factors of status, age, degree of intimacy, etc., but also, to some extent, on the temporary role of one person relative to another.[20] A lecturer might feel it reasonable to say to a student *Get that essay to me by next week*, but not *Make me a cup of coffee*. In the former case he would be exercising his legitimate authority over the student's academic behaviour; but in the latter case, he would be stepping outside that recognized role. Again, rights and duties are important in defining the standing of participants in relation to one another.

In English-speaking society, there is no pronoun distinction to signal this type of social relationship, but, as the above example already suggests, the amount of tact required in an impositive will be determined in part by the degree of respect implicit in *s*'s stance towards *h*.

We can now summarize the way these various parameters influence tact as follows:

  (i)   the greater the cost of A to h,
  (ii) the greater the horizontal social distance of h from s,
  (iii) the greater the authoritative status of h with respect to s,
  (iv) the greater will be the need for optionality, and correspondingly for indirectness, in the expression of an impositive, if s is to observe the Tact Maxim.

5.8 Tact and condescension

The final clause (iv) of the above generalization is not without exceptions, for although optionality implies indirectness, indirectness does not imply optionality. There are some impositives where indirectness does not contribute to tact, and even some where indirectness militates against tact. One exception already noted is a negative question such as *Can't you be quiet?*: the negative question is more indirect than the positive question, but is less tactful, since it reduces the amount of choice implied. This example also leads on to another kind of exception, such as *Must you make all that noise?*, in which indirectness leads to an ironic interpretation. Most interesting, perhaps, is a type of example not yet considered, where s uses a form of utterance which looks like a commissive, and which is nevertheless intended and interpreted as an impositive. A boss might say, with apparent indulgence, to his new secretary:

[58] Would you like to type these letters?

Another example, from an earlier era, is the permissive use of *may* in giving an order; for example, in a Victorian schoolboy-story, the headmaster might dismiss a boy by saying:

[59] You may go now, Smith.

On the face of it, the utterers of [58] and [59] are being polite in offering h a chance to do something gratifying. But in fact, a different analysis is required, for there is little doubt that [58] would be followed by the typing of the letters, and [59] by the immediate departure of the boy. It is often felt that a sentence like [58] is objectionable precisely because it trades on the authoritative status of s. Since s's position is such that h cannot but acknowledge his authority, h feels obliged to accept the 'offer', and hence s is free to enjoy the pleasure of condescension. Here the excessive politeness of s does not make use of the Irony Principle.

Rather, the Hinting Strategy comes into force:

  (i) *s* is apparently being polite in offering *h* the choice of doing *A*, in a manner which suggests that *A* is pleasant.

[(ii) But *A* is not pleasant.]

(iii) However, *s*'s remark can only be relevant if *s* wants *h* to do *A*.

(iv) And, since *s* has authority over *h*, *h* is required to do *A*.

This strategy on the part of *s* seems reasonable only if we again suppose the existence of a social 'balance-sheet' between *s* and *h*. By appearing to give *h* a choice, *s* appears to increase the credit balance in his own favour. This advantage is spoiled, however, if *h* recognizes that *s*'s tact is insincere. The danger is that *s* will merely makes an impression of condescension. In these cases, as in cases of irony, being too polite can mean being impolite.

Notes

1. See Brown and Levinson's discussion (1978:71–3) of intrinsic FTAs (= face threatening acts).
2. In his 1979 revision of the 1975 article 'A taxonomy of illocutionary acts', Searle changes the term 'representative' to 'assertive'. Here I use the terminology of the later version. Other, related taxonomies are those of Austin (1962:152–63), and Bach and Harnish (1979:41–55).
3. Mention should be made of the importance of socially assumed rights and duties as factors entering into the evaluation of the weightiness of *s*'s imposition upon *h*. See further note 17 below.
4. On these implications of negative questions, and the relation of negative questions to negative propositions, see Leech (1974:318–20).
5. *Cf* Brown and Levinson's (1978) distinction between 'on the record' and 'off the record' in communicative acts.
6. An earlier account of such pragmatic paradoxes is given in Leech (1980 [1977a]:108).
7. This account differs from that of Searle (1969:66), who defines a question as a type of illocutionary act, and then finds it necessary to separate 'real questions' (where *s* wants to find out the answer) from 'exam questions' (where *s* knows the answer already). It is better to follow Levinson (1978) in showing that questions, although logically they have a common basis, perform a wide range of pragmatic functions.
8. On the concept of *mand, cf* Lyons (1977:751): 'Mands differ from statements in that their tropic is to be interpreted as "so be it", rather than "it is so".' Lyons's threefold distinction (borrowed from Hare 1970) between phrastic, tropic, and neustic only partially cor-

responds to the threefold distinction between syntactic, semantic, and pragmatic abstractions that I have presented here.

9. 'Propositional content' is Searle's (1969) term. Kempson (1975:43–4) adopts Stenius's (1967) term 'sentence-radical'.

10. On this approach to questions, *cf* Hudson (1975) and Leech (1981). Searle (1969) applies the concept of *propositional function* only to *wh*-questions.

11. It is necessary to distinguish between a 'logically well-formed answer' in this sense, and a 'pragmatically appropriate response' to a question. Examples [21] and [22] from Smith and Wilson on p 94 above illustrate the latter, but not the former.

12. Support for this point of view comes from the arguments of Bolinger (1977:152–82) and Downes (1977) in favour of the syntactic and semantic identity of the imperative and the infinitive.

13. Unreal or counterfactual conditional propositions and their truth values are discussed in McCawley (1981:311–26).

14. For factuality conditions imposed by predicates, see Leech (1980 [1977b]) and Leech (1981 [1974]:301–6).

15. The two sentences [44] are not pragmatically equivalent, nor are the two sentences [45]. The sentences *Will you . . .* and *Can you . . .* are more institutionalized as impositives than their 'paraphrases'. In addition to this, Sadock (1974:78) also argues that the pairs are clearly distinct on syntactic grounds. He thus claims that in one sentence the request illocution is encoded in the grammar, whereas in the other sentence it is not. While acknowledging that such differences do exist, I am interested here in focusing on the equivalence in sense, and to some extent in force, between these sentences, rather than emphasizing their dissimilarily. See 8.7 below for further reference to Sadock's theory of indirect illocutions.

16. The commercial analogy has also been exploited by Brown and Levinson (1978) in their interpretation of communicative acts as involving exchange of 'goods and services'. A commercial model is also supported by the observation that some illocutions such as promises and bets require, for their successful performance, a contractual relation between *s* and *h*. See Fotion (1982).

17. The importance of rights and obligations in the assessment of cost or benefit, and hence of politeness, is evidenced by an example I owe to Jennifer Thomas. Suppose a passenger *p* asks a driver *d* to stop the bus at a bus-stop. Very little politeness is required for this speech act, because it is the driver's job (*ie* his occupational duty) to let passengers get off at bus-stops. But now suppose that *p* asks *d* to stop the bus outside *p*'s house, where there is no bus-stop. In this case a great deal of politeness, as well as other redressive behaviour such apologizing and explaining, may be required. In both cases the amount of trouble or effort on the part of the driver is the same; but the imposition is far greater in the case where the driver is asked to do something 'as a personal favour'.

18. Preserving equilibrium also seems to be an important aspect of other

kinds of human communicative behaviour. See Argyle and Dean (1965) on the preservation of equilibrium in the distancing of one participant from another in interactive behaviour.

19. Brown and Gilman's scales of power and solidarity have been applied to politeness by Brown and Levinson (1978:79–89).

20. Brown and Gilman (1960:261) cite as a 'favourite example' the shift of French mountaineers from *vous* to *tu* after a 'certain critical altitude' is reached.

Chapter 6

A survey of the Interpersonal Rhetoric

Lady Bracknell: ... Is this Miss Prism a female of repellant aspect, remotely connected with education?
Chasuble (somewhat indignantly): She is the most cultivated of ladies, and the very picture of respectability.
Lady Bracknell: It is obviously the same person.
[Wilde, *The Importance of Being Earnest*, Act III]

In describing the Interpersonal Rhetoric I have so far concentrated on the Cooperative Principle and one maxim of the Politeness Principle, *viz* the Tact Maxim. By restricting the range of discussion in this way, I have tried to show, through illustration, the explanatory value of a rhetoric of which Grice's CP is just one component. I have also mentioned an Irony Principle (4.1); but it is now necessary to consider what other principles and maxims must be postulated in order to explain the relation between sense and force in human conversation. In short, I shall try to fill in some gaps in my introductory diagram of the Interpersonal Rhetoric (Fig. 1.4). This will take me on to more speculative ground, but will nevertheless establish, in outline, quite a rich system of principles and maxims.

6.1 Maxims of politeness

Apart from the Tact Maxim, there are a number of maxims dealing with polite behaviour. Before describing them, I shall note, as a general point, that politeness concerns a relationship between two participants whom we may call *self* and *other*. In conversation, *self* will normally be identified with *s*, and *other* will typically be identified with *h*; but speakers also show politeness to third parties, who may or may not be present in the speech situation.[1] The label *other* may therefore apply not only to addressees, but to people designated by third-person pronouns. The importance of showing politeness to third parties varies: a key factor is whether or not the third party is present as a bystander; another is whether the third party is felt to belong to *s*'s or to *h*'s sphere of influence. To take a clear case: s has to be more polite in referring to h's spouse than in referring to s's own spouse. Even in this area, however, there are cross-cultural variations: in some societies, a man discussing his wife will treat her as '*self*', and therefore feel free, perhaps even obliged, to denigrate her; but in other societies, he will treat her as '*other*'.

The maxims of the PP tend to go in pairs as follows:

(I) TACT MAXIM (in impositives and commissives)
 (a) Minimize cost to *other* [(b) Maximize benefit to *other*]

(II) GENEROSITY MAXIM (in impositives and commissives)
 (a) Minimize benefit to *self* [(b) Maximize cost to *self*]

(III) APPROBATION MAXIM (in expressives and assertives)
 (a) Minimize dispraise of *other* [(b) Maximize praise of *other*]

(IV) MODESTY MAXIM (in expressives and assertives)
 (a) Minimize praise of *self* [(b) Maximize dispraise of *self*]

(V) AGREEMENT MAXIM (in assertives)
 (a) Minimize disagreement between *self* and *other*
 [(b) Maximize agreement between *self* and *other*]

(VI) SYMPATHY MAXIM (in assertives)
 (a) Minimize antipathy between *self* and *other*
 [(b) Maximize sympathy between *self* and *other*]

The statement of these maxims has been simplified for convenience: strictly, (I)(a), for example, should read: 'Minimize *the expression of beliefs which* express or imply cost to other', and the other maxims should be similarly expanded. In that they recommend the expression of polite rather than impolite beliefs, all of them come under the PP. The first four maxims go in pairs because they deal with bipolar scales: the cost–benefit and praise–dispraise scales. The other two maxims deal with unipolar scales: the scales of agreement and sympathy. Although there are various connecting links between the scales, each maxim is distinct in that it refers to an evaluative scale which is distinct from the scales referred to by the others. Whereas (I) and (II) respectively concern the cost of benefit of future action to *other* and to *self*, (III) and (IV) respectively concern the degree to which s's remarks convey some good or bad evaluation of *other* and of *self*. For example, the Approbation Maxim is exemplified in the intrinsic courtesy of congratulations, and the Modesty Maxim in that of apologies.

Although Searle's categories of illocution (5.2) correlate only roughly with different types of politeness, I have associated one or more of these categories with each maxim. Since his fifth category of 'declarations' does not involve politeness (5.1), however, this category is excluded from the list. In justifying these maxims I shall draw on various kinds of evidence: the evidence of pragmatic asymmetries between *s* and *h*, of implicatures, and of indirectness generally. (The Tact Maxim has already been fully illustrated in 5.3–5.8.)

Not all of the maxims and sub-maxims are equally important. Of the twinned maxims (I)–(IV), (I) appears to be a more powerful constraint on conversational behaviour than (II), and (III) than (IV). This, if true, reflects a more general law that politeness is focused more strongly on *other* than on *self*. Moreover, within each maxim, sub-maxim (b) seems to be less important than sub-maxim (a), and this again illustrates the more general law that negative politeness (avoidance of discord) is a more weighty consideration than positive politeness (seeking concord). One further difference in importance should be noted, although it is not reflected in the form of the maxims: politeness towards an addressee is generally more important than politeness towards a third party.

Once more we should bear in mind that these maxims are observed 'up to a certain point', rather than as absolute rules. It is particularly important to remember this with the weaker sub-maxims, those in square brackets, such as 'Maximize dispraise of self'. A person who continually seeks opportunities for self-denigration quickly becomes tedious, and more importantly, will be judged insincere. In this way the CP (Maxim of Quality) restrains us from being too modest, just as in other circumstances it restrains us from being too tactful.

6.1.1 The Generosity Maxim
MINIMIZE BENEFIT TO SELF: MAXIMIZE COST TO SELF

I have already mentioned the bilateral aspect of impositive and commissive speech acts. Bilaterality means that in practice, there is little need to distinguish the '*other*-centred' Maxim of Tact from the '*self*-centred' Maxim of Generosity. The asymmetry of [1] and [2] or of [3] and [4], for example, can be explained in terms of either of these maxims:

[1] [†]You can lend me your car. ([†]impolite)
[2] I can lend you my car.
[3] You must come and have dinner with us.
[4] [†]We must come and have dinner with you. ([†]impolite)

(*Note*: The dagger[+] indicates that this utterance is markedly less acceptable, in terms of absolute politeness, than the utterance with which it is paired; remember that we are still concerned with *absolute* rather than *relative* politeness.)

The offer [2] and invitation [3] are presumed to be polite for two reasons: firstly, because they imply benefit to *h*, and secondly and less crucially, because they imply cost to *s*. But in [1] and [4], the relation between *s* and *h* on both scales is reversed. On the other hand, sometimes the illocution is such that the Tact Maxim alone is relevant: a piece of advice such as *You can get them for less than half the price at the market* is meant to be beneficial to *h*, but does not imply any cost to *s* apart from the verbal effort to giving the advice itself. In yet other cases, the Generosity Maxim appears to apply without the Tact Maxim: for example, a request for a second helping is slightly more polite if *h*'s role as potential benefactor is suppressed: *Could I have some more X*? Marginally still greater politeness is achieved if reference is omitted to *s* as beneficiary: *Is there some more X*? But the hypothesis that the Generosity Maxim is less powerful than the Tact Maxim is supported by the observation that an impositive can be softened, and thereby made more polite, by omission of reference to the cost to *h*. This restricts the description of the action *A* to *s*'s benefit from the transaction:

[5] Could I borrow this electric drill?

is marginally more polite than *Could you lend me this electric drill*? And (say)

[6] I wouldn't mind a cup of coffee

is marginally more polite than *Could you spare me a cup of coffee*? This is because the illocutionary goals of [5] and [6] overtly compete with the Generosity Maxim, but not with the Tact Maxim. There is a converse tendency to suppress *s*'s part of the transaction in commissives:

[7] You could borrow my bicycle, if you like
   (*cf* I could lend you my bicycle, if you like).
[8] Would you like these pencils sharpened?
   (*cf* Would you like me to sharpen these pencils?)

The playing down of *s*'s beneficent role here is a mirror image of the strategy in [5] and [6]. The idea is that it is more polite, in an offer, to make it appear that the offerer makes no sacrifice, so that in turn it can become less impolite for *h* to accept the offer.

6.1.2 The Approbation Maxim

MINIMIZE DISPRAISE OF OTHER; MAXIMIZE PRAISE OF OTHER.

An unflattering subtitle for the Approbation Maxim would be 'the Flattery Maxim' – but the term 'flattery' is generally reserved for *insincere* approbation. In its more important negative aspect, this maxim says 'avoid saying unpleasant things about others, and more particularly, about *h*'. Hence whereas a compliment like *What a marvellous meal you cooked!* is highly valued according to the Approbation Maxim, †*What an awful meal you cooked!* is not. Similarly, it is acceptably polite to say (referring to the performance of a musician):

[9] *A*: Her performance was outstanding! *B*: Yes, wasn't it!

But suppose that *B* is the performer:

[10] *A*: Your performance was outstanding! *B*: †Yes, wasn't it!

In this case, *B* falls foul of the Modesty Maxim, to which we shall turn in the next section.

Since dispraise of *h* or of a third party is impolite, it is understandable that, as in the case of the Tact Maxim, various strategies of indirectness are employed in order to mitigate the effect of criticism:

[11] *A*: Her performance was magnificent, wasn't it! *B*: Was it?

Assuming that both *A* and *B* listened to the performance, *B*'s reply is evasive and implicates an unfavourable opinion. By questioning *A*'s statement, *B* implicates that he is not sure whether *A*'s judgement is correct. The impolite implicature derives from the unlikelihood that *B*'s question is simply a request for information, and from the fact that if *B* had been able, sincerely, to agree with *A*, *B* would (by the PP) have done so.

In this case, *B* apparently violates the CP (Maxim of Quantity). Grice gives another example of an uninformative reply: that of a person who writes a reference for a student applying for a philosophy job:

[12] 'Dear Sir, Mr. X's command of English is excellent, and his attendance at tutorials has been regular. Yours, etc.'

[Grice 1975:52]

In explaining the implicature of this violation of the Maxim of Quantity. Grice adds that *s* '. . . must . . . be wishing to impart information that he is reluctant to write down. The supposition is tenable only on the assumption that he thinks Mr. X is no good at philosophy.' I would add, to supplement Grice's gloss, that *s*'s reluctance to declare his opinion is due to the Approbation Maxim.

In other cases, the reluctance to criticize manifests itself in institutionalized forms of understatement:

[13] You could be more careful.
[14] Her performance was not so good as it might have been.
[15] A: Do you like these apricots? B: I've tasted better.

With reference to some scale of value, these sentences in effect say 'a higher position on the scale is possible'. But where the Approbation Maxim is in force, a failure to commit oneself to a favourable opinion implies that one cannot (truthfully) do so. In other words, the lack of praise implicates dispraise.

6.1.3 The Modesty Maxim
MINIMIZE PRAISE OF SELF: MAXIMIZE DISPRAISE OF SELF.
The Modesty Maxim, like the other maxims of politeness, shows itself in asymmetries:

[16] A: They were so kind to us.   B: Yes, they were, weren't they.
[17] A: You were so kind to us.   B: †Yes, I was, wasn't I.
[18] How stupid of me!   [18a] †How clever of me!
[19] †How stupid of you!   [19a] How clever of you!
[20] Please accept this small gift as a token of our esteem.
[21] †Please accept this large gift as a token of our esteem.

As [16] shows, it is felicitous to agree with another's commendation except when it is a commendation of oneself. Similarly [18] shows how self-dispraise is regarded as quite benign, even when it is exaggerated for comic effect. In [20], the understatement of one's generosity is shown to be quite normal, and indeed, conventional, in contrast to the exaggeration of one's generosity. As [17] and [21] illustrate, to break the first submaxim of Modesty is to commit the social transgression of boasting.

The following conversation between two Japanese women (quoted from Miller 1967: 289–90) exemplifies how a pragmatic 'paradox' can arise through the conflict of the Modesty and Approbation Maxims, just as it can (see 5.4) through the conflict of the Tact and Generosity Maxims when an offer is repeatedly declined. In this case, the pragmatic paradox takes the form of repeatedly denying the truth of a compliment:

A   A
mā, go-rippa na o-niwa de   My, what a splendid garden

gozāmasu wa nē. shibafu ga hirobiro to shite ite, kekkō de gozāmasu wa nē.

B

iie, nan desu ka, chitto mo teire ga yukitodokimasen mono de gozaimasu kara, mō, nakanaka itsumo kirei ni shite oku wake ni wa mairi-masen no de gozāmasu yo.

A

ā, sai de gozaimashō nē. kore dake o-hiroin de gozāmasu kara, hitotōri o-teire asobasu no ni datte taihen de gozai-mashō nē. demo mā, sore de mo, itsumo yoku o-teire ga yukitodoite irasshaimasu wa. itsumo honto ni o-kirei de kekkō de gozāmasu wa.

B

iie, chitto mo sonna koto gazāmasen wa.

you have here – the lawn is so nice and big, it's certainly wonderful, isn't it!

B

Oh no, not at all, we don't take care of it at all any more, so it simply doesn't always look as nice as we would like it to.

A

Oh no, I don't think so at all – but since it's such a big garden, of course, it must be quite a tremendous task to take care of it all by yourself; but even so, you certainly do manage to make it look nice all the time: it certainly is nice and pretty any time one sees it.

B

No. I'm afraid not, not at all . . . .

It appears that in Japanese society, and more particularly among Japanese women (see Miller, *ibid*: 290), the Modesty Maxim is more powerful than it is as a rule in English-speaking societies, where it would be customarily more polite to accept a compli-ment 'graciously' (*eg* by thanking the speaker for it) rather than to go on denying it. Here English-speakers would be inclined to find some compromise between violating the Modesty Maxim and violating the Agreement Maxim.

There is an obvious trade-off between different maxims of the PP, just as there is between the maxims of the CP. The Modesty Maxim sometimes comes into conflict with some other maxim, in which case we have to allow one maxim to take priority over the other. In [17], for example, *B* adheres to the Agreement Maxim at the expense of the Modesty Maxim, but in this situation the Modesty Maxim plainly carries greater weight. In the Japanese conversation above, *A partially* agrees with *B* over the work en-tailed by the garden, but then reiterates her compliment. In offer-ing food to a guest, a Japanese may say *Ohitotsu dōzo*[2] (literally 'Please [have] one'), thereby apparently minimizing generosity. But this may be seen as a result of attaching greater importance to modesty: to offer more than one is to suggest that one's food is worth eating. In contrast, an English-speaking host might well be considered niggardly if he passed round the peanut-bowl with the words: *Have a peanut!* It is normally considered to be more polite to offer a large quantity: *Have as many as you like.* The greater value attached to the Modesty maxim in Japanese culture is indicated further by the greater degree of understatement employed in giving presents. Whereas an English person may (as in [20]) call his gift 'small', the Japanese may go further, and say 'This is a gift which will be of no use to you, but . . .' A host may even go to the extreme of denying the existence of the food he is offering:

> Nani mo (meshiagaru mono wa) ari-masen ga, dōzo
> 'There is nothing (to eat), but please . . .'

In this way, a maxim of politeness may overrule the Maxim of Quality.

6.1.4 Other maxims of politeness

Although there is less evidence for other maxims, it is worth noting, for example, that there is a tendency to exaggerate agreement with other people, and to mitigate disagreement by expressing regret, partial agreement, etc. We must therefore talk in terms of a Maxim of Agreement. Compare the rudeness of the reply in [22] with the replies in [23]–[25]:

> [22] *A*: It was an interesting exhibition, wasn't it?
> 　　　*B*: †No, it was very *un*interesting.
> [23] *A*: A referendum will satisfy everybody.
> 　　　*B*: Yes, definitely.
> [24] *A*: English is a difficult language to learn.
> 　　　*B*: True, but the grammar is quite easy.
> [25] *A*: The book is tremendously well written.
> 　　　*B*: Yes, well written as a whole, but there are some rather boring patches, don't you think?

As [24] and [25] show, partial disagreement is often preferable to complete disagreement. We may also add a Maxim of Sympathy, which explains why congratulations and condolences are courteous speech acts, even though condolences express beliefs which are negative with regard to the hearer:

> [26] I'm terribly sorry to hear that your cat died.

This is polite, in contrast, for example, with †*I'm terribly pleased to hear that your cat died.* There is nevertheless some reticence about expression of condolences, since to refer to the propositional context X is in fact to express an impolite belief (see 7.4) in the sense of a belief unfavourable to h. Hence it might be preferable to say, instead of [26]:

[27] I'm terribly sorry to hear about your cat.

Such is the power of the Sympathy Maxim that, without further information, we interpret [27] as a condolence, *ie* as an expression of sympathy for misfortune, and [28] as a congratulation:

[28] I'm delighted to hear about your cat.

That is, we assume that the event alluded to in [27] is unfortunate (such as a death), and that in [28] is fortunate (such as the winning of a prize in the cat-show). Thus, the following exchange would be, to say the least, atypical of human conversation:

[29] *A*: I'm delighted to hear about your cat.
     B: What do you mean? He's just died.
     A: Precisely.

6.2 Metalinguistic aspects of politeness

Politeness is manifested not only in the *content* of conversation, but also in the way conversation is managed and structured by its participants. For example, conversational behaviour such as speaking at the wrong time (interrupting) or being silent at the wrong time has impolite implications. Consequently we sometimes find it necessary to refer to the speech acts in which we or our interlocutors are engaged, in order to request a reply, to seek permission for speaking, to apologize for speaking, etc.:

[30] *Could you tell me* what time the bus leaves, please?
[31] *May I ask* if you're married?
[32] *I must warn you* not to discuss this in public.
[33] *We regret to inform you* that the aspidistra stands are no longer obtainable.

Such utterances are 'metalinguistic' in that they refer, in the mode of *oratio obliqua* (8.3, 8.4), to illocutions of the current conversation. Sentences such as [31]–[33] have, in fact, been known as hedged performatives,[3] since they may be regarded as polite mitigations of utterances such as *I warn you that X, We inform you that X*. The avoidance of a direct-speech utterance can be one more example of a strategy of polite obliquity: [31], for example, is a more tactful variant of *Are you married*? Like other indirect impositives, [30] and [31] employ the Hinting Strategy:

obtaining the conversational cooperation of h, which is the ostensible function of [30], is a preliminary goal leading to the ultimate goal of obtaining information.

Why does a speaker sometimes find it advisable to use such metalinguistic strategies? Part of the reason is that speech acts are like other kinds of action in involving some cost of benefit to s or h. Minimally, for example, answering a question involves some cooperative effort on the part of the person addressed; and in addition, some questions, such as *How old are you?* or *Are you married?* may be felt to be a serious imposition in that they threaten the privacy of h.[4] In this light, [31] is felt to be to some extent a genuine request for permission: s seeks to be allowed to intrude on the private territory of h, and even though h would find it difficult to reply without giving the information desired, the *May I ask you...?* is more than a vacuous formality. It is understandable, then, that 'hedged performatives' are used as devices of politeness, especially when h is a person of a more authoritative status than s. We cannot automatically assume the right to engage someone in conversation, let alone to use that conversation as a means to our own ends. Even some ostensibly 'polite' illocutions, such as giving advice, may be judged to be impositions, requiring a preface such as *Could I suggest...?*, or *Might I just give you a word of advice?* The reason for regarding advice as impolite, of course, is that although the recommended action A may be considered beneficial to the addressee, the actual speech act of advising may offend both the Modesty and Approbation Maxims, because it takes for granted that s is superior in knowledge, or experience, or judgement, etc. to h. Unambivalently polite illocutions, on the other hand, may be introduced by a 'hedged performative' which stresses the desirability or even inevitability of the illocution:

I want to thank you...
We are delighted to announce...
I must tell you how much I admire your...

Bringers of bad tidings may find it advisable to express both the distasteful and the unavoidable nature of their task:

I'm sorry to have to tell you...
We regret to have to inform you that...
I must warn you that...

To engage a person in conversation, particularly if that person is a stranger or a superior (*ie* an addressee who is 'distant' in terms of the horizontal and vertical scales discussed in 5.7), may itself be regarded as an act of presumption, for conversation implies cooperation on the part of *h* as well as of *s*. This probably explains in part why, in the historical development of some languages (such as Italian, Portuguese, and German), polite forms of address have developed out of third-person pronouns and verb forms, as if *s* can only politely enter into conversation with *h* through the evasive tactic of pretending that *h* is a listener, but not an addressee. It may also explain in part the tact in English of indirect askings such as *I wonder if you would lend me your coat*. The implicature here seems to be that *s* does not feel entitled to ask *h* a question, and therefore expresses interest in knowing the answer to the question in a manner which suggests that it is no part of *h*'s responsibility to provide it.

The polite and impolite implications of silence must also be considered.[5] The adage on which the children of a previous age were reared, 'Don't speak unless you are spoken to', reminds us that silence may be the only polite form of behaviour available to someone of little status. But if one has been engaged in conversation by someone else, silence is a sign of opting out of a social engagement to observe the interpersonal rhetorical principles, and is hence in many circumstances a form of impoliteness. These contradictory implications of silence sometimes lead to a pragmatic impasse when two or more people engaged in conversation are joined by an outsider. The newcomer may feel it rude to interrupt the conversation, but the participants may feel it rude not to give the newcomer a chance to join in. The result may be an uncomfortable hiatus in the conversation.

The problem of how to end a conversation politely is familiar to every competent language user, and makes us aware of the close connection between politeness and the activity of talking merely to preserve sociability, the type of behaviour which Malinowski (1930) named PHATIC COMMUNION. We may, indeed, argue for an additional maxim of politeness, the metalinguistic 'Phatic Maxim' which may be provisionally formulated either in its negative form 'Avoid silence' or in its positive form 'Keep talking'.[6] It is the need to avoid silence, with its implication of opting out of communication, which accounts, at a rather trivial level, for the discussion of stock subjects such as the weather, and less trivially, for the occurrence of uninformative statements such as *You've had your hair cut!* As such remarks patently violate the Maxim of Quantity, here is yet another case where an apparent breach of the CP is to be explained in terms of another maxim – in this instance the Phatic Maxim. However, it is inadequate to describe phatic communion as simple avoidance of silence. More positively, such conversation, if it has no other illocutionary point, serves to extend the common ground of agreement and experience shared by the participants. Hence the choice of subject matter tends to be non-controversial, and to concentrate on the attitudes of the speakers, rather than on matters of fact. In this context, even *You've had your hair cut!* makes its contribution to the progress of the conversation, by making *h* aware that *s* has *noticed* something of which *s* is already aware, and by giving *h* an opportunity to elaborate on personal experience in a new direction. On the assumption that such exploration of common ground of experience and attitude is always possible, we might therefore treat avoidance of silence as a special case of the Agreement and Sympathy Maxims (6.1.4). But whether or not the Phatic Maxim is to be subsumed under these other maxims, it seems reasonable to argue that in this case, as in others, the apparent uninformativeness of language is to be attributed to other conversational principles, and is not to be regarded as evidence against the validity of the CP.

6.3 Irony and banter

The previous discussion of irony (4.1) has suggested that the Irony Principle (IP) takes its place alongside the CP and the PP in the Interpersonal Rhetoric.[7] This principle, however, is parasitic on the other two, in the following sense. The CP and the PP can be seen to be functional by direct reference to their role in promoting effective interpersonal communication; but the IP's function can only be explained in terms of other principles. The IP is a 'second-order principle' which enables a speaker to be impolite while seeming to be polite; it does so by superficially breaking the CP, but ultimately upholding it. Apparently, then, the IP is *dys*-functional: if the PP promotes a bias towards comity rather than conflict in social relations, the IP, by enabling us to bypass politeness, promotes the 'antisocial' use of language. We are ironic at someone's expense, scoring off others by politeness that is obviously insincere, as a substitute for impoliteness.

The insincerity may be more or less obvious; it may take the form of a breach of the Maxim of Quantity (as on *pp* 80, 82), or more often of a breach of the Maxim of Quality:

[34] That's all I wanted!
[35] With friends like him, who needs enemies?
[36] Bill wanted that news like he wanted a hole in the head.

Used ironically, [34] is taken to mean 'That's exactly what I did *not* want'. Here the falseness of the statement will probably be

made clear by a contradictory tone of utterance, more appropriate to the sentiment of 'That's the last straw'. In [35] and [36], the
Maxim of Quality is infringed by implicature rather than by direct
statement. But the insincerity of *s*'s purported opinion is clear
from its absurdity. Thus [35] purports to express a belief that
enemies are a good thing, and [36] presents a similarly favourable
view of holes in the head. An indirect violation of the Maxim of
Quality is also present in imperatives such as *Don't mind MĚ*
(*will you?*) addressed to a person who has just, say, rudely
barged into the speaker; or *DÒ help yoursélf* (*won't you?*), said
to someone who is only too obviously helping himself already. A
command, to be felicitous in a goal-oriented model, requires that
the addressee has not yet complied with it. This condition is
violated in the above examples. In a rather similar way, the
question *Do you have to spill ash on the carpet?* implicates the
speaker's belief that *h* may be incapable of avoiding the fault in
question. In each of these cases, therefore, *s* appears to make an
innocent assumption which is patently untrue, and by that means
implicates that the opposite assumption, which is impolite, is
true.

The ironic force of a remark is often signalled by exaggeration
or understatement, which makes it difficult for *h* to interpret the
remark at its face value. The speaker of [34], for example, pre-
tends to take up an extreme position in saying that *That's all* (*ie*
the *only* thing) *I wanted*. The ironic force would not have been
registered if *s* had simply said the opposite of the truth, as in
That's what I wanted. This instance of exaggeration may be coun-
terposed to an understatement such as *Some of his words were
not Sunday school words* (Mark Twain), which is also ironic, but
for the opposite reason. In this case it is the Maxim of Quantity,
not the Maxim of Quality that is most directly violated. By negative uninformativeness (see 4.5.1) *s* politely implicates that 'one
expects all of his words to be Sunday School words'. But clearly
this is a false expectation. Therefore we infer, as before, the
opposite state of affairs to be the true one: that the man was
given to using bad language. Unlike [34], this is not an untrue
proposition, but merely a highly uninformative one. Ironic understatement typically, by negation, makes a claim which is manifestly far weaker than a claim that could be made.

Irony varies in force from the comic irony of Mark Twain to
the more offensive irony of sarcastic commands such as *Do help
yourself*. Although it appears to be dysfunctional, in providing a
method of being offensive to others, the IP may well have a positive function in permitting aggression to manifest itself in a less

dangerous verbal form than by direct criticism, insults, threats, etc. Whereas an insult can easily lead to a counter-insult, and hence to conflict, an ironic remark is less easy to answer in kind. It combines the art of attack with an apparent innocence which is a form of self-defence. The function of irony may thus be tentatively explained as follows. If the PP breaks down, it is liable to break down on both sides: direct accusation leads to counter-accusation, threat to counter-threat, and so on. But because irony pays lip-service to the PP, it is less easy to break the PP in one's response to it. Hence the IP keeps aggression away from the brink of conflict.

If we acknowledge the existence of an Irony Principle, we should also acknowledge another 'higher-order principle' which has the opposite effect. While irony is an apparently friendly way of being offensive (mock-politeness), the type of verbal behaviour known as 'banter' is an offensive way of being friendly (mock-impoliteness).

The Banter Principle, as we may call it, is clearly of minor importance compared with other rhetorical principles we have examined. But it is manifested in a great deal of casual linguistic conversation, particularly among young people.[8] For example, in a game of chess, one person may say jokingly to another: *What a mean cowardly trick*! referring to a particular clever gambit. Or two friends may greet one another with remarks such as *Here comes trouble*! or *Look what the cat's brought in*! This principle might be expressed as follows:

'In order to show solidarity with h, say something which is (i) obviously untrue, and (ii) obviously impolite to h.'

Like irony, banter must be clearly recognizable as unserious. Since overpoliteness, as we have seen (p 82), can have the effect of signifying superiority or ironic distance, underpoliteness can have the opposite effect of establishing or maintaining a bond of familiarity. The reason is this. A low value on the scales of authority and social distance (5.7) correlates with a low position on the scale of politeness; that is, the more intimate the relationship, the less important it is to be polite. Hence lack of politeness in itself can become a sign of intimacy; and hence, the ability to be impolite to someone in jest helps to establish and maintain such a familiar relationship. The implicature derived from the Banter Principle is just the opposite of that derived from the IP (see p 83):

'What s says is impolite to h and is clearly untrue. Therefore what s really means is polite to h and true.'

We might go so far as to call the Banter Principle a 'third-order principle', because it may itself exploit irony. Banter could be described as mock-irony in cases like *A fine friend YÒU are!*, said jokingly (say) to a partner who has given away an advantage in a card game. The interpretation of this utterance requires a double reversal of values:

(i) You are a fine friend. (face-value)
(ii) By which I mean that you are NOT a fine friend. (Irony Principle)
(iii) But actually, you ARE my friend, and to show it, I am being impolite to you. (Banter Principle)

The 'higher-order' principles, in that they rely upon the implicatures of 'lower-order' principles, involve greater indirectness in the working-out of the force of the utterance, and are therefore less powerful in their effect. For this reason, we can place the PP, the IP, and the Banter Principle in a hierarchy of importance, corresponding to the order in which they have just been mentioned.

6.4 Hyperbole and litotes

Two ways of apparently violating the CP which deserve separate consideration are HYPERBOLE (overstatement) and LITOTES (understatement). Naming these devices by their classical names brings to mind their role in traditional rhetoric, and pertinently recalls the continuity between 'rhetoric' as it is understood here and 'rhetoric' as it has been variously understood since the time of Aristotle.

To understand these pragmatic strategies, we first have to appreciate that truthfulness is not always a matter of making a straightforward choice between truth and falsehood. Just as truth conditions are often to be represented in terms of values on a scale, so telling the truth may itself be judged as a matter of degree, according to how accurate *s* is in representing such scalar values. 'Hyperbole' refers to a case where the speaker's description is stronger than is warranted by the state of affairs described, and 'litotes' refers to the converse of this. A hyperbole such as *It made my blood boil* constitutes a violation, in some degree, of the Maxim of Quality, and a litotes such as *I wasn't born yesterday* constitutes in some degree a violation of the Maxim of Quantity. But as with irony, the violation of the CP is only a superficial matter: we would not apply these rhetorical terms to utterances in which overstatement or understatement was actually used to deceive the addressee. Moreover, as with irony, the best safeguard against deceit is to make sure the utterance is so much at variance with context that no one could reasonably believe it to be 'the whole truth, and nothing but the truth'. Hence hyperbole and litotes are further illustrations of the by now familiar pattern of conversational implicature: we reach the indirect force of *s*'s remark by means of an obvious face-value violation of the CP.[9]

We have already met cases where the justification for hyperbole and litotes is politeness. There will naturally be a preference for overstating polite beliefs, and for understating impolite ones: while an exaggeration such as *That was a delicious meal!* is favoured in praising others, an uninformative denial – a typical device of understatement – is frequently used in criticism: *I wasn't overimpressed by her speech*. The understating of praise will normally be directed towards *s* rather than towards *h*:

[37] That wasn't such a bad meal that I cooked.
[38] That wasn't such a bad meal that you cooked.

The grudging compliment of [37] is relatively acceptable as a form of self-congratulation; but [38] is glaringly impolite as a compliment to a hostess on her cuisine, more especially because the negative statement implicates that it was to be expected that the meal would be bad (see 4.5.1).

But not all cases of hyperbole and litotes can be explained by reference to their role in enhancing politeness. The frequency of overstatement in ordinary conversation has its testimony in many idiomatic expressions, as in *Her eyes nearly popped out of her head*; *It makes my blood boil*; *He was all ears*; *That'll cost the earth*; *I've been working my fingers to the bone*, etc.; also in the exaggerated use of universal quantifiers and references to the extremities of scales: *eg: I'm completely broke*; *There's absolutely nothing on the telly this evening*. Almost all these examples make reference to an absurdly extreme position on a scale; *eg: Her eyes nearly popped out of her head* refers to the highest conceivable point on a scale of surprise, and *It made my blood boil* refers to the highest conceivable point on a scale of anger.

A conversational principle which seems to underlie such cases is the principle which enjoins us to

'Say what is unpredictable, and hence interesting.'

At the risk of proliferating too many pragmatic principles, I shall tentatively propose, then, an Interest Principle, by which conversation which is interesting, in the sense of having unpredictability or news value, is preferred to conversation which is boring and predictable. One common way in which this principle manifests itself in our everyday linguistic experience is the temptation we feel, when retelling a personal anecdote, to embroider on the anecdote various kinds of elaboration and exaggeration. Another sign of this principle is the way in which hyperbolic expressions become weakened through a process of diminishing returns (in this respect they resemble euphemisms). If overstatements are used frequently, an addressee inevitably adjusts his interpretation so that they lose their interest value and become predictable. There is thus a perpetual tug-of-war, in human conversation, between the Maxim of Quality and the Interest Principle.[10]

If hyperbole is, in this sense, a natural tendency of human speech, it is difficult to understand why the opposite tendency of litotes is so often observed. Part of the explanation is that there is a dialectic between hyperbole and litotes somewhat parallel to that between politeness and irony. Just as irony is a 'second-order principle' which sacrifices politeness for the sake of the CP, so litotes is a 'second-order principle' which sacrifices the interest-ingness of overstatement for the sake of the honesty of under-statement. If hyperbole suffers from diminishing returns because of incredulity, it is a salutary tactic to move in the opposite direc-tion, and to restore credibility by using descriptions which so obviously fall short of what could be truthfully asserted that they cannot be supposed exaggerated. Litotes therefore regains the credit which goes with strict observance of the Maxim of Quality, and which is sacrificed by hyperbole.

To elucidate the motivation for litotes further, I shall call upon yet another principle: one that has been acknowledged by psychologists under the title of the 'Pollyanna Hypothesis'.[11] This states that people will prefer to look on the bright side rather than on the gloomy side of life, thus resembling the optimistic heroine of Eleanor H. Porter's novel *Pollyanna* (1913). Interpret-ing it in a communicative framework as a 'Pollyanna Principle' means postulating that participants in a conversation will prefer pleasant topics of conversation to unpleasant ones. The negative aspect of this principle is, of course, EUPHEMISM: one can dis-guise unpleasant subjects by referring to them by means of apparently inoffensive expressions (*eg* workers are 'made redun-dant' instead of being 'dismissed'). But another aspect is the tendency to understate the degree to which things are bad. Thus the 'minimizing' adverbials of degree *a bit*, *a little*, and *a little bit* are specialized towards negatively evaluated terms:

[39] The paint was a bit dirty.
[40] †The paint was a bit clean.

Another restriction, which seems to have become institutionalized in grammar, is that *a bit* and *a little* can occur with the negatively evaluative adverb *too*, but not with the positively evaluative adverb *enough*:

[41] She is *a little too* young for the job.
[42] *She is *a little* young *enough* for the job.

Another adverb which often implicates a negative evaluation is *rather*, which again tends to add a downtoning effect to the term it modifies:

[43] The employees were *rather unenthusiastic* about the move.
[44] The employees were *rather enthusiastic* about the move.

Although both [43] and [44] are perfectly grammatical, [44] is pragmatically abnormal in comparison with [43]. A third technique for understating pessimistic evaluation is the one we have already observed – the use of negation:

[45] The meeting was not particularly well attended.
[46] †The meeting was not particularly badly attended.

As a negative proposition is assumed to deny a positive expectation, [45] takes as its norm the corresponding positive proposition 'The meeting was particularly well attended'. Hence even if the meeting had been quite well attended, it would be truthful to assert [45]. In this way, the understatement disguises a bad report in a form which on the face of it permits a good interpretation. The unfavourable interpretation is arrived at indirectly, by implicature, and is thus weakened. The opposite proposition [46] is pragmatically less favoured, because it runs counter to the Pollyanna Principle. It would occur only in an unusual context, where for some reason bad attendance was expected.

We can see, then, that litotes is a way of underplaying aspects of meaning which are pragmatically disfavoured. In [45], it is the pessimistic judgement that the meeting was badly attended that is thus mitigated. In other examples, it is impoliteness that it is mitigated, as in the following examples of modest self-praise:

[47] Actually, I'm *rather* good at crossword puzzles.
[48] We're *rather* proud of our classless profession.

Hyperbole and litotes are not single pragmatic principles, but rather general tendencies which occur whenever some pragmatic principle brings about a distortion of the truth. The influence of the PP, for example, causes both polite overstatement and polite understatement. The influence of the Pollyanna Principle causes both optimistic overstatement and euphemistic understatement. But there is in addition a type of litotes (illustrated by [44]) which seems to function simply as an antidote to the opposite tendency to exaggerate in keeping with the Principle of Interest:

[49] She's *not* a *bad-looking* girl.
[50] There are some *rather splendid* murals on the North Wall.

Here the understatement, which untypically acts in mitigation of a favourable quality, appears to be a guarantee of the honesty of the speaker's opinion, reasserting, against the Principle of Interest, the value of the CP.

6.5 Conclusion

This chapter has moved from relatively firm ground – the maxims of politeness – to a more uncertain area where I have speculated on the role in conversational rhetoric of such traditional rhetorical devices as irony, hyperbole, and litotes. I have suggested how these can be broadly integrated into the Gricean paradigm of conversational principles and implicatures, thereby helping to account for indirect relationships between sense and force in ways which supplement the maxims of the CP and the PP. I can now present a summary of the principles and maxims of the Interper-

TABLE 6.1 Interpersonal Rhetoric

First-order principles	Higher-order principles	Contributory maxims
Cooperative Principle		Quantity Quality Relation Manner
Politeness Principle		{ Tact Generosity { Approbation Modesty Agreement Sympathy Phatic?
	Irony Banter	
Interest Principle Pollyanna Principle		

sonal Rhetoric as it has been enlarged by the additions of this chapter (Table 6.1). There is clearly a great deal to be done in elaborating this plan, and in solving some of the problems it raises. One of the problems is this: describing irony, hyperbole, and similar effects in terms of pragmatic principles emphasizes the social perspective on language at the expense of the psychological. Thus, for instance, the choice between hyperbole and litotes can in part be described in terms of a goal-oriented model, but must also take account of differences in the personality, the attitude, and so on of the language user. This is true of all components of the Interpersonal Rhetoric, but is probably less true of the CP and PP than of the other principles.

Another aspect of the subject which this chapter has neglected is the typological study of cultures and languages in relation to the Interpersonal Rhetoric. So far, our knowledge of intercultural differences in this sphere is somewhat anecdotal: there is the observation for example, that some eastern cultures (*eg* China and Japan) tend to value the Modesty Maxim much more highly than western countries; that English-speaking culture (particularly British?) gives prominence to the Maxim of Tact and the Irony Principle; that Mediterranean cultures place a higher value of the Generosity Maxim and a lower value of the Modesty Maxim. These observations assume, of course, that such principles, being the general functional 'imperatives' of human communication, are more or less universal, but that their relative weights will vary from one cultural, social, or linguistic milieu to another. Although these matters remain unclear in detail, the Interpersonal Rhetoric provides a framework in which they may be systematically investigated.

Notes

1. The existence of both second-person and third-person politeness is well demonstrated in languages where there exist special polite and honorific morphemes in relation to both addressee and referent. See Kuno (1973:18–22) on the honorific system of Japanese. Comrie (1976), in discussing languages with rich honorific systems, distinguishes between three separate axes of politeness: the speaker–addressee, speaker–referent, and speaker–bystander axes.
2. I am indebted to Hideshi Sato for this and the following Japanese illustrations.
3. The pragmatic and semantic implications of hedged performatives are explored in Fraser (1975).
4. Relevant here is Goffman's (1963, 1967, 1971) work on *face* and *territories of self*.

5. See Sacks, Schegloff, and Jefferson (1974) on turn-taking conventions.

6. On the communicative value of silence, see Verschueren (forthcoming), Chapter 3.

7. See note 2, Chapter 4, *p* 102.

8. A ritualized form of banter is the activity of 'sounding' (a ceremonial exchange of insults) practised in the black community of New York, as studied by Labov (1972). This language-game depends for its effect on the understanding that the allegations made by each party are recognized as untrue, and therefore on the fact that they cannot be mistaken for real insults.

9. Grice (1975:53) cites hyperbole and litotes (or meiosis) as floutings of the Maxim of Quality.

10. De Beaugrande and Dressler (1981: 144, 160, 213) examine 'interestingness' as a desideratum of a text. On the one hand, they associate it with unexpectedness and informativeness (*cf* the Maxim of Quantity), and on the other hand they see it as in conflict with 'knownness' (*cf* the Maxim of Quality).

11. The Pollyanna Hypothesis (Boucher and Osgood 1969) has been used to explain why words of pleasant associations predominate over those with unpleasant ones, and also why speakers tend to conceal the badness of things through negative expressions (see Clark and Clark 1977:538–9). Rather than reflecting a human tendency to be optimistic, it may represent the tendency to associate the normal with the good, and the abnormal with the bad. If so, a familiar case of competition between the Pollyanna Principle and the Interest Principle is found in (uncensored) newspapers and news broadcasts, where interestingness, and hence newsworthiness, is strongly associated with what is unpleasant. ('Bad news is good news.')

Chapter 7

Communicative Grammar: an example

JOHNSON: 'My dear friend, clear your *mind* of cant. You may *talk* as other people do: you may say to a man, "Sir, I am your most humble servant." You are *not* his most humble servant.... You tell a man, "I am sorry you had such bad weather the last day of your journey, and were so much wet." You don't care six-pence whether he was wet or dry. You may *talk* in this manner; it is a mode of talking in Society: but don't *think* foolishly.'

[James Boswell, *The Life of Johnson*, 15 May, 1783]

7.1 Communicative Grammar and pragmatic force

In the preceding chapters I have tried to develop in more detail the approach to pragmatics briefly stated in Chapters 1 and 2. My aim is now to give an example of how this approach works out in practice, by applying it to the pragmatics of negation and interrogation in English. The analysis will necessarily be rather informal, but it will be elaborated in more detail than has been practicable so far.

One of the implications of this model is that we can analyse any grammatical category (say negation, modality, or interrogation) on three distinct levels. The most familiar level to linguists is the syntactic: we can describe, for example, how to form negative sentences or clauses in English. The second level is the semantic: the level, that is, of sense rather than of force: here we consider, for example, the negative operator in relation to propositional logic. And the third level is the pragmatic: we have already considered, for example, one aspect of the pragmatics of negation in 4.5.1, where the sub-maxim of negative uninformativeness was discussed. We may describe as COMMUNICATIVE GRAMMAR an approach to grammar which aims to relate these three levels of description to each other.

In which direction should the analysis be made? Should we start with syntax, and work out from there to semantics and finally to pragmatics, or should we work in the opposite direction? In principle, there seems to be no good reason for preferring one order to the other; but in practice, it is natural to start with what is relatively well known and clear-cut – the syntax – and to go from there to what is relatively context-variable and unclear – the pragmatics. In deciding on this direction, we implicitly seem to take up the position of the addressee, who (as argued in 2.5.2) arrives at the force of an utterance by decoding its sense and then, by heuristic problem-solving, works out its force, or pragmatic interpretation. This interpretative direction is the one taken, for example, by Grice with his concept of conversational implicature, and by Searle in his discussion of 'indirect speech acts'. Methodologically, this seems to be the soundest way to approach the elucidation of pragmatic force, since if we agree (see 2.4) that pragmatics, like semantics, is a study of publicly conveyed meaning, rather than of the private thoughts or judgements of this or that person, then it is inevitable that we start with the text itself – what is publicly observable – and then attempt to reconstruct from this the meaning which is conveyed, given certain assumptions and certain kinds of knowledge shared by s and h. It is for this reason that I suggested in 1.4(i) that the best role for the pragmatic analyst is that of a bystander or observer: the third person in the exchange.

   Another reason for preferring to work from syntax to pragmatics, or (if you will) from form to function, is the difficulty of pinning down what the force of an utterance is, given (as argued in 3.4) that pragmatic force is essentially non-categorical and indefinitely variable according to context, and that pragmatic description involves indeterminacies and continuous values. In fact, before we embark on the task of exemplifying pragmatic analysis in more detail, the question must be considered: what form does the description of pragmatic force take? To provide a provisional answer, I shall bring together a number of observations which can be made about pragmatic force, on the basis of earlier chapters:

1. The force of an utterance U is defined, for our purposes, by a set of conversational implicatures F (I use 'implicature' in the broad sense of 'a proposition pragmatically inferred from (i) the sense of U, (ii) the assumption that s is observing, in certain respects and to certain degrees, the principles and maxims of the Interpersonal Rhetoric; (iii) contextual knowledge').

2. The set of implicatures F is ordered in such a way that for each implicature it is possible to trace a path whereby it can be inferred, perhaps via intermediate implicatures, to a certain degree of probability, from (i)–(iii) above. The length of this path is a measure of the indirectness of the implicature.

3. Each implicature has a degree of confidence associated with it; this degree of confidence might be formalized as a probability of the implicature's being part of what s meant to convey by U.

4. A subset of the set of implicatures F defines the illocutionary

force of U. This subset (which in the simplest cases has only one member) defines a means–ends analysis of which the uttering of U is the central action, and thereby defines the presumed illocutionary goal of s in uttering U.

5. Another (not always disjoint) subset of F defines in what respects and to what extent s is presumed to be observing the maxims of the Interpersonal Rhetoric. The implicatures in this subset define s's presumed *rhetorical* goals, such as observing certain maxims of the PP.

6. Many implicatures are associated with some value on a pragmatic scale. For example, an implicature in the form of a propositional attitude, such as 's believes that $[X]$', will be associated with a subjective value as to the degree of confidence of that belief. If such values are represented by Greek letters, α, β, . . . then an implicature should be more fully expressed in a form such as 's believes$^\alpha$ that $[X]$'. Similarly, if an implicature has to do with s's observance of the PP, then some value should be attached to the relevant attitudinal predicate to indicate *how* polite s is being. We have already sufficiently noted the scalar nature of politeness: one cannot reduce tact, for example, to a simple yes–no choice between 's is obeying the Tact Maxim' and 's is not obeying the Tact Maxim'. Also, the scalar nature of properties such as informativeness and truthfulness has already been noted in, for example, the trade-off between politeness and sincerity.

7. Some implicatures contain more than one attitudinal predicate, one proposition being embedded in another. For example, an implicature may read: 's assumes$^\alpha$ that $[h$ is being modest$^\beta]$'. In principle, this embedding of one propositional attitude in another can proceed indefinitely.

These general statements about force will do for the present. Obviously, a stricter formulation of the notion of 'pragmatic force' is possible, and I shall return briefly to that question in the final chapter. At present, it is probably the indeterminacy of that notion which will strike readers accustomed to more categorical theories, such as Searle's speech-act theory. I can only say that this indeterminacy is necessarily a prominent factor in any model which attempts to represent realistically how linguistic communication works.

Yet one further kind of indeterminacy must be mentioned: that which comes between Popper's expressive and signalling functions of language. In discussing meaning, we normally assume that what is expressed by s and what is signalled by s are equivalent: that what s plans to communicate, and what is actually conveyed to h are the same. This assumption is, indeed, built into the pragmatic definition of meaning (2.4). But there are two respects in which this match between s's meaning and h's meaning may fail. First, there may, as I have already argued, be an element of planned indeterminacy: the force of U may be to some extent left for negotiation between s and h. Second, there may be an element of unplanned indeterminacy: for example, in the discussion of the Maxim of Relation (4.3) I suggested that relevance is a matter of degree, and that to a certain point it is a matter of choice whether h recognizes s's remarks as relevant to a particular conversational goal or not. To take one of Grice's original examples (1975:54), supposedly an extract from a tea-party conversation:

> A: Mrs X is an old bag.
> (A moment of appalled silence)
> B: The weather has been quite delightful this summer, hasn't it?

In Grice's interpretation, B blatantly violates the Maxim of Relation, and hence implicates that A has committed a social gaffe. But another reading of it, perhaps less likely in this case, is that B is genuinely embarrassed by A's remark, and ineptly changes the subject, without intending that anyone should notice his embarrassment or displeasure. In either case, A's response may be of three kinds:

(a) A, coarse, thick-skinned fellow that he is, fails even to notice B's embarrassed change of subject.
(b) A notices B's inept change of subject, and attributes it to B's genuine embarrassment at A's remark.
(c) A notices B's inept change of subject, and attributes it to B's intention of drawing the company's attention to the fact that A has committed a social gaffe.

And of course, there are further possible responses, such as B's noticing the change of subject, but not regarding it in any way as a reaction to A's previous remark. One point made by this illustration is that what may be part of the intended meaning may not be a part of the conveyed meaning and vice versa. And a second point, more important for the present discussion, is that it is impossible to determine a boundary between an utterance whereby s implicates some proposition p (in this case 'A has committed a social gaffe') and an utterance which merely communicates the unintended information that s believes p. To revert to the simplest type of example: when is a yawn simply a *sign* of boredom, and when is it an intended *signal* of boredom? The fact that such indeterminacies are commonplace in communication should not, however, blind us to the fact that linguistic communication depends hugely on the assumption that what *s* means is interpreted as such by *h*. It is this overlap between 'intended' meaning and 'conveyed' meaning which is the central concern of pragmatics. The Maxims of Relation and of Manner are the guarantors of its centrality.

7.2 Remarks on pragmatic metalanguage

What kind of metalanguage is required for the description of pragmatic force? I have used, and will continue to use, ordinary English verbs and adjectives to denote the mental events and states (*eg* propositional attitudes) attributed to *s*. This practice is a matter of convenience, and should not be taken as more than a rough-and-ready method of description. For example, the choice of one volitional verb (such as *want*) rather than another (such as *intend*) suggests a qualitative distinction which may not be justified in pragmatic reality. Ultimately, a neutral metalanguage must be devised – one containing predicates which reflect the pragmatic significance themselves, and which is not tied to the senses of words of particular languages such as English.

One metalinguistic practice which will be avoided in pragmatic description here is the use of illocutionary or performative verbs, such as *offer, suggest, state*. This is perhaps rather surprising, since in the speech-act theory of Austin and Searle, in particular, such verbs play a crucial part in the metalanguage for discussing illocutionary force. But, as I have already indicated (2.2), I do not accept the view that illocutionary force can be adequately captured by reference to such categories as offers, suggestions, and statements. My position will be elaborated when I consider speech-act verbs in the next chapter. For the present, I assume that using English verbs such as *offer* is simply a shorthand way of describing illocutionary force, in the sense of the role that an utterance has in a means–ends analysis.

A final comment must be made on the metalanguage for describing pragmatic force. Implicatures which express propositional attitudes (such as '*s* believes that [*X*]') are themselves metalinguistic (or one may prefer to call them 'metapropositional') in that they refer to a proposition [*X*], which is in some way 'entertained' by *s*. Since the propositional content represented by *X* is generally derived from the sense of the utterance *U* whose force is being described, it follows that the pragmatic metalanguage must subsume, by metalinguistic inclusion, any expression used for representing the sense of utterances in the language. This recalls what I said earlier (3.2) when discussing the four worlds: that there is feedback from a higher function of language to a function lower on the hierarchy. In my earlier formulation, sense belongs to the higher ideational function (Popper's descriptive and argumentative functions) and force belongs to the lower interpersonal (Popper's signalling) function. Nevertheless, in terms of means–ends analysis, the 'higher' function is instrumental to the 'lower' (see 3.3.1). One might express this finding as follows: anything which can be meant in a grammatical (ideational) sense can also form part of meaning in a pragmatic (interpersonal) sense.[1]

Now that the concept of pragmatic force has been explored a little further, we can envisage what task of description is required of a Communicative Grammar that relates syntax, via semantics, to pragmatics. For completeness, I should also add that a Communicative Grammar in the fullest sense relates syntax not only to interpersonal pragmatics, but also to textual pragmatics. But this extra level can be omitted at this point. My present concern is to justify such a Communicative Grammar, by showing (with reference to my chosen topics of negation and interrogation) that if we separate these three levels of statement, and also show the relations between them, we are able to make generalizations which would otherwise be impossible. My method, as already stated, will be to begin with syntax.

7.3 Some aspects of negation and interrogation in English

7.3.1 Syntax
All of the combinations in Table 7.1 overleaf, except [2], are possible in English.[2]

On the other hand, only the italicized sentences [1], [4], [6] (and possibly [8]), are in any sense 'usual'. The usual cases can be accounted for by the syntactic redundancy rules:

[9] Rule I   negative   → non-assertive
                           (where negative = –affirmative)
    Rule II   interrogative → non-assertive
                           (where interrogative =
                           – declarative)
    Rule III otherwise   → assertive

TABLE 7.1

	Declarative	Affirmative	Assertive
[1] *George is sometimes late* / *The train has arrived already*	√	√	√
[2] **George is ever late* / **The train has arrived yet*	√	√	×
[3] *George isn't sometimes late* / *The train hasn't arrived already*	√	×	√
[4] *George isn't ever late* / *The train hasn't arrived yet*	√	×	×
[5] *Is George sometimes late?* / *Has the train arrived already?*	×	√	√
[6] *Is George ever late?* / *Has the train arrived yet?*	×	√	×
[7] *Isn't George sometimes late?* / *Hasn't the train arrived already?*	×	×	√
[8] *Isn't George ever late?* / *Hasn't the train arrived yet?*	×	×	×

But this analysis on the syntactic level does not account for the 'unusual' cases [3], [5], and [7], nor for the fact that the relation between the affirmative and negative questions [6], [8] is not parallel to that between affirmative and negative statements [1], [4].

7.3.2 Semantic analysis

These facts can be accounted for on the level of logical/semantic structure. On this level, the three syntactic oppositions correspond to three logical oppositions;

[10] *Syntactic oppositions*   *Logical oppositions*
     affirmative: negative $[pos (X)]$: $[neg (X)]$
     declarative: interrogative $[pos/neg (X)]$: $[? (X)]$
     assertive : non-assertive $[X^+]$: $[X^0]$

Here X represents the predication ('propositional content') shared by each member of a set of sentence types. The superscripts of X^+ and X^0 represent respectively the factuality operators 'fact' and 'non-fact' which are expressed, for example, through the choice of *some* and *any*, or between *sometimes* and *ever*. The question mark *?* is the question symbol which is a free variable ranging over {*pos, neg*} in *yes/no* questions. That is, the question mark indicates that the truth value associated with some X is undetermined: it is what Searle (1969:31) calls a propositional function (see 5.5). The 'standard' sentence-types [1], [4], and [6] can thus be associated with propositions and propositional functions as follows:

[1] George is sometimes late $[pos (X^+)]$
[4] George isn't ever late $[neg (X^0)]$
[6] Is George ever late? $[? (X^0)]$

These formulae exemplify logical restrictions on the combination of {*pos, neg*} with {$^+$, ^{0}}: positive affirmative propositions are factual (that is, they incorporate the claim that X corresponds to some state of affairs), whereas negative and interrogative sentences do not. These restrictions may be expressed by an appropriate reformulation of the redundancy rules in [9] as a set of logical rules:

[11] In any proposition $[p]$, *pos* co-occurs with X^+, *neg* co-occurs with X^0, and *?* co-occurs with X^0.

This explains why [2], combining *pos* with X^0, is ill-formed. The formulae for [1], [4] and [6] also exemplify the mutual exclusiveness of *pos, neg*, and *?*: naturally *pos* and *neg* are contradictory, and *?* is the variable which leaves *pos* and *neg* unspecified. A third point about these formulae is that they are enclosed by [ ], which indicate that the whole formula has the format of a proposition, something which may act as an argument of the predicates *TRUE, FALSE*. However, since strictly speaking only [1] and [4] represent propositions, it will be convenient (as in 5.5) to use the cover term 'propositional' for all three formulae [1], [4], and [6]. (However, whereas in 5.5 I indicated the contrast between indicative and non-indicative propositionals by the use of the symbols *I* and *N*, in this analysis this distinction is omitted as irrelevant.)

The problem to be considered now, however, is how to provide a logical analysis of the remaining sentences [3], [5], [7], and [8]. In providing an answer, I shall try to show that a satisfactory solution from the logical point of view is also the key to the pragmatic interpretation of such sentences. By way of anticipation, it is as well to notice here the rather special pragmatic implications of these 'less usual' sentence types by considering further examples. Suppose that a customs official, instead of asking his routine question [12], asks instead one of the questions [13]–[15]:

[12] Have you anything to declare?   *cf* [6]
[13] Have you something to declare?   *cf* [5]
[14] Haven't you anything to declare?   *cf* [8]
[15] Haven't you something to declare?   *cf* [7]

Immediately the relationship between the customs official and his interlocutor is placed on an abnormal, non-routine, and perhaps rather sinister footing. Here are possible contexts:

[13] Customs official sees a woman hovering uneasily between the 'Nothing to Declare' and the 'Something to Declare' exits. He suspects that she has something dutiable in her luggage, and wants to encourage her to make a clean breast of it.

[14] Customs official sees the woman struggling past with vast quantities of suitcases, etc. He cannot believe that among all that luggage she has nothing that should be declared. He challenges her.

[15] Customs official sees the woman walking through the 'Nothing to Declare' exit with jewellery spilling out of her handbag. He is as good as accusing her of smuggling.

Further examples show that these special question-types are closely connected with politeness:

[16] Will you have anything to eat?

[17] Will you have something to eat?
[18] Won't you have anything to eat?
[19] Won't you have something to eat?

If these are invitations from a hostess to a guest, [16], although it is the most regular kind of question, is the least polite, whereas [19] is the most polite. Here the implications of personal disposition are the opposite of those of [12]–[15]. On the other hand, when the hostess addresses her guest as follows, only [21] can count as an expression of polite regret, and [22] is downright rude:

[20] Are you leaving yet?
[21] Are you leaving already?
[22] Aren't you leaving yet?
[23] Aren't you leaving already?

To explain such overtones, let us first return to the logical analysis. An initial attempt to formulate the 'unusual' types of sentence would be a mechanical translation of the syntactic features into their logical correspondents:

[3a] George isn't sometimes late.	$*[neg\ (X^+)]$
[5a] Is George sometimes late?	$*[?\ (X^+)]$
[7a] Isn't George sometimes late?	$*[?\ neg\ (X^+)]$
[8a] Isn't George ever late?	$*[?\ neg\ (X^0)]$

These formulae have asterisks, because they are clearly ill-formed according to the logical constraints mentioned: [3a], [5a], and [7a] combine ? or neg with factuality; [7a] and [8a] combine ? with neg. This face-value ill-formedness is, in fact, an explanation of why they are 'less normal'. Their logical form has to be more complicated, and their pragmatic implementation more oblique, than those of more regular sentences such as [1], [4], and [6].

A clue to their logical form is that some, at least, of these sentences, have the nature of what have been called SECOND-INSTANCE utterances; that is, they presuppose a context in which they make reference to some previous utterance. This is clearest in the case of [3a], which could be contextualized as follows:

[24] *A*: I'm sorry to hear that George and Bill are sometimes late for work.
    B: George isn't *sometimes* late, he's *always* late!

Similarly in [13], a non-smuggler might angrily retort to the customs official:

[25] No, I *don't* have something to declare!

But in the other examples, it is not necessary that a second-instance utterance should repeat, in whole or in part, a previous utterance: it is only necessary for the proposition 'resurrected' by the second-instance speaker to have been believed or entertained in the relevant context. In this broader sense, such utterances might be called 'metapropositional' rather than 'metalinguistic': they express a propositional about a propositional.[3]

Once it is accepted that propositionals may make reference to other propositionals, the logical analysis of these sentences proceeds according to the rules:

[26] a X^+ must occur within the immediate scope of *pos*.
      b If two symbols from the set {*pos, neg, ?*} occur together in the same propositional, one of them must be attached to the main propositional, and the other to an included (embedded) propositional.
      c The free variable *?* cannot occur within the scope of *pos* or *neg*.

In fact, these are minimal extensions of the logical constraints mentioned earlier, in [11]. Rule *a* simply repeats the logical constraint mentioned in [11] – that X^+ can occur in the same propositional as *pos*, but not in the same propositional as *neg* or *?*. Similarly, *b* is a way of making sense of the already mentioned mutual exclusiveness of *pos, neg*, and *?*, by attaching them to different propositionals, such that one propositional is included within the other. With these two rules, we get the following revised formulae:

[3b] $[neg\ [pos\ (X^+)]]$ [7b] $[?\ [neg\ [pos\ (X^+)]]]$
[5b] $[?\ [pos\ (X^+)]]$ [8b] $[?\ [neg\ (X^0)]]$

Included propositions are delimited by [ ]; notice that the rule has applied twice in the case of [7b].[4]

This analysis, however, is still less than satisfactory. Firstly, it postulates a dual interpretation of *?* and *neg*, in line with the well-known distinction between internal and external negation. It has been argued that this distinction is unnecessary, and indeed it would be a pity not to give a unitary definition of negation and interrogation. This distinction arises because *?* and *neg* have two kinds of operands: in the most usual case they operate on predications (X^0) and in the less usual case they operate on propositions. We can, however, make the less usual case into a special case of the more usual, by recalling that propositions are defined as taking the predicate *TRUE* or *FALSE*. The insertion of *TRUE* between each included proposition and the preceding operator, so that ($TRUE$ [p]) becomes a predication (an instantiation of (X)), reduces the two kinds of negation/interrogation to one. Such an analysis is what underlies sentences such as [27]:

[27] It is true that I drank your beer. ($TRUE$ [p]$^+$)

And we note, in corroboration, that [27], like [3], [5], [7], and [8], is a second-instance sentence, assuming that the proposition 'I drank your beer' has already been entertained in the context. This now means that the formulae [3b]–[8b] can be finally re-written as:

[3c] [neg ($TRUE$ [pos (X^+)]^0)]
'It is not true that George is sometimes late.'
[5c] [? ($TRUE$ [pos (X^+)]^0)]
'Is it true that George is sometimes late?'
[7c] [? ($TRUE$ [neg ($TRUE$ [pos (X^+)]^0)]^0)]
'Is it true that it is not true that George is sometimes late?'
(*ie* 'Isn't it true that George is sometimes late?')
[8c] [? ($TRUE$ [neg (X^0)]^0)]
'Is it true that George isn't ever late?'

This reformulation, incidentally, deals with another weakness of the analysis of [3b]–[8b]: there was no explanation, in that analysis, of why the operators *pos, neg,* and *?* only occur in one scope-ordering, *viz:* '*pos* within (*neg* within) *?*'. This ordering, under the new formulation, is the only one which is well formed according to the rules: *pos* must be innermost when X is factual (X^+), and *?* must always be outermost, because $TRUE$ must be predicated of a full proposition, not of a propositional function.

I therefore judge that [3c]–[8c] are the simplest, in the sense of most general, rule-governed analyses of logical types that they represent. But as written formulae, they are far from simple, and so for convenience of reference, I shall abbreviate them as follows (adding a further example of each sentence-type):

Abbreviations:

[1d]	*pos X*	*eg* She bought some flowers.
[3d]	*neg TRUE pos X*	*eg* She didn't buy some flowers.
[4d]	*neg X*	*eg* She didn't buy any flowers.
[5d]	*? TRUE pos X*	*eg* Did she buy some flowers?
[6d]	*? X*	*eg* Did she buy any flowers?
[7d]	*? TRUE neg TRUE pos X*	*eg* Didn't she buy some flowers?
[8d]	*? TRUE neg X*	*eg* Didn't she buy any flowers?

7.3.3 Pragmatic analysis

7.3.3.1 Positive propositions

I shall begin the pragmatic analysis with the straightforward cases [1d], [4d], and [6d]. For maximum generality, no specific prior knowledge will be assumed about the context. Nevertheless, certain minimal pragmatic assumptions may be made: *eg* that the utterance has both a speaker (*s*) and a hearer (*h*), and that both *s* and *h* understand its sense. A further assumption is that *s* is observing the CP. Thus, for [1d], the most direct pragmatic interpretation is roughly as follows:

[1e] A. *pos X*   (sense – given)

    B. *s* says to *h* that *X* (minimum contextualization)

    C. B has the goal of making *h* fully aware (*ie* informing *h*) that *X* (minimum illocutionary assumption)

    D. *s* believes that *X* (Quality)

    E. *s* believes that *h* is not aware that *X* (Quantity: corroborative condition)

    F. *s* believes that it is desirable for *h* to be aware that *X* (Relation: corroborative condition)

   (On 'minimum illocutionary assumption' and 'corroborative condition', see 2.5.2.)

In terms of heuristic problem-solving (see Fig. 2.4 *p* 41), the minimally contextualized speech act B presents the addressee with a problem of interpretation. To solve the problem, *h* puts forward the 'default' hypothesis C (corresponding to Searle's 'essential condition'). Certain inferences D, E, and F are drawn from the combination of C and the Cooperative Principle. These are: D (corresponding to Searle's 'sincerity condition'), and E and F (corresponding to Searle's 'preparatory conditions'). Of these three, D is derived via the Maxim of Quality, E via the Maxim of Quantity, and F via the Maxim of Relation. These are 'corroborative conditions' because they are ancillary consequences of C which, if they obtain, confirm the hypothesis C. That is, if the function of B is informative (which is the most likely hypothesis), then *s* must believe (assuming the CP) that *X*, that *h* is not aware that *X*, and that it is desirable for *h* to be aware of *X*. The CP here constitutes a background premiss from which the more specific conclusions D, E, and F are provisionally drawn. These conclusions may be called 'context-sensitive' in the sense that contextual evidence may cause them to be abandoned. I have suggested that they are likely to be the least risky assumptions that can be made, and that they are accepted 'by default' if there is no evidence to the contrary.

The analysis draws on Grice's conversational implicatures, and makes them do, in a sense, the work of Searle's speech-act rules. As far as Grice is concerned, D–F can be considered implicatures, although they are not the kind he most discusses: implicatures which arise from an apparent violation of the CP. Implicatures in the present model are, however, all in the last resort provisional, and liable to subsequent cancellation. Moreover, I have extended the Maxim of Quantity so that it applies to the choice of whether to say anything at all. 'Do not make your contribution more informative than is required' means, in the limiting case, 'Do not assert anything at all, unless you have some information to impart'. Therefore the fact that s makes an assertion is in itself grounds for assuming E. This is one reason for speaking, and the other makes an appeal to the Maxim of Relation: in cooperatively informing h of X, h should believe that s has some goal in saying X, ie that it is desirable from s's point of view for h to be aware of X.

7.3.3.2   Negative propositions
Negative propositions follow the same interpretative pattern as positive ones, except that for X in [1e], the negation of X is substituted in each line of the interpretation, and except that an additional implicature is derived. This is the implicature by negative uninformativeness (see 5.4.1), that s in uttering neg X believes that prior to the uttering of neg X, s or h has had the disposition to believe that X. Thus we add to the end of the interpretation, in the case of the negative proposition, the implicature:

[4e] G. s has had, or believes that h has had, the disposition to believe that X.

7.3.3.3 Ordinary yes–no questions
Straightforward questions such as [6] may be pragmatically interpreted as follows:

[6e] A. $? X$ (sense – given)
B. s puts the question $? X$ to h (minimum contextualization)
C. B has the function of getting h to inform s whether X is the case   (minimum illocutionary assumption)
D. s does not know whether X is the case   (Quantity)
E. s believes that h knows whether X is the case (Relation)
F. s wants to know whether X is the case   (Relation)

Since the logical analysis of *yes–no* questions characterized them as 'defective propositions', *ie* propositions lacking a positive or negative sign, it is reasonable to argue, via the Maxim of Quantity, that unless *s* does not know whether *X* is the case, *s* is breaking the CP. Hence D, which Searle treats as a preparatory condition for questions, is a natural implicature. There may, of course, be other reasons for leaving the positive/negative value of *X* unspecified, especially in special settings such as judicial cross-examinations, classroom elicitations, and examination questions. Searle, by way of justifying D as a condition for questions, acknowledges a difference between 'real questions' and 'exam questions'. But this oversimplifies and overcompartmentalizes in a way that is avoided if the word 'question' is restricted to its logical sense. All that is claimed in [6e] is that a *yes–no* question, as a logical category, finds its most likely implementation in circumstances where *s* does not know the answer.

With the provisional identification of the question with an information-seeking speech act in C, the Maxim of Quality and the Maxim of Relation allow us to check this assumption in D, E, and F.

7.3.3.4 *Loaded yes–no questions*

Leaving aside the assertive negative proposition [3] (which is a rather different problem)[5], I turn now to the more complex 'loaded questions' [5], [8], and [7] – in that order. Some general strategy for interpreting second-instance sentences is required for all these cases, and the correct approach seems to run roughly as follows. Second-instance questions contain a face-value infringement of the Maxim of Manner, in that regarded purely as information elicitations, they are logically more complex and oblique than is necessary. This is because there is a logical equivalence between every one of these second-instance questions and a simpler question in which the predicate *TRUE* does not occur. Consider:

$$[5\mathrm{f}] \quad ?\ \textit{TRUE pos } X \Rightarrow \begin{cases} \textit{pos TRUE pos } X \equiv \textit{pos } X \\ \textit{neg TRUE pos } X \equiv \textit{neg } X \end{cases}$$

In [5f] the two propositions to the right of the arrow are the alternative logical answers to the question on the left of the arrow, and these two answers are logically equivalent to the simpler propositions *pos X* and *neg X*. The situation is the same for [8] and [7], except that the positions of *pos X* and *neg X* are reversed:

[8f] ? TRUE neg X $\Rightarrow$ $\begin{cases} pos\ TRUE\ neg\ X \equiv neg\ X \\ neg\ TRUE\ neg\ X \equiv pos\ X \end{cases}$

[7f] ? TRUE neg TRUE pos X $\Rightarrow$
$\begin{cases} pos\ TRUE\ neg\ TRUE\ pos\ X \equiv neg\ X \\ neg\ TRUE\ neg\ TRUE\ pos\ X \equiv pos\ X \end{cases}$

If we define questions as 'logically equivalent' whenever there is a one-to-one relation of truth-value equivalence between their answers, then all these questions are logically equivalent to the simple question ? X. That is, no information can be elicited by these questions which cannot be equally well elicited by a much simpler question. According to the Maxims of Manner, therefore, we expect to find some reason for this wilful obliquity. What can it be? What distinguishes these from ordinary questions like [6] is that they refer to one or more propositions. A reference to a proposition presupposes that the proposition exists, *viz* exists in somebody's mind. Hence a minimum pragmatic inference about second-instance questions is that the propositions to which they refer 'exist in the context'. This must generally mean that they exist in the speaker's or the hearer's mind, as an assumption.[6] I shall call this inference the SECOND-INSTANCE IMPLICATURE.

The analysis of [5] proceeds along these lines. Since [5] is a special case of [6], the analysis repeats that of [6], substituting *TRUE pos X* for X throughout. However, since *TRUE pos X* is logically equivalent to X, we can also reverse the substitution process by replacing *TRUE pos X* simply by X. The extra second-instance implicature G is added:

[5e] A. ? TRUE pos X (*eg: Did she buy some flowers?*) is equivalent to ? X.
Therefore B–F in [6e] apply to
? TRUE pos X as well.
IN ADDITION:
G. *s* assumes, or believes *h* to assume, that X (Manner, second instance)

G explains why assertive questions such as [5] tend to be called 'questions with a positive bias', or 'questions expecting the answer *Yes*'.

Similarly for the negative question [8] (? *TRUE neg X*). In this case, the included proposition is negative, and so the second-instance implicature takes the form of G':

[8e] A. ? TRUE neg X (*eg: Didn't she buy any flowers?*) is equivalent to ? X.
Therefore B–F in [6e] apply to
? TRUE neg X as well.

IN ADDITION:

G' s assumes or believes h to assume that *neg X, ie* that X
is not the case. (Manner, second instance)

H. s has had, or believes h to have had, a disposition to
believe that X. (Quantity, negative uninformativeness)

The further implicature H is added by virtue of the sub-maxim of
negative uninformativeness. Thus a negative question such as
Didn't she buy any flowers? expresses two contrasting expectations: one (the cancelled expectation) that she bought some flowers, and a second (the actual expectation), that she didn't buy any
flowers. It is for this reason that such questions typically connote
surprise, or even disbelief in what appears to be the case. (*eg:
Aren't you ashamed of yourself?* – 'I would expect you to be
ashamed of yourself, but apparently you're not.')

The negative assertive question [7] *Didn't she buy some flowers?* adds yet one further degree of obliquity. Once again, the implicatures of ordinary questions apply here too, *? TRUE neg
TRUE pos X* being mutually substitutable with *? X* in A–F of
[6e]. To these we add the three implicatures G', H, and I:

[7e] A. *? TRUE neg TRUE pos X* (*eg: Didn't she buy some
flowers?*) is equivalent to *? X*.

G' s assumes or believes h to assume that *neg TRUE pos
X, ie* that X is not the case. (Manner, second instance)

H. s has had, or believes h to have had, a disposition to
believe that TRUE *pos X*. (Quantity, negative uninformativeness)

I. s or h assumes (in conflict with G') that X. (Manner,
second instance)

The negative assertive question is treated in the same way as the
negative non-assertive question, except that the additional
second-instance implicature I is derived from the second included
proposition. Pragmatically, the main difference between the two is
that [7] expresses a stronger commitment to the positive proposition, the assumption in I cancelling the assumption in G'.
There is a stronger connotation of disbelief in [7] than in [8], and
moreover [7] tends to occur where the proposition *pos X* has
actually been asserted or presupposed in the context. The difference is brought out in [22] and [23]: *Aren't you leaving yet?* could
be an exasperated question to a guest who has outstayed his welcome: 'I hoped/expected that you would have left, but it appears
that you haven't', whereas *Aren't you leaving already?* could not
be used in that context: its user assumes that 'You are leaving

already' is likely to be true, rather than just a fervent wish. It is understandable, in this light, that negative assertive questions like [7] and [23] often effectively cease to become information-eliciting utterances (questions in Searle's sense), and become an indirect and slightly tactful way of expressing disbelief in what *h* has said or implicated.

It will be noted that in [7e] implicature I is actually inconsistent with implicature G'. This is an important point about the present use of the term 'implicature': that one implicature of an utterance may actually cancel out another implicature of the same utterance. The cancelled implicature does not, however, cease thereby being part of the meaning of the utterance.

7.4 Implicatures of politeness

This leads back to the question of politeness. Questions such as [16]–[19] are, for reasons explored in 5.3, typically interpreted as offers, and it is noticeable that the loaded questions [17]–[19] are more polite as offers than [16]:

[16]	Will you have anything to eat?	*? X*
[17]	Will you have something to eat?	*? TRUE pos X*
[18]	Won't you have anything to eat?	*? TRUE neg X*
[19]	Won't you have something to eat?	*? TRUE neg TRUE pos X*

We have seen that there is an essential asymmetry in polite behaviour, in that whatever is a polite belief for the speaker tends to be an impolite belief for the hearer, and vice versa. This asymmetry is exemplified in the very nature of offers: it is polite to offer someone something, but it is also often more polite to decline an offer than to accept it. As the term 'polite belief' itself suggests, such beliefs are what a speaker purports to believe, rather than what he actually believes, which may be quite different.

The assertive question [17] is more polite than the ordinary question [16], because it implicates (see G in [5e]) a polite belief:

[17a] *s* assumes [or believes *h* to assume] that *h* wants something to eat.

The material in square brackets may be ignored for the present –

see below. Typically, [18] is also more polite than [17], for
reasons which are more complex. A negative question, as we
have seen, implicates an actual negative assumption and a cancelled positive belief. These two implicatures correspond to the
hearer's 'polite belief' and the speaker's 'polite belief' respectively. Thus [18] is doubly polite because it pays the hearer the compliment of assuming he is being polite. It gives the hearer a
chance to withdraw or suppress a polite refusal:

[18a]   s [assumes or] believes h to assume that h doesn't want
        anything to eat. This cancels or supersedes a disposition
        by s [or an assumed disposition by h] to believe that h
        does want something to eat.

But [19] is even more polite, because it countermands the hearer's polite assumption (or the hearer's anticipated refusal) by an
equally strong polite assumption on the part of the speaker: the
speaker refuses, as it were, to accept the politeness of the hearer,
since to do so would involve himself in being impolite at a further
remove:

[19a]   s [assumes or] believes h to assume that h doesn't want
        anything to eat. This cancels or supersedes a disposition
        by s [or an assumed disposition by h] to believe that h
        does want something to eat, and in turn is cancelled by
        an assumption by s [or an assumed assumption by h] that
        h does want something to eat.

The words in square brackets in [17a]–[19a] are in practice excluded from the interpretation of these polite questions, although
according to my previous account of the second-instance implicature, they should be a possible component. The significant thing
is that these are in practice excluded because they represent *impolite beliefs*. We now see how the PP interacts with the CP, causing an impolite part of the interpretation to be suppressed.

Another significant point is: these analyses show a connection
between politeness and obliquity (indirectness). Because [17a]–
[19a] are in effect restricted to the implicature of polite beliefs, we
can observe how every additional implicature adds an extra degree of politeness. A principle at work here is that of 'reciprocity
of perspectives' as well as asymmetry of politeness: to be really
polite, one must assume that the hearer is also being polite, and
must forestall his politeness. This leads in theory to an infinite regress of politeness, of which the first three stages are represented
in [17a]–[19a]. Thus we may derive from the progressive addition
of implicatures in [17a]–[19a] a corresponding set of 'politeness
implicatures':

[17b] s is observing the PP.
[18b] s is observing the PP.
   s assumes that h is observing the PP.
[19b] s is observing the PP.
   s assumes that h is observing the PP.
   s assumes that h assumes that s is observing the PP.

The increase of politeness from [17] to [19] is measured in terms of the number of iterations of the PP

Without analysing in detail the customs official examples [10]–[13], we may note that in this case obliquity works in the opposite direction: because 'You have something to declare' is an impolite belief, the more indirect kinds of question are progressively more impolite, more threatening, than the ordinary *yes–no* question.

This analysis shows how the pragmatic interpretation of an utterance is built up from (a) a minimum illocutionary assumption, and (b) implicatures, including implicatures of politeness, which follow from, or accompany, this assumption. (In a more indirect case, this assumption may be rejected in favour of another.) In this way, the addressee reconstructs the meaning as planned by the speaker.

7.5 Conclusion

The separation of semantics from pragmatics is justified if it can be shown that there are different kinds of regularities to be observed on each of these levels, and that the relation between these two kinds of regularity can be explained in a principled way. This is what I have tried to demonstrate in this chapter.

On the semantic level, rules can be formulated to account for the logical relations between affirmative and negative, assertive and non-assertive, and declarative and interrogative sentences, and to account for the apparent asymmetry of these categories in syntax. On the pragmatic level, generalizations can be made about the way in which the CP and the PP determine the form of linguistic behaviour in relation to communicative function. It is clear that these two classes of regularity are of a very different nature, and yet their synthesis through the problem-solving strategies of pragmatic interpretation is able to show how sentences which are syntactically alike (such as different kinds of negative questions) may have widely varying and contrasting pragmatic interpretations.

Another point I have tried to demonstrate through the analysis of this chapter is that it is unnecessary for pragmatics to include special speech-act rules, such as those stipulated by Searle. Conditions such as Searle's essential conditions, preparatory conditions, and sincerity conditions of illocutions do not have to be independently stated, since comparable (though probabilistic) conditions can in any case be arrived at by virtue of the sense of the utterance and the maxims of the CP. As Miller and Johnson-Laird put it (1976:636), 'given a set of conversational maxims, a literal interpretation of the utterance, and a specification of its context of use, it is in principle possible to infer its illocutionary force'.

Notes

1. This finding contrasts significantly with Searle's 'Principle of Expressibility' (1969:19–21), at least in the particular form of it he applies to speech acts: 'for any possibe speech act, there is a possible linguistic element the meaning of which . . . is sufficient to determine that its literal utterance is a performance of precisely that speech act'. In effect, where Searle says that whatever can be pragmatically meant can be grammatically said, I am claiming that whatever is grammatically said can be (part of what is) pragmatically meant.

2. *George is ever late* is, of course, grammatical if *ever* is understood in the archaic sense of 'always'.

3. The idea of 'second instance' comes from Bolinger (1965[1952]). The difference between the 'metalinguistic' and 'metapropositional' categories is that in the former case the actual words purportedly used in the 'source utterance' are quoted, while in the latter case only the sense of what was assumed to be said or thought is reproduced. The difference, that is, is parallel to that between direct and indirect speech (*oratio obliquo*), or that between the form and content modes of mention (see Leech 1980[1977b]).

4. The formulae [3c]–[7c] are not in themselves derivable from the rules. But if we note that only one scope-ordering is possible (*viz*: '*pos* within (*neg* within) *?*'), then these are the only formulae which are well-formed. See *p* 163 below for an explanation of this.

5. The assertive negative proposition [3] *George isn't sometimes late* is different from the other second-instance cases because it only allows the strictly metalinguistic interpretation which is clarified by the use of quotation marks: *George isn't 'sometimes late'* (see note 3 above). In this case, the truth value of the assertive proposition is quite different from that of the corresponding non-assertive one. As example [24] above shows, 'George isn't "sometimes late"' is logically consistent with 'George is always late', but 'George isn't ever late' is not.

6. Second-instance implicatures form a class of implicatures, or (to put it another way) an implicature strategy which, as in the cases of hyperbole and irony, one might dignify with the label 'principle' or 'maxim'. I have not succeeded in giving a convincing explanation of how second-instance implicatures arise, but I suggest that they derive

from the fact that second-instance expressions, like direct and indirect speech quotations, actually *name* a particular utterance-token. Logically, therefore, they are analogous to a definite expression introduced by *the*: for example, *Is George sometimes late?* could be revealingly paraphrased: *Is the proposition-token 'George is sometimes late' true?* And as with definite expressions in general, it is assumed that s and h, by virtue of shared contextual knowledge, can identify which proposition-token is meant. (On the relevance of the type-token distinction here, see Leech (1980 [1977]:33–9).)

Chapter 8

Performatives

Q: We have cats the way most people have mice.
                                   [Signed] Mrs C. L. Footloose
A: I see you have. I can't tell from your communication, however, whether you
wish advice or are just boasting.

                                   [James Thurber, *The Owl in the Attic*]

This chapter, my last dealing with the Interpersonal Rhetoric, will
continue the polemical note sounded at the end of the preceding
one. It will try to justify the approach I have taken towards illocutionary force against competing positions. The competing positions I shall consider are: firstly, 'orthodox speech-act theory' in
the mould of Austin and Searle, and secondly, the performative
hypothesis of Ross, Lakoff, Sadock, and others.

A key point in my argument will be the need to make a radical
separation between the analysis of illocutions and the analysis of
illocutionary verbs.

8.1 The Performative and Illocutionary-Verb Fallacies

I would like to oppose two theses which I regard as fallacies, and
which have influenced thinking about illocutionary force, particularly through the work of Austin and Searle. The 'ILLOCUTION-
ARY-VERB FALLACY' is the view that the analysis of illocutionary
force can be suitably approached through the analysis of the
meaning of illocutionary verbs such as *advise*, *command*, and
promise. On the face of it, this appears to be a reasonable
approach. But according to the view I have developed, it leads to
the error of 'grammaticizing' pragmatic force. Whereas the sense
of illocutionary verbs is part of grammar, to be analysed in categorical terms, illocutionary force is to be analysed in rhetorical
and noncategorical terms. When we are analysing illocutionary
verbs, we are dealing with grammar, whereas when we are analysing the illocutionary force of utterances, we are dealing with
pragmatics. It is easy to confuse these two things, because one is
part of the metalanguage for the other: that is, when we discuss

or report illocutionary acts in ordinary discourse (*eg* in saying *John asked Theodore to open the window*) we inevitably find ourselves doing so in terms of the illocutionary verbs which the English language provides for this purpose, such as *ask* and *report*. I have, however, made it clear (see especially 2.2) that illocutionary force, particularly because of its indeterminacy and scalar variability, is more subtle than can be easily accommodated by our everyday vocabulary of speech-act verbs. Thus if we associate, as I have done, illocutionary force with the plan (revealed in means–ends analysis) which *s* attempts to fulfil by communicating the message of *U* to *h*, then the type of analysis illustrated in Chapters 6 and 7 indicates that force must be studied in part in non-categorical, scalar terms. For example, the difference between 'ordering' and 'requesting' is partly a matter of the scale of optionality (how much choice is given to *h*), and the difference between 'requesting' and 'offering' is a matter of the cost–benefit scale (how far is *A* to the cost/benefit of *s/h*) (see 5.3, 5.7).

A special case of the Illocutionary-Verb Fallacy is what may be called the PERFORMATIVE FALLACY. This is the thesis that a performative, an utterance containing an explicit performative verb, is the canonical form of utterance, the yardstick in terms of which the forces of other utterances are to be explicated. It is this fallacy which leads one to say that an ordinary non-performative sentence like [1] has a meaning which can be made explicit by adding some performative prelude as in [2a] or [2b]:

[1]   He did not do it.
[2a] I state that he did not do it.
[2b] I maintain that he did not do it.

The strictest form of the Performative Fallacy is the assumption that corresponding to every non-performative utterance like [1], there is a performative utterance like [2a] or [2b] which makes its force explicit.

Another special case of the performative fallacy is the PERFORMATIVE HYPOTHESIS of Ross (1970) and others, that the main verb of the underlying semantic structure of every sentence is a performative, *ie* that 'deep down' in its deep structure, every sentence like [1] has a form something like [2a].

8.2 The speech-act theories of Austin and Searle

Both Austin and Searle flirt with the Performative Fallacy, and end up embracing the Illocutionary-Verb Fallacy.[1] I believe that these two things are connected. That is: the interest that they have in performatives implicitly influences them into assuming that a careful analysis of the meaning of illocutionary verbs can lead to the understanding of illocutionary force. This, however, is historical hindsight.

The original idea in Austin's *How to Do Things with Words* (1962) was that performative utterances ('performatives' for short) are fundamentally different from constative (or descriptive) utterances. Whereas constative utterances could be evaluated in traditional terms of truth and falsehood, performatives were neither true nor false: instead, they were to be regarded as felicitous or non-felicitous. But examples such as [1] and [2a] above led Austin to the eventual conclusion that all utterances are 'performative' in the sense of constituting a form of action, rather than simply a matter of saying something about the world. Austin underlined this by drawing a parallel between 'explicit performatives' such as

[3] I promise that I shall be there.

and 'primary performatives' (or 'primary utterances') such as:

[4] I shall be there.

Finally, as is well known, Austin concluded that in all regular utterances like [3] and [4], whether they have a performative verb or not, there is both a 'doing' element and a 'saying' element; and this led him to shift to a distinction (1962:109) between locutionary acts ('roughly equivalent to uttering a certain sentence with a certain sense and reference') and illocutionary acts ('utterances which have a certain (conventional) force'), and to supplement these categories with the further category of perlocutionary acts ('what we bring about or achieve *by* saying something'). It was, however, by assuming the performative to be the explicit, test case, of an illocution that Austin proceeded to his classification of illocutionary acts. This classification (into 'Verdictives' 'Exercitives', 'Commissives', 'Behabitives', and 'Expositives') is a prime example of what I have just called the 'Illocutionary-Verb Fallacy': Austin appeared to assume throughout that verbs in the English language correspond one-to-one with categories of speech act.

When a similar classification was put forward by Searle, in 'A taxonomy of illocutionary acts', he expressly disassociated himself from Austin's assumption of such a correspondence between verbs and speech acts: 'Differences in illocutionary verbs are a good guide, but by no means a sure guide to differences in illocutionary acts' (1979 [1975a]:2). Nevertheless, it is clear throughout this paper that Searle is thinking in terms of illocutionary verbs. Although we may agree that his taxonomy is more successful and systematic than Austin's, we soon find him harking back to the performative as the canonical form of each illocution, and as the basis for his classification: 'I now propose to examine the deep structure of explicit performative sentences in each of the five categories.' Searle does not justify this proceeding,[2] but takes it for granted presumably in accordance with the 'principle of expressibility' ('The principle that whatever can be meant can be said') which he adopts with similar lack of justification in *Speech Acts* (1969:19–21). The 'principle of expressibility' is a convenient thesis if one wishes to argue that it is always possible to elucidate the illocutionary force of an utterance by prefixing an appropriate performative. In other respects, too, Searle appears to rely upon the 'Performative Fallacy' while not overtly acknowledging it. He allows that illocutionary force may be expressed by a number of 'illocutionary-force indicating devices' (1969:30) including intonation, punctuation, etc., as well as performative verbs; but in practice, the use of devices other than performatives is not developed or illustrated in his work. Similarly, he admits that there is 'enormous unclarity' in the assignment of utterances to illocutionary categories, and yet insists that: 'If we adopt illocutionary point as the basic notion on which to classify uses of language, then there are a rather limited number of basic things we do with language.' So Searle sticks to a categorical theory of speech acts, in spite of the obvious difficulties of deciding when a given utterance fits into one category rather than another.

My arguments against the Illocutionary-Verb Fallacy have so far been descriptive: the categorical 'pigeon-holing' of speech acts which this entails simply regiments the range of human communicative potential to a degree which cannot be justified by observation. Let me now turn to a more theoretical point. In referring to human conversational behaviour, as to other areas of experience, our language provides us with categorical distinctions. But it is to commit a fundamental and obvious error to assume that the distinctions made by our vocabulary necessarily exist in reality. Language provides us with verbs like *order*, *request*, *beg*, *plead*, just as it provides us with nouns like *puddle*, *pond*, *lake*, *sea*, *ocean*. But we should no more assume that there are in pragmatic reality distinct categories such as orders and requests than that there are in geographical reality distinct categories such as puddles, ponds, and lakes. Somehow, this assumption slips unnoticed into Searle's introduction to his taxonomy:

> What are the criteria by which we can tell that of three actual
> utterances one is a report, one a prediction and one a promise? In
> order to develop higher order genera, we must first know how the
> species *promise, prediction, report*, etc. differ from one another.
>
> (1979 [1975a]:2)

But it would be strikingly inappropriate if one were to begin a
treatise on expanses of water on the world's surface in this way:

> What are the criteria by which we can tell that of three actual expanses
> of water, one is a puddle, one a pond, and one a lake? In order to
> develop higher order genera, we must first know how the species
> *puddle, pond*, and *lake* differ from one another.

In defence of Searle it could be argued, first, that the comparison
is unfair: if one had chosen monkeys and giraffes (say) instead of
ponds and puddles, the example would have been less ridiculous.
But my reply is (a) that one has no right *in advance* to assume
that such categories exist in reality (although one might discover
them by observation); and (b) that in actuality, when one *does*
observe them, illocutions are in many respects more like puddles
and ponds than like monkeys and giraffes: they are, that is
to say, distinguished by continuous rather than by discrete
characteristics.

   A second argument in defence of Searle's categorical position
is that pragmatic reality is very different from geographical reality: that since language is from the pragmantic point of view a
societal phenomenon (belonging, in the terms of 3.2, to 'World 3'
rather than to 'World 1'), there is more reason to suppose that, in
this case, language reflects precisely the distinctions that do exist
in social reality. Indeed, it might be maintained (by a social
variant of the Sapir–Whorf hypothesis) that the distinctions that
a language draws between various kinds of speech act become, by
that very fact, significant distinctions in social communication.
But again, my reply is that we cannot assume in advance such an
isomorphism between language organization and social organization, any more than we can (say) in the case of kinship terminology. Swedish distinguishes lexically some kinship categories (*eg*
between paternal and maternal grandfathers) which are not distinguished by the English lexicon. Similarly French makes a distinction, which English does not, between male and female
cousins. But it would surely be rash to assume, in these cases,
that the lexical distinctions correspond to underlying differences
of social organization. Once again, I would argue that one cannot
assume the homology of linguistic and social organization *in advance*; the only way of justifying such a view would be to make in-

dependent studies of the use of language, and of the way English (or some other language) *describes* the use of language, before coming to the conclusion that the two things are homologous. And the evidence so far presented suggests that in general they are not.

8.2.1 Declarations

There do appear to be some cases where the categorical distinctions of the grammar/lexicon correspond to categorically defined speech acts: these are the speech acts that Searle calls 'DECLARATIONS'.[3] For example, on the whole we can tell exactly, if we know the conventions, when a speech act such as naming a ship, making a vow, sentencing a criminal, or of bidding at an auction is performed, and when it is not. This type of conventionalized and compartmentalized linguistic behaviour is, however, the exception rather than the rule.

Interestingly enough, declarations such as these were the first types of speech act to occur to Austin (1962:5) when he set out to investigate performatives. These highly conventional speech acts are those of which it is almost possible to claim (as Searle points out, 1979 [1975a]:16) that 'saying makes it so'. In these verbal rituals, the performative is often an important ingredient: *I name this ship* ..., *I bid* ..., *I vow* ..., *I bequeath* ..., etc. This is because on the whole it is important for society, or some social group, to know precisely when that category of speech act has been performed.

Declarations are exceptional in more than one way. To show one of their exceptional features, it is necessary to return to the discussion of means–ends analysis in 2.5.1. The simplest case of a means–ends analysis I gave there was a non-linguistic example (see Fig. 2.1, *p* 36), that of switching on a heater in order to get warm. I also pointed out that the same goal could be achieved by

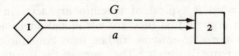

I   = initial state (The bridge is not open)
a = speech act: *I hereby declare the bridge open*
2   = final state (The bridge is open)

FIGURE 8.1

language – for example by saying to someone else *Switch on the heater* – but that this was more indirect (see Fig. 2.2, *p* 37). Almost invariably, in fact, language is to be regarded as an indirect, rather than a direct means of accomplishing some extralinguistic goal: the illocutionary goal of getting *h* to appreciate one's goal is a necessary preliminary to getting that goal achieved. Declarations, however, unlike most other speech acts, are a direct means to a goal, and can thus be represented by the very simplest of means–ends diagrams (see Fig. 8.1, *p* 179). Of course, there is more to officially opening a bridge than saying the right words: the words have to take place in the right setting (*eg* the speech act must be public, and at the right place and time for a bridge-opening). In this respect, a declaration is rather like a sacrament: it is an outward and audible sign that an abstract (psychological, social, or spiritual) action is being performed. It should be stressed that the action which is performed in making a declaration is basically social: in formally opening a bridge, for example, one makes it 'open' in the sense that it is henceforth *permissible* to use the bridge. (Any *physical* action accompanying the declaration, such as cutting a ribbon, is simply ceremonial and sacramental, like the speech act itself.) This is not to deny that the social change brought about by a declaration can be very important. It can be as important as declaring war, getting married, or buying a house. But if the end-state is physically different from the initial state, the declaration will not (according to the belief systems which most of us would claim to share in today) be efficacious on its own in bringing it about. It is no good saying, for instance, *I declare this door open* as a means of physically opening a door. The only speech act which could accomplish such a feat would be a supernatural one (like Ali Baba's *Open Sesame*), and this indeed exemplifies the close connection between declarations and magical speech acts such as casting spells.

Hence declarations, interesting though they are, do not by any means represent what is typical of illocutionary acts. In fact, there is reason for arguing that they are not illocutionary acts at all. Instead, they are conventional rather than communicative acts: the linguistic parts of rituals.[4] The sense of the words may, but need not, indicate their part in the performance: if the conventions were suitably altered, one could name a ship by reciting a poem, or by eating a cream bun. Such examples are reminders that linguistic declarations (as Searle himself notes) are often paralleled by non-verbal declarations, like the raising of an umpire's finger, or the bang of an auctioneer's gavel. As Searle points out, declarations have no sincerity conditions; the only way in which they can fail to take effect is through the failure of one or more of the accompanying conditions of the ritual (for example, when a marriage is performed by a layman impersonating a priest). Searle is right in saying that 'Declarations are a very special category of speech acts' (1979 [1975a]:18–19). They are 'performative', in the sense of 'action-performing', in a more obvious sense than is true of illocutionary performatives like 'I promise to be there'. From now on, I shall exclude declarations from my discussion of performatives and of illocutionary force, and will concentrate on performatives which are illocutionary, and which explicitly or implicitly describe some speech act.[5]

8.3 Illocutionary performatives: descriptive and non-descriptive approaches

I have spent some time on declarations in order to focus attention on their differentness, and will now go on to argue that the performative verb construction, with which they are strongly associated, is exceptional too. The performative, far from being something which underlies every single utterance, is something highly unusual in itself: it occurs, understandably enough, when a speaker needs to define his spech act as belonging to a particular category. In this way, the officer who says to a soldier *I order you to stand up* is making clear the official definition of his illocution as an order, just as he would retrospectively if he said: *Stand up – and that's an order*. The fact that the utterance is so defined may have clear consequences in itself: for example, disciplinary action. A related observation, brought out by this example, is that a performative is metalinguistic: it is, both syntactically and semantically, a kind of reported-speech (*oratio obliqua*) utterance. To say this is simply to point out the parallel between pairs such as:

	s	$IA(t)$	h	U
[5]	I	order	you	to stand up
[6]	He	ordered	them	to stand up

Both [5] and [6] name a speech situation, of which the components are

[7]	s	= speaker	h = addressee
	IA	= illocutionary act	U = utterance
	t	= time of speech act	

On the other hand, a performative is a very special reported-

speech utterance, because the speech situation which it names is
its own speech situation.

The metalinguistic character of performatives is in fact the key
to their nature: because they impose a label on themselves, they
not only make clear their own (illocutionary) force, but also
categorize it. Thus *Sit down* could have a variable and partly
indeterminate force which might, in different circumstances, be
called an invitation, a suggestion, an offer, or an order; but *I order
you to sit down*, by defining itself as an order, allows no such
ambivalence. This makes it clear why the Performative Fallacy is
an important error: it is an attempt to impose on all utterances a
categorical structure which only a small number of special metalinguistic utterances possess.

What I have been working round to is a DESCRIPTIVE view of
performatives, as contrasted with the non-descriptive view taken
by Austin, Searle, and others.[6] Austin contrasted the action-like
quality of performatives with the description-like quality of constatives. But the descriptive view of performatives levels out this
contrast in the opposite direction to that eventually chosen by
Austin: it is the view that performatives, like all other sentences
in declarative form, are propositions. True, they are a rather
unusual propositions; but they are, nevertheless, propositions,
capable of being true or false.

Considering the question whether performatives have a truth
value, it is not easy to reach agreement on the actual facts of
usage. On behalf of the non-descriptivist view, it can be claimed
that a performative like [8] cannot be denied, but that what
appears at first blush to be a denial of the performative is actually
a denial of the proposition it contains:

[8] I maintain that the United Nations is nothing but a talking-
     shop.
[9] Oh no, it isn't – it's the last hope of civilized man.

Thus [9] is not a denial of [8], but rather of the included proposition 'The United Nations is nothing but a talking-shop'. On the
other hand, the descriptivist can argue that a performative *may*
be denied in special circumstances:

{ [10] I sentence you to death.
{ [11] Oh no, you don't. The death penalty has been abolished,
         and anyway, you're not a judge.
{ [12] I hereby agree with you that the United Nations is just a
         talking-shop.
{ [13] Oh no, you don't. You don't agree with me, because my
         opinion is quite different from what you imagine.

What is clear is that circumstances in which performatives can plausibly be denied are very difficult to find. The descriptivist does not dispute this, but rather finds a pragmatic explanation of why it is so. The descriptive/non-descriptive argument about performatives is therefore yet another example of the archetypal debate about whether a given phenomenon should be handled by grammar or by pragmatics. The descriptivist adopts a complementarist position, arguing that the peculiarity of performatives is predictable from their sense and the relation between this and their force; the non-descriptivist adopts a 'semanticist' position, maintaining that the peculiarity of performatives is a matter of their fundamental logical status.

The difficulty with the non-descriptive position is that it needs a great deal of special pleading. How is it possible that a performative, which is syntactically and (arguably) semantically just like a proposition – in fact, just like a reported-speech proposition – should turn out to be not like a proposition at all? It was perhaps easier for Austin to take this line than for the present-day linguist. For a philosopher of his generation, it was easy to see one's task as the disentangling of the snares that ordinary language lays for the unwary thinker. He was happy to describe performatives as utterances which happened to be 'masquerading' in the 'disguise' of descriptive statements. But for us, it is more difficult to believe that language somehow maliciously deceives the analyst in this way. Surely performatives, which are like propositions in all other noticeable particulars, must also be like propositions in having a truth value? The descriptivist, who accounts for performatives both semantically and syntactically as a subset of *oratio obliqua* propositions, has a simpler view of language than the *non*-descriptivist, who must maintain that the remarkable resemblances between illocutionary performatives and *oratio obiqua* utterances are fortuitous.[7]

Hence the onus is very much on the non-descriptivist to prove that these things which look so much like propositions are really so different. For the descriptivist, however, it is enough to show that the peculiarity of performatives is explicable in terms of the assumptions one may reasonably make about their pragmatic interpretation, given that they are a special type of *oratio obliqua* utterance. This is what I shall now attempt to do.

Syntactically, a regular illocutionary performative utterance has certain well-known characteristics:

(i) The verb of the main clause is an illocutionary verb.
(ii) This verb is in the simple present tense.
(iii) The subject of this verb is in the first person.

(iv) The indirect object of this verb, if one is present, is *you*.
 (v) Optionally, this verb is preceded by the adverb *hereby*.
(vi) The verb is followed (except in elliptical cases) by a re-
       ported-speech clause.

Semantically, characteristics (ii)–(v) add up to a specification for
an *oratio obliqua* proposition which is reflexively indexical: in all
these ways, a performative contains references to the current
speech situation. This much follows from the regular senses of the
present tense, of first- and second-person pronouns, and of the
adverb *hereby*. The self-naming nature of performatives will be
shown more carefully in what follows.

8.4 Illocutionary performatives and *oratio obliqua*

Seeing that most illocutionary performatives are *oratio obliqua*
utterances, we have first to examine *oratio obliqua* as a phenomenon in itself, before we can explain such performatives. To
this end, let us compare the DIRECT SPEECH example [14] with the
indirect speech or *oratio obliqua* analogue [15] adding to these
the parallel performative example [16]:

[14] I will telephone you.
[15] Bill assured Pat that he would telephone her.
[16] I assure you that I'll telephone you.

The relation between [14] and its speech situation is shown in
Fig. 8.2.

[14] s_1 IA_1 (t_1) h_1 U_1
                                        ‾‾‾‾‾‾‾‾‾‾‾‾‾‾‾‾‾‾‾‾‾‾‾‾
                                        I will telephone you
                                        ↓   ↓   ↓
                                        s_1 (t_2) h_1

[where t_2 is later than t_1]

FIGURE 8.2 Direct speech

(Here the arrow ↓ represents reference, and shows that the pronouns *I* and *you* refer respectively to the speaker (s_1) and to the
hearer (h_1). The symbols s_1 (speaker), IA_1 (illocutionary act), t_1
(time of utterance), h_1 (hearer) and U_1 (utterance) define the
speech situation (*cf* 1.4) in which the utterance [14] occurs.) But
for an *oratio obliqua* example like [15], a more complex representation is needed: we have to distinguish between the PRIMARY

SPEECH SITUATION, that in which [15] itself occurs, and the SECONDARY SPEECH SITUATION, *ie* the speech situation which is described by [15]. In Fig. 8.3, these situations are distinguished by different subscripts: *eg*: s_1 signifies the s of the primary situation (the implicit 'I'), and s_2 signifies the speaker, Bill, of the secondary situation. In [15], the s, IA, t, and h of the secondary utterance are actually named in the subject, verb, tense, and indirect object of the main clause, and (to complete the description of the secondary speech situation), the content of the secondary utterance U_2 is described by the complementizer clause *that he would telephone her.*

[15] $s_1\ IA_1\ (t_1)\ h_1$ $\overline{\qquad\qquad U_1 \qquad\qquad}$

Bill assured Pat that he would telephone her
↓ ↓ ↓ ↓
$s_2 IA_2(t_2)\ h_2$ ↓
                $\overline{\qquad U_2 \qquad}$

$\overline{\qquad}$ 's_2 TELEPHONE h_2 at t_3'

[where t_2 is earlier than t_1, and t_3 is later than t_2]

FIGURE 8.3   *Oratio obliqua*

To complete the paradigm, let us consider a similar representation (Fig. 8.4) for the performative [16]. Following the descriptive view of performatives, we show [16] as a special case of the *oratio obliqua* utterance as shown in Fig. 8.3: the only difference between [15] and [16] is that in the latter case the secondary situation is identical to the primary situation.

[16] $s_1\ IA_1(t_1)\ h_1$ $\overline{\qquad\qquad U_1 \qquad\qquad}$

I assure you that I'll telephone you
↓ ↓ ↓ ↓
$s_2\ IA_2(t_2)\ h_2$ ↓
                $\overline{\qquad U_2 \qquad}$

$\overline{\qquad}$ 's_2 TELEPHONE h_2 at t_3'

[where $s_2 = s_1$, $h_2 = h_1$, $t_2 = t_1$, $IA_2 = IA_1$, $U_2 = U_1$ and t_3 is later than t_2]

FIGURE 8.4   Performative *oratio obliqua*

The identity of the primary and secondary speech situations is shown by the five equations at the bottom of Fig. 8.4: $s_1 = s_2$, $h_1 = h_2$, $t_1 = t_2$, $IA_1 = IA_2$, and $U_1 = U_2$. These equations already indicate that indexically speaking, [16] is equivalent to its nonperformative analogue [14]. To justify the descriptive account of performatives, therefore, all that is required is the justification of each of these five equations, given that a performative such as [16] has the normal grammatical characteristics of a performative. We may start with the easiest equations to justify, *viz* the first two, $s_1 = s_2$ and $h_1 = h_2$. These equations follow simply from the normal interpretations of the first- and second-person pronouns *I* and *you*. The remaining three equations are not quite so straightforward, and need to be justified by separate arguments, presented in the following three sections A-C.

A. $t_1 = t_2$ 'TIME OF PRIMARY SITUATION = TIME OF SECONDARY SITUATION'

Ostensibly there is no problem in justifying (A). The fact that the illocutionary verb is in the present tense seems to mean that it describes a speech act taking place at the present time, *ie* at the time of the primary speech act. But this is not the whole explanation. A verb in the present tense need not refer to an event happening at the time of speech, as is clear from an example like *I knock off work early on Fridays*. This sentence is likely to be uttered at a time other than knocking-off time on a Friday, and it is not likely that the event it describes in the present coincides with the speech event of uttering the sentence itself. The reason, clearly, is that the sentence has a habitual interpretation.

There is also, however, a non-habitual or punctual interpretation of the present tense with action verbs. This 'instantaneous present' means that the event described takes place (*ie* begins and ends) at the very time of speaking, and for pragmatic reasons, this in turn tends to imply that the event described is brief (otherwise, the non-punctual or progressive aspect would be used). Thus the instantaneous sense of the present tense occurs (for example) in sports commentaries as in *Johns passes the ball to Waters*, but not in the description of longer events: *He reads a book* must be given a habitual interpretation, whereas *He is reading a book*, which refers to an actual present activity, also implies that the activity has been in progress before the moment of speech, and will continue in progress after it. Because the conditions for its occurrence are difficult to satisfy, the 'instantaneous present' is rather rare.[8] But those conditions are indeed ideally satisfied in the case of a self-naming utterance, for inevitably, in such a case, the event described is simultaneous with the act of description itself.

Another kind of situation in which the 'instantaneous present' occurs is in the enactment of ceremonies, where the speaker performs a ritual action and describes himself as performing it at the same time:

[17] I *give* you this ring
    (gives ring)   – in a marriage ceremony.
[18] I *sign* you with the cross
    (makes the sign) – in a baptism.

Such examples make it easy to see that the instantaneous present that occurs in performatives is no different from the instantaneous present that occurs in descriptions of non-verbal actions. Both have a somewhat dramatic, ritualized effect, and both can be accompanied by *hereby*. Compare, for example, *I hereby give you this ring* (referring to a motor act) with *I hereby give you my word* (referring to the verbal act of making a promise).

There is no claim, however, that a sentence like [16] or [18] is necessarily performative. Unless the adverb *hereby* is added, the simple present can still be grammatically ambiguous between the habitual and instantaneous interpretations, as we have already seen with *I declare the meeting open* (*p* 180). But to justify the equation $t_1 = t_2$ as part of the interpretation of a performative, I merely need to show that given the grammatical properties of performatives, that equation is possible (and reasonably likely), not that it is necessary. Following the complementarist view, I want to argue that performative utterances are identified as such in pragmatics; but at the same time, I want to show (and have shown in this particular) that the performative interpretation of a sentence follows unproblematically from its grammatical form and sense. The next equation to justify is:

B. $U_1 = U_2$ 'PRIMARY UTTERANCE = SECONDARY UTTERANCE'
This equation appears paradoxical. How can an utterance like [19] refer to itself?·

[19] I promise [that I will telephone you].

Surely the recognized manner of referring to an utterance is to quote the actual words of which it is composed – and how can an utterance quote itself? The answer lies in the difference between the two modes of reporting illustrated in [20] and [21]:

[20] I told her: 'I'll telephone you later.'
    (direct speech)
[21] I promised her that I'd telephone her later.
    (*oratio obliqua*)

With direct speech, the reporter is committed to giving a verbatim report of what was said; in *oratio obliqua*, he is not so committed: rather, he is committed to giving a description of the utterance's meaning (in either a semantic or pragmatic sense of 'meaning'). Unlike [20], [21] could be a correct report of an utterance such as *O.K., I'll phone you in a few minutes*, or *Don't worry – I'll call you around eight*. There is no need for the words used in the secondary utterance to appear in the primary utterance. In this sense, *oratio obliqua* is metapropositional (see 7.2) rather than strictly metalinguistic.[9] From a grammatical point of view, then, there is nothing to prevent a performative like [19] from giving a true report of itself. It remains to be shown that U_1 = U_2 is plausible not only on grammatical, but on pragmatic grounds. To show this I shall adopt an informal *reductio ad absurdum* tactic. Assume first the negative situation, where $s_1 = s_2$, $h_1 = h_2$, and $t_1 = t_2$, but where $U_1 \neq U_2$. Could one, in principle, conceive of a speech situation of which these specifications were true? It is just about imaginable that s, in addressing h in a spoken utterance U_1, could simultaneously write a different message (U_2) to h, and moreover that s could use U_1 as a means of referring to U_2. Or the same thing could happen the other way round, if U_1 were the written utterance and U_2 the spoken utterance. But in practice, such a linguistic juggling act is seldom if ever observed. The nearest approach I have found to such an unlikely event occurs in this passage from *Julius Caesar*, Act IV, Scene i:

> *Octavius*: Your brother too must die. Consent you, Lepidus?
> *Lepidus*: I do consent –
> *Octavius*:   Prick him down, Antony.
> *Lepidus*: Upon condition Publius shall not live,
>   Who is your sister's son, Mark Antony.
> *Antony*: He shall not live; *look, with a spot I damn him.*

While making the written sign which condemns Publius, Antony describes that same act by speaking the words: *with a spot I damn him*. But this is a declaration rather than an illocutionary performative, and besides, the use of the non-progressive present in such cases would not occur so readily today as it did in Shakespeare's English. It is absurd to suppose that people who utter performatives normally find themselves writing a simultaneous message on a piece of paper. As a matter of pragmatic plausibility, then, it is virtually inescapable that if $s_1 = s_2$, $h_1 = h_2$, and $t_1 = t_2$, then $U_1 = U_2$.

C. $IA_1 = IA_2$ 'ILLOCUTIONARY ACT OF U_1 = ILLOCUTIONARY ACT OF U_2'

It need not take long to justify the remaining equation, $IA_1 = IA_2$. For if the primary and secondary utterances are identical, the primary utterance cannot consistently refer to itself as having an illocutionary force other than the illocutionary force that it has.

Again, for the sake of argument, let us suppose the contrary. Suppose that s, in uttering [19] *I promise that I will telephone you*, really, in his heart of hearts, is not promising at all (having no intention of performing the action mentioned), but is simply making a suggestion. Then we might argue that U_1 is not a promise, but that U_2 is (*ie* that $IA_1 \neq IA_2$). But even if this were consistent with the use of term *promise*, it would in fact be absurd. For it would follow that if U_2 were not a promise, then U_1, which is identical to U_2, would not be a promise either. (The performative proposition *I promise... would simply be untrue*). So when a performative verb is used in a sentence like [19], it must be being used to describe the illocutionary force of the utterance of which it is a part. This conclusion is entirely convincing from a pragmatic point of view: on the rather rare occasions when performatives are used, they evidently have the function of rendering explicit, in situations where clarity and explicitness are important, the illocutionary force of the utterances containing them.

8.5 The pragmatics of illocutionary performatives

What I have argued in 8.4 is not only that the descriptive theory of performatives is possible, but that it is the only plausible interpretation there is, once one accepts that the present tense of the performative verb is non-habitual. In accordance with the complementarist position, however, my argument is that a performative utterance derives its property as a performative from pragmatics, as well as from semantics. (For this reason, I use the term 'performative utterance' rather than 'performative sentence'). Semantically, it is a proposition with a present-tense verb, and is ambiguous between the habitual and instantaneous interpretations. But pragmatically, it is a self-naming utterance which has the force indicated by its main verb. Thus the performative wears its illocutionary heart on its sleeve, whereas for non-performative utterances, the illocutionary force has to be inferred pragmatically (*ie* is implicit rather than explicit).

One thing which pragmatics has to explain, in this account, is the relation of a performative to its non-performative analogue: *eg* between [22] and [23]:

[22] I admit that Gus is greedy.
[23] Gus is greedy.

Since this relation has been assumed to be one of equivalence, and has thereby been made much of in standard treatments of performatives, the first point to make here is that in the complementarist view, as has been made clear, this is not an equivalence relation. None the less, there is a kind of rough equivalence to be explained: *eg* that the speaker of [22], like the speaker of [23], commits himself to the truth of the proposition that 'Gus is greedy'. (This rough equivalence would, however, be much less apparent if the performative verb in [22] were, say, *suggest* or *guess* rather than *admit*).

Since a performative is semantically a proposition, the derivation of its force from its sense follows the pattern already proposed for affirmative declarative utterances (7.3.3.1). We assume, by the Maxim of Quality, that if s is obeying the CP, s is telling the truth, *ie* that s is being sincere in designating the illocution as a 'promise', an 'admission', etc. The Maxim of Quality must be held to apply to such cases in default of evidence that s is being insincere, which would be difficult if not impossible to obtain. (Compare the problem of disconfirming propositional attitude statements such as *I believe that dinner is ready*). Moreover, if the description of the illocution is sincere, this has implications for s's commitment to the truth of the secondary utterance. For example, it is part of the sense of an assertive illocutionary verb like *admit* that any proposition 's admits [that P]' means that if s is being sincere, s believes P to be true. Hence the fact that both [22] and [23] imply that s believes that 'Gus is greedy' can be explained by pragmatic inference as follows:

That [23] implies s believes 'Gus is greedy' is due to
 (i) the normal interpretation of positive propositions, assuming the Maxim of Quality (see 7.3.3.1).
That [22] implies s believes 'Gus is greedy' is due to (i) above, and also to
 (ii) the sense of *admit* as an English illocutionary verb, and
(iii) the logical principle of transitivity of reflexive belief, (see Ch. 4, note 7), that if x believes that x believes that Y, then x believes that Y.

The derivation runs as follows, given that the non-performative interpretation of [22] has been ruled out:

A. s_1 believes that [s_1 admits that Gus is greedy] is true (Maxim of Quality)

B. s_1 believes that [s_1, if observing the Maxim of Quality, believes [that Gus is greedy]] (from A, and the dictionary sense
of *admit*)

C. s_1 believes that [s_1 believes that Gus is greedy] (from B and
the Maxim of Quality)

D. s_1 believes [that Gus is greedy] (from C and transitivity of reflexive belief)

This type of argument can be used to show that the same implicatures are derivable from the performative and its non-
performative analogue, on the assumption that the performative
is in logical terms a proposition just like any other proposition.
On the other hand, it is also clear that the performative conveys
some elements of meaning which are not conveyed by its analogue. For example, from the sense of the verb *admit*, [22] also
entails that *s* believes that [Gus is greedy] is in conflict with other
beliefs which *s* maintains (see 9.5). This element of meaning,
which is explicitly conveyed by [22], could only be weakly implicated, or indicated though context, in the case of [23]. In this
way, the descriptive view of performatives accords with the
observation that

(a) performatives are often partly equivalent to their non-
performative analogues, but

(b) performatives express additional meaning which, if conveyed
at all, is only conveyed implicitly by their non-performative
analogues.

What I have proposed, then, is that to interpret performatives,
we have to interpret the illocutionary verb as part of the propositional sense of the utterance, and then, assuming that a performative is a self-naming proposition, the remainder of the
interpretation follows according to general patterns of inference
such as are exemplified in Chapter 7. We started from the pre-
mise that there is no essential difference between illocutionary performatives and other *oratio obliqua* propositions. The explanation works in the opposite direction from that associated with
'standard' speech-act theory: whereas for Austin and for non-
descriptivists, the meaning of the non-performative is reached via
the performative, in the present account the meaning of the performative is arrived at as a special case of the interpretation of
non-performatives. Since non-performatives are obviously simpler and more usual than performatives, the latter explanation is
more satisfactory on common-sense grounds, as well as for the
other reasons I have given.

8.6 The performative hypothesis

The arguments I have put forward against the Illocutionary-Verb
Fallacy apply *a fortiori* to the PERFORMATIVE HYPOTHESIS of Ross
(1970) and others. As already explained, this is the hypothesis
that in its underlying structure, every sentence has a higher clause
with the properties of a performative. In effect, this hypothesis
implies that a sentence like [24] has something like [25] as its
deep structure:

[24] Be careful.
[25] I IMPERE you [that you be careful].

(Here IMPERE is meant to be a generalized imperative verb: the
actual identity of the performative verb, or even whether it has
an overt surface-structure form at all, is not essential to the
hypothesis.) The equivalence between the performative and its
non-performative analogue is here achieved by the straightforward device of syntactic transformation: an optional PERFORMA-
TIVE-DELETION transformation which converts a sentence like [25]
into a sentence like (*You*) *be careful*. Hence, according to this
hypothesis, all sentences are 'deep down' performatives. The explicit performatives, like [26], are simply those exceptional sentences to which performative deletion has not applied:

[26] I order you to be careful.

It is assumed that this transformation, like others within a generative semantics framework, does not change meaning. The hypothesis therefore requires acceptance of the simplistic view that there
is a precise correspondence between the meanings of performatives and of their non-performative analogues. Another consequence of the hypothesis is that illocutionary force is defined in
grammatical terms, as explained by Sadock (1974:19):

[27] ... illocutionary force is that part of the meaning of a
     sentence which corresponds to the highest clause in its
     semantic representation.

It is plain that the performative hypothesis is in conflict with
everything I have argued (especially in Ch. 2) about the pragmatic
nature of illocutionary force, and the distinction between semantics and pragmatics.

It would take too long to present here even a small number of
the arguments which have been propounded both in favour of
and against the performative hypothesis. After the hypothesis
was put forward in the late 1960s, it flourished vigorously for a

few years, but was also subjected to severe attacks by a large number of critics, Searle, interestingly enough, being one of the most severe of them (see Anderson 1971; Fraser 1971; Searle 1979 [1975c]; Leech 1980 [1976]; Holdcroft 1978; Gazdar 1979). Even so, the performative hypothesis cannot be dismissed as being of historical interest only, as publications still appear in which it is assumed to be true, or at least taken seriously.[10]

Thus, although there would be no point in marshalling either old or new arguments against the hypothesis here, there is some value in briefly considering why the performative hypothesis arose, and why the obvious appeal it had for many linguists in the early 1970s did not persist. The original arguments in favour of the hypothesis were regarded as 'syntactic' arguments (see Ross 1970 for fourteen such arguments). Even at the outset of its popularity, Ross admitted that the performative hypothesis could be replaced by a 'pragmatic hypothesis' which would be as explanatory as the performative hypothesis, and possibly more so. But Ross regarded the 'pragmatic hypothesis' as being incapable of proper formulation, because it required the postulation of entities such as 'speaker' and 'hearer' which somehow existed 'in the air', outside the structure of the sentence (*ibid*. 254–8). The pragmatic hypothesis would, in fact, have replaced the deep-structure tree diagram (like that of [25]) postulated by the performativists by a diagram (like that of Fig. 8.4) in which the performative subject and verb, etc. would be replaced by pragmatic entities such as *s* and *IA*. Once this step had been taken, the performative hypothesis would have become unnecessary. But for many linguists of the early 1970s it was difficult to conceive of any linguistic explanation which did not take place within the framework of grammar. Hence Ross's correct insight – that the pragmatic hypothesis would be preferable to the performative hypothesis – was subsequently ignored both by himself and by others.

8.7 The extended performative hypothesis

The most extreme manifestation of the performative hypothesis is a variant of it developed in most detail by Sadock (1974 – but see also various contributions in Cole and Morgan 1975), and which may be called the EXTENDED PERFORMATIVE HYPOTHESIS. This is the hypothesis that the illocutionary force not only of a direct speech act, but also of an indirect speech act, can be appropriately formalized in a performative deep structure. For example, an

indirect request such as [28a] would be derived from a deep structure roughly like [28b]:

[28a] Can you close the window?
[28b] I request that you close the window.

Although Sadock does not claim that all indirect illocutions can
be explained in this way, he does claim that some can, and
moreover that it is possible to provide a set of criteria for deciding whether the underlying performative represents the indirect
illocutionary force or not. The criteria in question are 'syntactic'.
For example, the fact that [28a] can contain a mid-occurrence of
please is treated as a sign of its underlying status as a request:

[28c] Can you *please* close the window?

But such criteria as are offered are difficult to apply. If, for instance, [28a] is changed into a slightly different example with roughly the same force, may the word *please* still be inserted?

[29a] Would it be possible for you to close the window?
[29c] Would it *please* be possible for you to close the window?

And what about:

[30] ?? Are you *please* able to close the window?

In this area, acceptability judgements about sentences are particularly uncertain, which is itself a sign that we are dealing with
questions of pragmatics rather than grammar. But Sadock is on
less shaky ground when he points out that the extent to which indirect illocutions can be dealt with in grammar constitutes a gra-
dient of 'idiomatization', rather like the scale of 'idiomatization' in
the lexicon reflecting the way metaphors become institutionalized
by historical evolution. This process of 'idiomatization' (or
pragmatic specialization, as I called it in 2.3) accounts for the
occurrence of hybrid sentences which appear to combine the
grammatical characteristics associated with different kinds of
utterance. *Shut the window, can you*? combines features of a
command and a question. *Let's have a look at the hand, may I*?
combines features of a suggestion and of a request. *I'd like to
know, please, what are you going to say*? combines features of a
statement and a question. Such hybrids do occur quite frequently,
and it is a merit of Sadock and like-minded linguists that they
have focused on these anomalies and also labelled them by pic-
turesque portmanteau terms such as 'whimperative' and 'quec-
larative' (Sadock 1974:80, 105). The trouble is, however, that
although they are supposed to provide grammatical motivation

for the extended performative hypothesis, such sentences do not lend themselves to generalization in any kind of grammatical framework, being essentially exceptions to general rules. It is no wonder that Sadock and others advocating this hypothesis never got round to formulating the precise details of deep structures and transformations which it required.[11] To borrow Austin's term, an indirect illocution is a case of a sentence 'masquerading' as a sentence of a different type. From the grammatical point of view this masquerade must appear as unmotivated perversity, a needless complexity of language; while from the pragmatic point of view it can hopefully be explained in terms of the general principles of rational, purposive human behaviour.

In all significant respects, the present account is completely at odds with the extended performative hypothesis. First, the hypothesis implies that indirect force[12] can be adequately represented by a performative verb – an approach which totally fails to deal with the subtlety of indirectness in human communication. Secondly, it treats the distinction between direct and indirect force as simply an all-or-nothing matter (either a question is 'deep down' a request, or it is not), while I have argued that it is a matter of degree. Thirdly, no attempt is made to give a functional motivation for the relation between sense and force: for the extended performative hypothesis, it is just an arbitrary fact of grammar that a request can be rendered by means of a *Can you?* question, but not (say) by means of a *Shall I?* question. Fourthly, the relation between the direct and indirect force of an utterance (*eg* between *Can you squeeze through?* as an information question and as a request for action) is seen as a grammatical ambiguity, rather than as a matter of two coexisting meanings, one being conveyed by virtue of the other. In all these respects, I would argue that the extended performative hypothesis fails to account for fairly obvious and commonplace observations about how linguistic communication works. It was, to my mind, this elaboration of the performative hypothesis which showed most plainly the inadequacy of the attempt to squeeze pragmatics into the unyielding mould of grammar.

8.8 Conclusion

Within 'standard' speech-act theory, the classification of illocutionary acts has been an important pastime of those wishing to make a thorough survey of 'the things one can do with words'. Such a classification, as provided notably by Austin and Searle, is inevitably regarded as a taxonomy (a system of categories and subcategories). Moreover, the taxonomy has tended to reflect the assumption that the existence of an illocutionary performative verb justifies the existence of an illocutionary category.

My position is quite different from this, but oddly enough, my interest in the meaning and classification of speech-act verbs is almost as great as those of Austin, Searle, and others who have followed their example. The subject – the classification of verb meanings – remains the same, but there is a significant shift of viewpoint: I want to study these meanings not as a key to the nature of illocutionary *acts*, but as the key to how people (using the English language) *talk* about illocutionary acts. Already, in the discussion of the verb *admit* in 8.4, we have seen the relevance of verb meanings to the understanding of performatives. In the next chapter, this study of speech-act verbs in taken further. At this point, therefore, we are strictly speaking leaving pragmatics for semantics. But since we will be dealing with the part of semantics which acts as a metalanguage for pragmatics, the difference will not be so obvious as one might expect.

Notes

1. In Searle's case the embrace was clandestine, and explicitly disowned in Searle (1979 [1975a]). See the discussion below.
2. Searle is thinking in terms of a transformational grammar in which each type of performative sentence will have a fairly standard deep structure representation, various syntactic variations being introduced by transformations. Why does Searle restrict his attention to performatives, when he could just as easily broaden his scope to consider the use of illocutionary verbs in general? The reason appears to be that he is still somewhat under the influence of the Performative Verb Fallacy.
3. Searle (1979 [1975a]: 16–20). For declarations, it is significant that Searle does postulate a deep structure containing a performative even for non-performative utterances: for *You're fired* he postulates the following analysis:
   I declare: your employment is (hereby) terminated.
   This underlines the essentially 'performative' nature of declarations, in contrast to other kinds of speech act.
4. *Cf* the distinction drawn by Bach and Harnish (1979:108–19) between communicative and conventional illocutionary acts. The latter correspond largely to Searle's declarations.
5. It is worth bearing in mind that some verbs capable of being used performatively do not necessarily describe a speech act (*eg: object*), and also that some expressions describing speech acts are not verbs (*eg: to give one's word = to promise*).
6. Recent contributions to the descriptive–non-descriptive controversy are Harris (1978) and Spielmann (1980).

7. The non-descriptivist might in this respect be compared with an anti-Darwinian for whom the theory of natural selection could be used to explain relations between non-human species, but could not be used to explain anything about *homo sapiens*.

8. See Leech (1971:2–3; 1980 [1976]:66) on the instantaneous present and its relevance to performatives. We cannot understand 'instantaneity' and 'simultaneity' in this connection in a literal and physical sense. Notice, for example, that speakers use the instantaneous present in *I tell a lie* to describe an utterance spoken recently, although strictly a past tense or present perfective verb would be more appropriate.

9. See note 3, *p* 172. Austin draws a related distinction between phatic and rhetic acts (1962:95).

10. A recent and fairly sympathetic account of the performative hypothesis (also called the performative analysis) is given in McCawley (1981:210–15).

11. A critique of the extended performative hypothesis from this point of view is given in Leech (1977: esp. 143–5).

12. To be accurate, Sadock (1974:77–9) entertains three different hypotheses, called the SM ('surface-meaning'), UM ('use-meaning'), and MM ('meaning-meaning') hypotheses, of which only one assumes that the indirect illocution is always present in the sentence in the form of a deep structure performative. This he contrasts with Gordon and Lakoff's (1971) formalism of transderivational constraints. All of Sadock's hypotheses, however, take for granted the representation of illocutionary force by means of a deep structure performative.

Chapter 9

Speech-act verbs in English

Don't tell your friends about your indigestion:
'How are you!' is a greeting, not a question.

[Arthur Guiterman, *A Poet's Proverbs*]

In studying speech-act verbs, we shall find useful the distinctions which Austin, Searle, and others have made in their classification of speech acts themselves. This is no accident, and no cause for apology: for my argument has been that speech-act philosophers, in appearing to study speech acts, have tended to concentrate their attention on the meanings of speech-act verbs. Moreover, it is plausible to assume, without taking up any doctrinaire position, that there is likely to be a close similarity between the sorts of distinctions which are important in the analysis of speech-act verbs, and the sorts of distinctions which are important in the speech-act behaviour these verbs are used to describe. It would be perversely anti-Whorfian to suppose that, on the contrary, the verbs with which our language equips us for discussing communicative behaviour require us to draw distinctions which are not significant in the behaviour itself. The functional theory put forward in Chapter 3 (*pp* 47–62), indeed, gives reason for supposing otherwise. But one substantial difference between talking about speech acts and talking about speech-act verbs is, of course, that the distinctions which are non-categorical or scalar in the former case are categorical in the latter case. As Searle says (and we may follow him this far), 'Differences in illocutionary verbs are a good guide, but by no means a sure guide, to differences in illocutionary acts' (1979:2).

Another difference is that in talking of speech-act verbs we necessarily concern ourselves with particular verbs in particular languages. I shall be discussing speech-act verbs of English (by no means exhaustively) in this chapter, and make no claim to be dealing with the universal principles of linguistic behaviour.

9.1 Locutionary, illocutionary, and perlocutionary

A fitting way to begin the study of speech-act verbs is with the well-known distinction Austin makes between three kinds of speech act: a LOCUTIONARY act (performing the act *of* saying something), an ILLOCUTIONARY act (performing an act *in* saying something), and a PERLOCUTIONARY act (performing an act *by* saying something). For example:

LOCUTION: s says to h that X.
(X being certain words spoken with a certain sense and reference)
ILLOCUTION: In saying X, s ASSERTS that P.
PERLOCUTION: By saying X, s CONVINCES h that P.

The chief value of the distinction, for Austin, as for the present study, is that it enables us to separate the middle category – the one with which the theory of speech acts is centrally concerned – from the other two.[1]

In the first place, however, let us rethink this triple classification in terms of the process model of communication put forward in Chapters 2 and 3. Returning to Fig. 3.3 (*p* 59), we may provisionally identify the locutionary act with the transmission of the message (ideational communication), and the illocutionary act with the transmission of discourse (interpersonal communication). The only modification of this statement is that the 'illocutionary goal' of a discourse has been distinguished, in earlier chapters, from other social goals – the 'social goals' of maintaining cooperation, and politeness, etc. For this reason, the means–ends diagram (Fig. 9.1) shows more than one goal-arrow con-

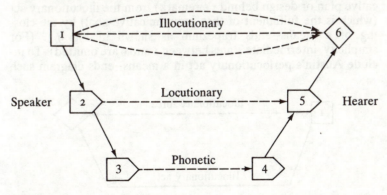

FIGURE 9.1

necting the initial and final states. The bottom line of Fig. 9.1, corresponding to the *text* in Fig. 3.3, *p* 59 can appropriately receive the label 'phonetic', following Austin's term *phonetic act* for the actual physical execution of the utterance. Figure 9.1 could also be filled out with additional parallel lines corresponding to what Austin calls rhetic and phrastic acts (or, in the terms of the discussion on *pp* 57–60, the semantic and syntactic levels of coding). But the main point is that the different kinds of speech act can be interpreted as comprising a hierarchy of instrumentality, one act forming a link in a chain of events which constitute another act, further up the hierarchy. (We will come to the perlocutionary act in a moment.)

But there is another aspect of the interpretation of Fig. 9.1 which needs consideration. As a means–ends diagram, Fig. 9.1 shows the illocution and locution as goals rather than as actions. Only if the sequence of events 2—3—4—5 takes place, so that the hearer decodes the message appropriately, will the locutionary act be performed; and only if the sequence 1—2—3—4—5—6 takes place will the illocutionary act be performed, and the utterance be understood to be a promise, or a claim, or whatever it is intended to be. In describing the rules for illocutionary acts, Searle assumes the 'normal input and output conditions' obtain, *eg* that *s* and *h* speak the same language, that *h* is not deaf or out of earshot; he also assumes that *s* and *h* are operating with the same conditions for the interpretation of illocutionary acts. We may make the same assumptions, and say that unless these conditions obtain, the illocutionary act, whatever *s*'s intention may be, will not be effectively performed. Thus Fig. 9.1 may be shown to distinguish illocutionary force (which is the communicative plan or design behind *s*'s remark) from the illocutionary act (which is the fulfilment of that communicative goal) by the closing of a means–ends trapezium as shown in Fig. 9.2. (For simplicity, intermediate states between 1 and 6 are omitted). To include Austin's perlocutionary act in a means–ends diagram such

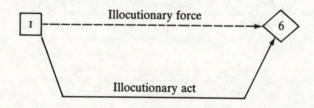

FIGURE 9.2

as Fig. 9.1, one can simply add one further layer to the hierarchy
as shown in Fig. 9.3. (I do not use the labels 'perlocutionary
force' or 'locutionary force' for the horizontal goal-arrows in
Fig. 9.3, but some more neutral word like 'plan' may be preferred. The term 'act', however, as in Fig. 9.2, can properly be
applied only to the sequence of events enacted in order to reach
the goal from the initial state; *ie* the perlocutionary act is represented, in Fig. 9.3, by the sequence 1—2—3—4—5—6—7—8,
the illocutionary act by the sequence 2—3—4—5—6—7, and
the locutionary act by the sequence 3—4—5—6.)

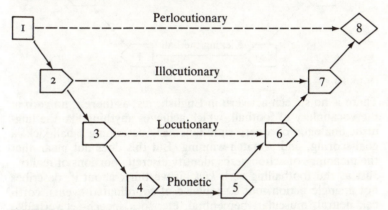

FIGURE 9.3

Although it is convenient and traditional, the practice of talking about linguistic behaviour as consisting of individual 'acts' is
somewhat misleading and possibly confusing. When we describe a
speaker, in Austin's terms, as simultaneously engaged in three
kinds of speech act (locutionary, illocutionary, and perlocutionary), this is rather like describing an event in a football match as
follows:

The centre-forward has kicked the ball; moreover, he has
scored a goal; and furthermore, he has won the match!

Linguistic behaviour, like football, is made up of complexes of
activity, rather than of single events, and it is often preferable, as
in the means–ends model, to describe more abstract events as
made up of chains of more concrete events, as in Fig. 9.4. The
atomistic tendency to think of linguistic activity in terms of individual and separable acts has, I believe, been encouraged by the
covert or overt assumption (which we have already encountered
as the source of the Illocutionary-Verb Fallacy) that the language

we possess for talking about speech behaviour must be a faithful reflection of its nature. We normally describe acts singly – one per proposition or clause – and the verbs we use in this description are easily imagined to have mutually exclusive reference.

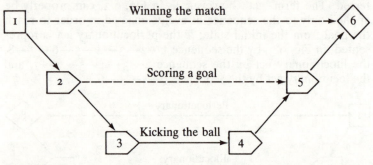

FIGURE 9.4

There is no speech-act verb in English, just as there is no verb in the vocabulary of football, which achieves anything like the linguistic analogue of a verb simultaneously describing a ball-kick, a goal-scoring, and a match-winning. But this does not mean that the meanings of action verbs identify discrete 'portions of reality'. Just as the footballing verb *kick*, if we think about it, describes not a single action, but a sequence of coordinated events, cortical, neural, muscular, perceptual, etc. so a speech-act verb like *thank* implies a whole set of coordinated actions, some of which may be appropriately described by other speech-act verbs such as *say* or *utter*. Here is a further reason, then, for not taking the correspondence between speech-act verbs and the reality they describe for granted.

If we think of a perlocutionary act quite generally as the action (or activity complex) of achieving something by means of speech, then not all perlocutionary acts are appropriately represented in the means–ends diagram of Fig. 9.3. The figure represents only a perlocutionary effect which follows as an intended result of the hearer's interpretation of the speaker's illocutionary goal. The verb *inform*, for example, normally denotes a speech act which intentionally brings about in *h* a state of knowledge which did not exist before.[2] The verb *convince* denotes a speech act which results in a new state of opinion. Still other perlocutionary verbs imply a more active response from *h*. Thus while *ask* denotes an illocutionary act which has, as a success condition, a decision by *h* to carry out the action that *s* intends, the perlocutionary verbs *prevail upon* and *incite* incorporate that success condition as part of their meaning:

Joe incited Bill to rob the bank

entails that Bill subsequently adopted Joe's goal of robbing the bank. But

Joe asked Bill to rob the bank

means only that if Bill subsequently determined to rob the bank, then Joe's request was successful. These and other perlocutionary acts so far discussed are described by causative verbs which normally incorporate the intended results of illocutionary acts.

There are, however, other kinds of causative verbs which have been assumed to denote perlocutionary acts. A distinction may be made, for example, between effects which are planned, and those which are not. When *s bores* or *embarrasses* or *irritates* his audience, most likely the result is unintended, and therefore does not form part of a means–ends analysis. Further, there are effects of greater or of less directness: the ultimate result of a *reproach* may be to bring about a desired *reformation* of *h*'s behaviour; but an intermediate result will be that of making *h* feel guilty or sorry. The means–ends analysis of indirect illocutions (4.3) has already anticipated such a chain of causes and effects. However, it is unnecessary to be too deeply concerned with these distinctions: perlocutionary effects do not form part of the study of pragmatics, since pragmatic force has to do with goals rather than with results.

9.2 A survey of speech-act verb classes

9.2.1 Illocutionary and perlocutionary verbs
The contrasts between illocutions, perlocutions, and other speech-act categories have typically been illustrated by lists of verbs and verb-like expressions; for example:

ILLOCUTIONARY: *report, announce, predict, admit, opine, ask, reprimand, request, suggest, order, propose, express, congratulate, promise, thank, exhort.*
PERLOCUTIONARY: *bring h to learn that, persuade, deceive, encourage, irritate, frighten, amuse, get h to do, inspire, impress, distract, get h to think about, relieve tension, embarrass, attract attention, bore.*

[adapted from Alston 1964:35]

My purpose now is to survey the major kinds of speech-act verb that exist, defining speech-act verbs as verbs which have, as a primary part of their meaning, a predicate of speaking. But especially I shall want to see how illocutionary verbs can be distinguished from other categories. This is not as easy a task as might be supposed, since the boundaries of verb meanings tend to be unclear, as is the boundary of the speech-act verb category itself. Many verbs which are cited in lists are not really speech-act verbs at all. Thus, in Alston's lists above, *deceive* and *amuse*, although they resemble perlocutionary verbs in being causative, actually denote psychological effects which can be attained either by linguistic or by non-linguistic means.[3] Similarly, verbs like *conclude* and *reveal*, which appear in lists of illocutionary acts,[4] primarily denote events of an intellectual nature, and only optionally involve linguistic events which cause or manifest such events. Compare:

[1] The observers *concluded* that the climate was slowly changing.

[2] The lecturer *concluded* that the climate was slowly changing.

Concluded could well be glossed in [1] as 'reached the conclusion that', and in [2] as 'said in conclusion that'. In this way, the intellectual sense of *conclude* (*ie* drawing a conclusion from evidence, or from premises, by argument) could be distinguished from the speech-act sense. But to complicate matters further, *concluded* in [2] could also be meant in the intellectual sense, *ie* 'The lecturer explained the conclusion to which the logical argument of his lecture was pointing.' We have therefore to allow for problems of blurring and overlap between speech-act and non-speech-act verbs.

Similarly, we have to reckon with verbs which shift between the illocutionary and perlocutionary classes. A slight difference is discernible between verbs like *inform* and *tell*, which appear to imply the fulfilment of the perlocutionary goal of 'causing *h* to know something', and those like *report* and *ask*, which seem not to take for granted the success of the illocution. But is this difference clear-cut? One useful test for distinguishing illocutionary from perlocutionary verbs is to place the verb in the context 'try to VERB':

[3] She *tried to persuade* me to accompany her.

[4] She *tried to ask* me to accompany her.

In the case of the perlocutionary verb of [3], *try* implicates (see *pp* 87–8) that the illocution failed to achieve its intended perlocutionary effect. But in the case of the illocutionary verb of [4], this obvious kind of interpretation is not available; instead, we have to conclude that the illocutionary act misfired in some way – probably because Searle's 'normal input and output conditions' were for some reason not satisfied. Thus 'tried to ask' suggests that (say) *h* was not listening, could not be found, or could not understand *s*'s use of language.

This test, which is clear enough for *ask* and *persuade* in [3] and [4], is less clear for verbs like *inform, tell,* and *report*, because it is more difficult here to envisage cases in which the illocution was performed, but where the intended perlocution failed to come off. But perhaps we may detect a difference parallel to that between [3] and [4], though less obvious, between [5] and [6]:

[5] Sir Bors *tried to report* to the king that the battle was lost.
[6] Sir Bors *tried to tell* the king that the battle was lost.

While [5] favours the interpretation that Sir Bors could not (say) find the king or gain an audience (illocutionary failure, due to deficient 'input or output conditions'), [6] allows the interpretation that Sir Bors, although he spoke to the king, could not get him to accept the truth of his report (perlocutionary failure).

9.2.2 Classifying illocutionary verbs

Such examples, however, are still rather unclear: that is no certain way of circumscribing the class of illocutionary verbs 'from the outside'. A more promising way of trying to define it is to seek an extensional definition, in terms of its subcategories. Here we will also meet some difficulty, but at least we can turn for help to the various taxonomies of illocutionary acts which have been proposed by Austin (1962), by Searle (1979 [1975a]), and by Bach and Harnish (1979). These taxonomies have a strong family resemblance, which at face value suggests that they may be near the truth.[5] Searle's taxonomy, which has already been introduced in 5.2, will provide a useful starting point – so long as we continue to remember that his concern is with illocutionary acts, and only incidentally with the corresponding classes of illocutionary verbs.

As the meanings of these illocutionary categories have already been outlined on *pp* 105–07, it will be better to concentrate first on the syntactic characteristics of these verbs,[6] before moving on to their semantic analysis in 9.4.

1. ASSERTIVE VERBS normally occur in the construction '*S* VERB (. . .) that *X*', where *S* is the subject (referring to the speaker), and where 'that *X*' refers to a proposition: *eg: affirm, allege, assert, forecast, predict, announce, insist.*
2. DIRECTIVE VERBS[7] normally occur in the construction '*S* VERB (*O*) that *X*' or '*S* VERB *O* to *Y*', where *S* and *O* are subject and object (referring to s_2 and h_2 respectively), where 'that *X*' is a

non-indicative *that*-clause, and where 'to *Y*' is an infinitive clause; *eg: ask, beg, bid, command, demand, forbid, recommend, request*. Unlike the *that*-clauses following assertive verbs, these non-indicative *that*-clauses contain a subjunctive or a modal like *should*, since they refer to a mand (see 5.5) rather than to a proposition; *eg: We requested that the ban (should) be lifted*.

3. COMMISSIVE VERBS normally occur in the construction '*S* VERB that *X*' (where the *that*-clause is again non-indicative), or '*S* VERB to *Y*', where 'to *Y*' is again an infinitive construction; *eg: offer, promise, swear, volunteer, vow*. Commissive verbs, which form a relatively small class, resemble directive verbs in having non-indicative complementizers (*that*-clauses and infinitive clauses), which necessarily have posterior time reference (*ie* time reference later than that of the main verb). There is therefore a case for merging the directive and commissive verbs into one 'superclass'.

4. EXPRESSIVE VERBS normally occur in the construction '*S* VERB (prep) (*O*) (prep) *X*n', where '(prep)' is an optional preposition, and where *X*n is an abstract noun phrase or a gerundive phrase; *eg: apologize, commiserate, congratulate, pardon, thank*.

Searle's fifth category of DECLARATIONS has already been considered in some detail (see 8.2.1), and it has been seen that declarations do not have an illocutionary force as it has been understood in this study (see 2.3.4). Rather, declarations are conventional speech acts, and derive their force from the part they play in a ritual.[8] In any event, most of the verbs associated with declarations (such as *adjourn, veto, sentence*, and *baptize*) essentially describe social acts, rather than speech acts (where 'social acts' means 'World 3 acts' in the sense of Table 3.1, *p* 52).

Searle's first four categories, therefore, will provide the nucleus of the set of English illocutionary verbs. Although they are not unproblematic and not exhaustive, they do define a rather homogeneous group of verbs with definable semantic and syntactic characteristics. But there is one group of verbs, question-introducing verbs like *ask, inquire, query* and *question*, which does not fit easily into any of them, although often treated as a subclass of directives. Because they are distinguished by their selection of an indirect question as complementizer, however, I prefer, for syntactic and semantic reasons, to recognize for these a fifth category of ROGATIVE verbs, which, like that of commissive verbs, is small but reasonably well-defined.

There are also verbs of referring, classifying, and predicating which, although they appear in lists of illocutions and performative verbs,[9] do not fit the category of illocutionary verbs according to present criteria. These are words such as *name, class, describe, define, identify*, and *attribute*. Some of them, like *classify* and *identify*, are not speech-act verbs at all, but rather 'cognitive verbs', describing the human processing of thoughts and experiences. Others, like *define*, stand for linguistic acts which are LOCUTIONARY (to do with 'said' meaning) rather than illocutionary. They carry no implication that *s* is communicating with an addressee: it is quite possible to *define, describe* or *refer* to things without there being an addressee to take note of the fact. The difference between such verbs and illocutionary verbs can be detected again by the test of using 'try to VERB' as a context:

[7] I tried to thank/congratulate/pardon the driver.
[8] I tried to define/name/refer to the driver.

Both [7] and [8] implicate that there are something wrong with the process of encoding or decoding ('normal input or output conditions'). But for the illocutionary verbs of [7], the hitch could be imagined as happening at *h*'s end: perhaps *h* was too far away to hear, did not take any notice, etc. But for the verbs in [8] the hitch must be located in *s*'s encoding process. For example, *I tried to define my feelings* suggests that I failed to find a suitable verbal representation of my feelings, rather than that the addressee, because of (say) impaired hearing, failed to make sense of my words.

9.2.3 Problems of classification and their solution

Mention must be made of two problems which arise with the four illocutionary categories I have borrowed from Searle. The first problem is that of polysemy. Some verbs are versatile enough to fit both syntactically and semantically into more than one category. *Advise, suggest*, and *tell*, for example, can be either assertive or directive:

She $\left\{ \begin{array}{l} \textit{advised} \text{ us} \\ \textit{suggested} \\ \textit{told} \text{ us} \end{array} \right\}$ that there had been a mistake.

She $\left\{ \begin{array}{l} \textit{advised} \text{ us to arrive early.} \\ \textit{suggested} \text{ that we (should) arrive early.} \\ \textit{told} \text{ us to arrive early.} \end{array} \right.$

This means that the lexicon of speech-act verbs must include mul-

tiple entries, which is not surprising, since it is the case for the
lexicon of English as a whole. What is less easy to account for is
the aspects of these words' meanings which seem to remain constant from one sense to another; for example, *suggest* both as an
assertive and as a directive implies a tentative illocution, in contrast to *tell*. There are also cases like *warn*, which belongs both to
the assertive and the directive category:

> They *warned* us that food was expensive.
> They *warned* us to take enough money.

But in this case, whatever the syntactic construction, the illocutionary meaning is simultaneously both assertive (warning *h* that
something will happen if...) and directive (warning *h* to do
something about it). That is, we must regard *warn* as a verb de-
noting a single compound speech act. Other verbs, notably,
threaten, are similar.[10] The main point, however, is that illocutionary verbs are capable of polysemy, and therefore that our
classification is not so much a classification of verbs, as of verb
SENSES.

   A second problem is that some verbs, like *greet* (which is simply followed by a direct object), do not take any of the clausal
complementizers described in 9.2.3, although semantically they
might be supposed to imply one. To deal with this, we could
stipulate as Searle does, that the syntactic frames associated with
each verb category are 'deep structures' which may appear in surface structure in various disguises. This would explain not only
the nonconformity of *greet*, but also the ability of other verbs,
such as *advise*, to occur without the normal complementizer
pattern.[11] For instance, the occurrence of *advise* followed only by
a direct object, as in *The doctor advised a rest*, would derive from
some such deep structure as *The doctor advised h to take a rest*.
My solution (which in practice may not seem very different) is to
replace this 'deep structure' analysis by an analysis at the level of
semantic representation (see 2.1, 5.5), where we are no longer
concerned with speech-act verbs, but rather with the speech-act
PREDICATES which they realize, and where the reported utterance
is represented by a metapropositional argument. Now, there is no
reason to expect that the speech-act verb expresses just the
speech-act predicate and no more. Its definition may incorporate
other aspects of the underlying semantic representation, and may
include part or all of the specification of the utterance content.
Superficially, [9] and [10] look dissimilar:

[9]   Joan *greeted* Obadiah.
[10] Joan *congratulated* Obadiah on winning the race.

But it is arguable that the semantic representation of [9] contains a component of 'expressing pleasure in X', just as [10] does. With *greet*, though, the sense of 'expressing pleasure in meeting h' is all part of the meaning of the verb, while with *congratulate*, the verb tells us merely that the event X is something pleasant for h, and the exact nature of X has to be made explicit, if explicitness is required. It must be accepted, then, that the superficial syntactic form of a sentence is not necessarily a good guide to the semantic structure implied by a given illocutionary verb. *Greet* is to be treated as an expressive verb, even though it lacks the typical syntactic indicators of that category. By the same token, we should be prepared to fit into the taxonomy expressions which do not belong to the syntactic class of verb, or which do not consist of a single word at all. There is no verb in English, for instance, paralleling *greet* and translating the Latin verb *valedicere* 'to say farewell'. But this lexical gap can be plugged easily enough by the use of a phrase: *say farewell/goodbye*. Similarly, *promise* can be paraphrased by the phrase *give one's word*.

These problems with syntactic definitions of Searle's illocutionary categories can be solved, therefore, if the categories are identified as having existence on the semantic, rather than the syntactic level. This has an additional advantage, which would be missed even by a 'deep structure' analysis, which is that elements of meaning which cannot with any certainty be assigned to a single lexical item can be given a representation in the meaning of the construction. *The doctor advised a new treatment* can be regarded as an abbreviation either of *The doctor advised h to undergo a new treatment*, or of *The doctor advised h to receive a new treatment*, or many other alternatives. But there is no need, in the analysis proposed here, to choose between these paraphrases. Thus instead of talking about 'illocutionary verbs' we should strictly be talking about 'illocutionary predicates', and the same goes for the five subcategories 'assertive verbs', etc. At this level, using a notation based on that introduced in 5.5, the five categories may be redefined by their conformity to the following formulae:

ASSERTIVE:	$(s_2 \quad IP \quad [P])$
DIRECTIVE and COMMISSIVE:	$(s_2 \quad IP \quad [M])$
ROGATIVE:	$(s_2 \quad IP \quad [Q])$
EXPRESSIVE:	$(s_2 \quad IP \quad (X))$

[where s_2 = secondary speaker; IP = illocutionary predicate; P = proposition; M = mand (see 5.5); Q = question; and X = propositional content (predication).]

Most illocutionary predicates (IPs) have at least two arguments: one argument identifying a speaker (s_2 above), and another argument identifying an utterance, in the *oratio obliqua* mode. On this basis, assertive predicates introduce reported statements, directive and commissive predicates introduce reported mands, and rogative predicates introduce reported questions.[12] The exceptional category in this respect is that of expressive predicates, which do not report the utterance itself, but rather presuppose an event to which the utterance expresses an attitude. This event is represented, in the formula, by a propositional content X, enclosed in round brackets which distinguish it from the metapropositional arguments of the other categories of predicate. Other defining conditions which are not shown in the formulae above are those which distinguish directive from commissive predicates. In the former, the mand has s_2 (the secondary speaker, *ie* speaker of the reported utterance) as its agent, while in the latter, the mand has h_2 (the secondary hearer) as its agent. Also, for both directives and commissives, the time reference of M is posterior to the time reference of the accompanying IP, while for expressive predicates, the time reference of X is non-posterior (see *p* 218).

Expressive predicates imply that s_2 presupposes the truth of the proposition corresponding to X, and this is an important difference reflected in the status of the complementizers in [11] and [12]:[13]

[11] She complained *that he ate too much*.   (assertive)
[12] She reproached him *for eating too much*. (expressive)

If the main verb in [11] is negated, this destroys the implication that s_2 believes the proposition 'He ate too much' to be true; whereas if the main verb in [12] is negated, that implication is generally felt to remain:

[11a] She did not complain *that he ate too much*.
[12a] She did not reproach him *for eating too much*.

Both *complain* and *reproach*, in a broad sense, refer to speech acts which express s_2's attitude to h_2's behaviour; but in a stricter logical sense, *complain* in [11] is assertive, while *reproach* in [12] is expressive. *Complain*, in fact, is one of a group of verbs which appear to be a mixture of the assertive and expressive categories: others are *boast, rejoice, grumble*, and *lament*. When these verbs preceded a *that*-clause, it seems best to analyse them as having the sense of 'to assert in a VERBing manner', where 'VERB' is the corresponding expressive sense of the verb. Like *warn*, they appear to convey two kinds of illocutionary meaning at once.

The above semantic account of *IP*s and the illocutionary verbs expressing them shows, in the first place, how illocutionary categories can be reduced to a small number of logical types. It is chiefly on this basis that the rogative *IP* deserves its place as a separate category, because it selects an indirect question as its argument. As a corroboration of this logical basis for *IP*s, it is also significant that each *IP* category corresponds closely to a category of psychological predicates. CREDITIVE predicates (or PROPOSITIONAL ATTITUDE predicates) like 'believe' and 'assume' correspond to assertive predicates: both kinds introduce a reported proposition as an argument. This and the other correspondences are set out in Table 9.1.

TABLE 9.1

ILLOCUTIONARY PREDICATES		PSYCHOLOGICAL PREDICATES	
Category	*Examples*	*Category*	*Examples*
A Assertive	REPORT ANNOUNCE	Creditive	BELIEVE, ASSUME
B Directive	URGE, COMMAND	Volitional	WISH, (BE) WILLING, INTEND, (BE) DETERMINED
C Commissive	OFFER, PROMISE		
D Rogative	ASK, INQUIRE	Dubitative	WONDER, DOUBT
E Expressive	EXCUSE, THANK	Attitudinal	FORGIVE, (BE) GRATEFUL

The following sentences illustrate the constructions associated with each type:

A. {
1. Jim *reported* that no one had arrived (ASSERTIVE)
2. Jim *believed* that no one had arrived (CREDITIVE)

B. {
1. Sheila *urged* me to do the shopping (DIRECTIVE)
2. Sheila *wanted* me to do the shopping (VOLITIONAL)

C. $\begin{cases} 1. \text{ Bill } \textit{offered} \text{ to drive} \\ \quad \text{us home} \\ 2. \text{ Bill } \textit{was willing} \text{ to drive} \\ \quad \text{us home} \end{cases}$ $\begin{cases} \text{(COMMISSIVE)} \\ \\ \text{(VOLITIONAL)} \end{cases}$

D. $\begin{cases} 1. \text{ Sid } \textit{inquired} \text{ what you} \\ \quad \text{were doing} \\ 2. \text{ Sid } \textit{wondered} \text{ what you} \\ \quad \text{were doing} \end{cases}$ $\begin{cases} \text{(ROGATIVE)} \\ \\ \text{(DUBITATIVE)} \end{cases}$

E. $\begin{cases} 1. \text{ Freda } \textit{pardoned} \text{ me for telling} \\ \quad \text{a lie} \\ 2. \text{ Freda } \textit{forgave} \text{ me for telling} \\ \quad \text{a lie} \end{cases}$ $\begin{cases} \text{(EXPRESSIVE)} \\ \\ \text{(ATTITUDINAL)} \end{cases}$

These syntactic correspondences are not accidental. The 'speech-reporting' and 'thought-reporting' functions are logically parallel in that they deal with the same kinds of *oratio obliqua*: reported propositions for Type A, reported mands for Type B, and so on. But the connection between the examples A–E above is actually more intimate than this: in every case, Sentence 2 reports a mental state which is implicated to belong to the speaker (s_2) in Sentence 1. Take Sentences A 1 and A 2 as an example: if the Maxim of Quality is being observed by Jim, then if A 1 is true, then A 2 is true. If s_2 is speaking sincerely, each kind of illocutionary act description can be said to 'meta-implicate' the corresponding mental state description.

9.2.4 Phonically descriptive and content-descriptive verbs

From now on, I shall revert to the practice of discussing verb types, rather than predicate types. Although it is technically more appropriate to discuss illocutionary meanings in terms of predicates, there is the advantage of familiarity in sticking to 'illocutionary verb', 'assertive verb', and similar expressions. The polysemy of verbs will not result in confusion, as I shall always consider verbs in relation to a particular sense illustrative of a particular illocutionary category.

Before summarizing this survey of different classes of verb related to illocutionary verbs, it is as well to mention a class of speech-act verbs which are rarely confused with illocutionary verbs, being associated with direct speech rather than *oratio obliqua*. I have called these PHONICALLY DESCRIPTIVE verbs (Leech 1980 [1977b]:67), in contrast to the CONTENT-DESCRIPTIVE verbs of which illocutionary and perlocutionary verbs are both subtypes. Their meaning, that is, has to do with the *manner* of utterance, rather than the *matter*. Examples are *grunt, hiss, mumble, mutter, shout, whine, whisper*. For such verbs (most of which can also be used in reference to non-vocal noises), it is usually possible to paraphrase a clause 's_2 VERB Y' by 's_2 SAY Y in a VERBING manner'; *eg*:

[13] Boris mumbled 'Goodbye' ≡ Boris said 'Goodbye' in a mumbling manner.

Phonetically descriptive verbs are generally more acceptable with direct speech than with *oratio obliqua*:

[14] 'That was a mistake', mumbled/gasped/   [MORE LIKELY]
squeaked/stuttered Maggie.

[15] Maggie mumbled/gasped/squeaked/   [LESS LIKELY]
stuttered that that was a mistake.

Conversely, illocutionary verbs are inclined to be more acceptable with *oratio obliqua* than with direct speech:

[16] Walter ordered/urged/implored   [MORE LIKELY]
me to go away.

[17] 'Go away,' ordered/urged/   [LESS LIKELY]
implored Maggie.

These preferences are not surprising, since direct speech and *oratio obliqua* give respectively a formal and a semantic/pragmatic description of the utterance they report. Between these two types there is a NEUTRAL type, containing speech-act verbs such as *say, repeat*, and *reply*, which seem to occur equally readily with direct speech and with *oratio obliqua*. Although *repeat* ('say again') and *reply* ('say in answer') have a more specific meaning than *say*, the features of meaning they add to *say* do not describe either the matter or the manner of the speech act, but rather describe the way in which this speech act fits into a sequence of speech acts. In this sense they are neutral between the phonically descriptive and the content-descriptive categories.

Figure 9.5 (*p* 214) summarizes the various kinds of verb which have been mentioned in this survey.

9.3 Is there a separate class of performative verbs?

One obvious omission from the foregoing classification of speech-act verbs is that of the performative verb. Discussions of performatives have often assumed that there is a special category of verbs distinguished by their ability to be used performatively, and this is made explicit by those adherents of the performative hypothesis (see 8.6), such as Ross (1970) and Sadock (1974), who

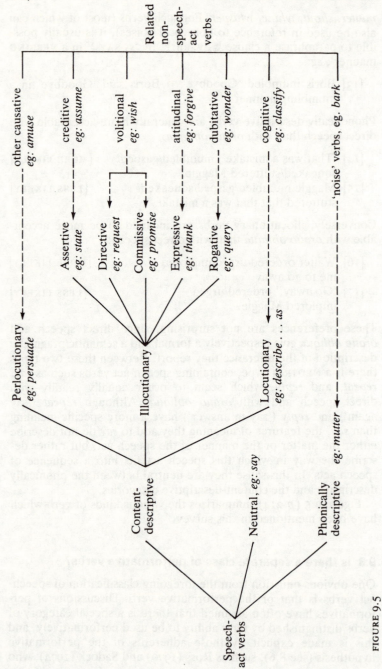

FIGURE 9.5

have marked such verbs by a special feature + PERFORMATIVE in the lexicon of the language in question. Searle (1979 [1975a]:7) similarly assumes an independent 'performative' criterion for classifying illocutions.

My argument will be that we do not need such a feature, which is an unnecessary complication of the grammar and of the lexicon. There is no need to suppose that speakers of a language like English have to learn precisely which verbs they are permitted, by the grammar of the language, to use as performatives. If it can be shown that 'performativity' as a characteristic of verbs can be predicted from other characteristics, the grammar of the language will be to that extent simplified. This is, I would claim, another respect in which linguists (particularly those of the generative semantics persuasion) have 'overgrammaticized' their data (see 3.5), assuming that a grammatical explanation has to be given for things which are better explained pragmatically.

To justify this view, I first go back to the *descriptive* account of performatives presented in 8.3–8.5. There it was argued that performatives are simply self-naming utterances, in which the performative verb actually refers to the act in which s is involved at the moment of speech. On this basis, we might begin by assuming that all speech-act verbs are potential candidates for the performative role of self-reference. In actual fact, however, the topmost and bottommost verb classes in Fig. 9.5 do not generally act as performatives:

[18] ??I (hereby) *persuade* you to be quiet.
      (PERLOCUTIONARY VERB)
[19] ??I (hereby) *whisper* 'You be quiet'.
      (PHONICALLY DESCRIPTIVE VERB)

The reasons for this are not so much grammatical as pragmatic. It is pragmatically uncooperative (and incidentally impolite) to use a perlocutionary verb like *persuade* performatively, because one cannot do so truthfully, without guaranteeing in advance that h's response will be in accordance with s's wishes.[14] Felicitous use of [18] would be restricted to a hypothetical world in which h were an automaton under the 'thought-control' of s. Significantly, however, there is nothing odd about using perlocutionary verbs in so-called 'hedged performatives' (see 6.2), since here there is no taking for granted of the illocutionary effect:

[20] May I *persuade* you to eat more cake?
[21] We must *remind* you that dogs are forbidden.

A different kind of pragmatic argument accounts for the non-occurrence of [19]. A phonically descriptive verb as performative nas no motivation in terms of the Maxims of Quantity and Quality, because *h* will always know, on hearing *s*'s performative utterance, whether *s*'s phonic characterization of the utterance is correct or not. Thus if *s* says [19] in a whisper, *h* will know that [19] is true; whereas if *s* says [19] while bellowing into *h*'s ear, *h* will know it to be false. In this respect, a phonically descriptive verb used as a performative is the opposite of an illocutionary verb so used: in the latter case, the truth value of the performative will rarely if ever be verifiable by the addressee, and hence the performative prefix *I VERB you...* will always be informative to some degree or other.

All the other kinds of speech-act verb in Fig. 9.5 can act as performatives – notably, of course, the illocutionary categories – except for some cases which, again for pragmatic as well as semantic reasons, would be felicitous as performatives only in strange circumstances, if at all.[15] Among these are verbs like *allege* and *boast*, which imply an unfavourable opinion of *s*'s speech act, and verbs like *insinuate, imply,* and *hint,* which require that the proposition they introduce should be conveyed implicitly or indirectly.

[22] ??I hereby allege that the money was stolen.
[23] ??I hereby hint that your slip is showing.

On the positive side, we also have to add to the set of verbs capable of acting as performatives those verbs, like *caution, nominate, resign, bid,* and *baptize,* which occur in declarations. These verbs are partially self-referring (in that, for example, *part* of the act of resigning may consist in saying the words *I resign...*); but essentially they denote ritual social acts rather than speech acts.

The conclusion, then, is that the set of performative verbs coincides with the set which is the union of the set of speech-act verbs and the set of verbs used in declarations, except for those speech-act verbs which for one reason or another are infelicitous in a self-referential function. Linguists have tended to judge the grammaticality of performative verbs out of context; but it is worth pointing out that the acceptability of these verbs can vary greatly from one cultural context to another.[16] To judge performatives in purely grammatical terms is an error in this respect, as well as for reasons already noted (8.3–8.6).

9.4 A semantic analysis of some illocutionary verbs

The remainder of this chapter will be largely devoted to an out-

TABLE 9.2

	[X is the event described in the propositional content]	(a) Does X follow the speech act?	(b) Is s or h involved in X?	(c) If X follows the speech act, is it conditional or unconditional?	(d) Is X ↑s, ↓s, ↑h, or ↓h? (see p xiii)	(e) What attitude is implicated?
Directive	a. TELL / COMMAND / ORDER / DEMAND	Yes	h	Uncond.	↓h (↑s)	Intention that h do X
	b. ASK / REQUEST / BEG	Yes	h	Condit.	↓h (↑s)	Wish that h do X
	c. ADVISE / RECOMMEND / SUGGEST	Yes	h	Condit.	↑h	Belief that X will be good for h
	d. INVITE	Yes	h	Condit	↑h ↓s	Willingness for h to do X
Commissive	e. OFFER	Yes	s	Condit.	↑h ↓s	Willingness to do X
	f. PROMISE / UNDERTAKE / VOW	Yes	s	Uncond.	↓s (↑h)	Intention to do X
	g. THREAT	Yes	s	Condit.	↓h (↑s)	Insistence that h do X
Expressive	h. CONGRATULATE	No	(h)	—	↑h	Pleasure at X
	i. THANK	No	(h)	—	↑s	Gratitude for X
	j. APOLOGIZE	No	s	—	↓h	Regret that X
	k. PARDON	No	h	—	↓s	Forgiveness for X
	l. CONDOLE / COMMISERATE WITH	No	(h)	—	↑h	Sympathy with h over X
	m. LAMENT	No	(s)	—	↓s	Sorrow over X
	n. BOAST	No	(s)	—	↑s	Exultation over X

line analysis of the meanings of a representative set of illocutionary verbs. The technique of analysis will be similar to that of
componential analysis, *ie* I shall isolate a number of discrete variables in terms of which the meanings of the verbs contrast. A
selection of the verbs in the assertive, directive, commissive, and
expressive categories will be examined. The similarity between
the variables applicable to the last three categories is evident
from the fact that they can be conveniently included within a
single table, Table 9.2 on *p* 217.

In Table 9.2, the words in the left-hand column, such as TELL,
ASK, and ADVISE, should be interpreted as verbs used *in a particular sense* and *in a particular syntactic/semantic context*. Thus,
although the verb *suggest* can occur both as a directive and as an
assertive verb, in the table it is clear that it is the directive sense
that is being represented. There are a number of additional
points to be made about the interpretation of Table 9.2, and
these are now enumerated.

1. Column (a)

This column distinguishes expressive verbs from directive and
commissive verbs. The contrast is between 'posterior' and 'non-
posterior' time. The present and past (as measured from the time
of the reported utterance) are lumped together, and opposed to
the future. Thus directives and commissives can only involve future events, whereas expressives can refer to either present and
past, but not to future:

*I promise that $\begin{cases} \text{you have been having fun.} \\ \text{you are enjoying yourselves.} \end{cases}$
*Mary thanked us for coming to see her next week.[17]

The main contrast on the time continuum for purposes of tense
and aspect is between past and non-past; it is therefore rather
surprising that the main temporal contrast, for the purposes of
defining illocutionary verbs, is between future and non-future.
This is true not only for commissive, directives, and expressives,
but also for assertives (see 9.5).

2. Column (b)

This column distinguishes between directive and commissive
verbs. Some illocutionary verbs, notably directives, make reference to an event (X) for which h is assumed to be responsible. In
other cases, such as congratulations, h is not necessarily involved
as an agent, but nevertheless participates in the event. (These latter cases are marked (h) in Table 9.2.). Both these types of

'addressee-oriented' illocutionary verbs must be contrasted, however, with corresponding types of 'speaker-oriented' illocutionary verbs, such as *promise, offer*, and *apologize*. It is important, in distinguishing speaker-orientation and addressee-orientation in this sense, to note that involvement of *s* or *h* (as the case may be) is implied even where it is not explicitly signalled in the complement.

[24] The colonel ordered *that the bridge be destroyed*.
[25] I promise *that you will get your reward*.

It is understood, in [24], that *h* is the person who has to see to the destruction of the bridge, even though *h* is not mentioned. Similarly, in [25], it is understood that *s* will see to *h*'s reward. Because of this, it is important that the definition of factors like speaker and addressee-orientation should be tied to *X* as the *event* referred to by the complement, rather than to the semantic structure of the complement itself.

3. Column (c)
This column is relevant only to those verbs whose event *X* takes place after the speech act. For those verbs marked 'conditional', *s* intends that the event will not take place unless *h* indicates agreement or compliance. For those marked 'unconditional', *s* intends uptake by *h* to be taken for granted. Thus the difference between a command and a request, on this dimension, is between a directive with which *s* assumes *h* will comply, and a directive which *s* assumes, or rather purports to assume, will only take effect if *h* agrees. For reasons made clear in the discussion of optionality (5.6–5.7), this distinction is an important correlate of courtesy. A comparable contrast exists between *promise* and *offer*. Whereas in pragmatic reality the 'conditionality factor' is a scale of *how much* choice is allowed to *h*, in illocutionary semantics it is a simple 'yes or no' choice between using one lexical item rather than another. In the set of conditional directives, however, there are some verbs (*beg, plead, implore*) which presuppose that *s* is in a disadvantageous relation to *h*, and therefore imply a greater choice on *h*'s part.

4. Column (d)
The symbols used here are the same as those used in 5.7. In a general sense, ↑*s* means 'desirable for *s*', ↑*h* means 'desirable for *h*', ↓*s* means 'undesirable for *s*' and ↓*h* means 'undesirable for *h*'. However, the meaning can be made more precise according to what scale of value is appropriate (see 5.7, 6.1.1–6.1.4).

For directives and commissives, the cost–benefit scale (see 5.3) is relevant, and therefore the meanings of the symbols can be more precisely stated as 'beneficial to *s/h*' and 'costly to *s/h*', according to the interpretation of commissives and impositives discussed in Chapter 5. For expressives, other scales are relevant, in accordance with the Approbation and Modesty Maxims discussed in 6.1.2 and 6.1.3. With *commiserate* it is assumed that *X* is *unfortunate* for *h*, while with *congratulate* it is assumed that *X* is *creditable to h*. As Table 9.2 shows, for some verbs contrasting values for *s* and *h* seem to be required (*cf* 5.7), while for others one value suffices.

5. *Horizontal Groupings*
Table 9.2 does not indicate more subtle features of meaning which distinguish the 'quasi-synonymous' verbs grouped together horizontally. Nor does it give an exhaustive list of verbs included in each group. Just one example of semantic contrasts outside those represented in the table is that between *command*, with its implication that *s* is a person in authority over *h*, and *demand*, which has the opposite implication that *s* is not in authority over *h*:

> The colonel *commanded* that the bridge (should) be destroyed.
> The residents *demanded* that the eyesore (should) be removed.

If the main verbs in these sentences changed places, the effect on both sentences would be incongruous: we would have to think much harder to find a suitable context for them. But for reasons to be given in (8) below, the resulting sentences would not be ungrammatical.

6. *Minimal Pairs*
As it stands, however, Table 9.2 is detailed enough to illustrate how 'minimal pairs' may be detected in speech-act semantics. We can say, for example, that *tell* and *ask* differ from one another, according to the table, merely in terms of the conditionality of the response. That is, in

> Guy *told*/*asked* Hugo to feed the hamster

told implies that Guy means Hugo to do the deed unconditionally, while *asked* implies that Guy means Hugo to exercise choice over whether or not to do it. The fact that this distinction carries with it pragmatic consequences regarding politeness and the relation between Guy and Hugo is not included in the definitional contrast. A parallel minimal pair is that of *promise* and *offer* as commissives:

My sister *promised/offered* to buy the tickets.

Here, the semantic contrast is a matter of conditionality as before, but the ancillary pragmatic consequences are quite different. These examples show clearly the difference between the categorical distinctions of semantics, and the scalar variables of pragmatics. We may be uncertain, in an actual conversation, of whether *I'll buy the tickets* is meant as a 'promise' or an 'offer', because the difference between those two is a matter of gradience (on the scale of optionality). But if we report such a speech act, we may find ourselves in a position of describing it either as a 'promise' or as an 'offer' and thereby having to impose a categorical interpretation upon it. A different kind of minimal pair is that between *offer* and *invite*, where the principal contrast is a matter of whether s or h is to be the agent of the future action X. (In addition, *invite* can have the more specific meaning of 'invite h to visit or to be the guest of s'). Although it cuts right across the directive/commissive boundary, this difference between s-orientation and h-orientation can be an almost imperceptible one in reality:

Matt *offered* to lend me his bicycle.
Matt *invited* me to borrow his bicycle.

These two sentences are virtually synonymous, because the difference between s-orientation and h-orientation is largely neutralized in the case of 'transaction' verbs like *lend* and *borrow*.

7. 'Accidental Gaps'
The componential analysis also reveals 'accidental gaps' in the lexicon of illocutionary verbs. Among the expressives, for example, the combination of two choices in Column (b) and four main choices in Column (d) leads to eight theoretical types of speaker–addressee involvement, of which only seven are listed in Table 9.2. The missing one is the combination of s in Column (b) and $\uparrow h$ in Column (d): a speech act concerning an event X which is initiated by s and which benefits h. On the face of it, there is a good pragmatic reason for the lack of an illocutionary verb with these characteristics. Such a speech act would appear discourteous, since it would allude to h's indebtedness to s, and would be the converse of thanking. Observation shows, however, that there is such a speech act: its function is the polite one of responding to an expression of thanks by h. The polite 'acknowledgement of thanks' is highly institutionalized in some languages (*eg* German *bitte (sehr)*), but is less institutionalized in English, where the lack of a verbal response to thanks is often noted. In

the interests of tact, such a speech act typically belittles the cost of the act X to s, by claiming either that X was desirable for s (*It's a pleasure*), or that X was a small matter (*It was nothing, Not at all*, etc.). It is perhaps not surprising that this speech act, which depends for its effect on the minimization of s's contribution, is not coded in the lexicon of English.

8. Interpretation of Scales

My last observation on Table 9.2 has to do with the interpretation of the evaluation scales in Column (d). For example, how do we recognize where X is costly or beneficial to s or to h, and hence, whether (say) *offer, invite,* or *ask* is an appropriate verb? Clearly the content of the complementizer clause is essential to this judgement, so that (for example) [26] is likely to be judged more felicitous than [27]:

[26] Ada *offered* to clean out the stables.
[27] Ada *invited* me to clean out the stables.

But this judgement is a subjective one, based on what people tend to regard as pleasant and as unpleasant. There is no reason for regarding a sentence like [27] to be ungrammatical, since there is nothing *linguistically* odd about someone who enjoys cleaning out stables. Taking this principle of subjective judgement further, we can even think, if we try, of sensible interpretation for more improbable examples:

[28] The children *promised* to be as bad as they could.
[29] The millionaire *apologized* to me for making me his heir.
[30] Max *congratulated* Walter on getting mauled by a lion.
[31] I *advised* Sarah to make me an interest-free loan of £3,000.
[32] Bob *threatened* that if Mary misbehaved, he would give her anything she asked for.

I challenge (performatively!) the reader to think of a plausible context for each of these sentences, within a time-limit of five seconds. If other flights of imagination fail, one can always contextualize the example by means of an eccentric wealthy uncle, or a religious devotee who believes that the more one suffers in this world, the more one is rewarded in the next. But an interesting question is: Whose judgement of desirability or undesirability is decisive in the reporting of an illocutionary act? For example, if the verb is *congratulate*, is it the judgement of the reporter (s_1), or of the congratulator (s_2) or of the congratulatee (h_2) that is in question? *Prima facie*, it is h_2, the person in respect of whom the evaluation is made (*ie* the person who is referred to as ↑ *h* in Column (d) on Table 9.2) whose judgement is implicated in the choice of verb. Thus [30] suggests that Walter (perhaps because of a generous insurance policy for lion-tamers) will regard being mauled by a lion as desirable. But this is a superficial view. More precisely, [30] implies that Max (s_2) *believes that X* is desirable for Walter (h_2). So if Walter has discontinued his generous insurance policy, but Max (his fellow lion-tamer) does not realize this, Max can still be said to congratulate Walter (albeit mistakenly), and [30] can still be an accurate report of that congratulatory illocution. More precisely still, we may say that judging whether a report of an illocutionary verb is true typically rests on a threefold evaluation, *viz* s_1's (the reporter's) judgement of what s_2 judges to be h_2's judgement of X.

9.5 Assertive verbs

Assertive verbs have been omitted from the preceding analysis. Although they form the most numerous illocutionary category, they lend themselves less easily to systematic analysis. This is probably because, unlike the other illocutionary categories, they generally assume an equal relation between s_2 and h_2. Of the columns in Table 9.2, however, one scale is relevant to assertive verbs, and this is Column (a), dealing with time reference. The question of whether the event described (X) is posterior or nonposterior is quite important to the status of an assertion, and on this basis we may distinguish PREDICTIVE assertive verbs (like *predict, foretell, forecast*) from RETRODICTIVE ones (like *report, narrate*, and *recount*):[18]

[33] The economics experts predicted that inflation would decrease.

[33a] ?*The economics experts predicted that inflation had decreased.

[34] The economics experts reported that inflation had decreased.

[34a] ?*The economics experts reported that inflation would decrease.[19]

Other distinctions of some importance are (a) that between 'making *P* publicly known' (*declare, proclaim, announce*) and 'making *P* privately and obliquely known' (*intimate, imply, hint*); and (b) that between 'confident assertion' (*affirm, aver, avouch, confirm, certify*) and 'tentative assertion' (*suggest, hypothesize, postulate*). Additionally, it can be said that whereas some assertive verbs (such as *announce* and *report*) are concerned with unidirectional passing of information about the world of reality, others (such as *claim* and *disagree*) may be called ARGUMENTATIVE, since they express the relation between the current truth claim and other truth claims made by *s* or *h*. In an argument, each participant may be said to have a 'position', which is the set of logically interrelated beliefs which the participant is concerned to justify and defend. Thus the verb *claim* 'lays claim to' a given proposition as belonging to, or supporting, *s*'s position; and *admit* 'allows' something belonging to one's adversary's position to be true. In this way, assertive verbs may assume an interactive character similar to that of commissive, directive, and expressive verbs. The following list of tentative definitions illustrates how argumentative verbs may be defined in terms of opposed positions (*s* = speaker and *a* = adversary; note that *a* and *h* 'hearer' are not necessarily the same).

1. '*s* CLAIMS that *P*' entails:
   '*s* ASSERTS that *P*' and '*P* is part of *s*'s position'.
   (also: *submit, posit*)
2. '*s* ADMITS that *P*' entails:
   '*s* ASSERTS that *P*' and '*P* is part of *a*'s position' and '*P* contradicts some aspects of *s*'s position'.
   (also: *concede, acknowledge, allow, confess, grant, owe*)
3. '*s* MAINTAINS that *P*' entails:
   '*s* ASSERTS that *P*' and '*a* has claimed or implied that NOT-*P* is part of *a*'s position'
   (also: *insist*)
4. '*s* AGREES that *P*' entails:
   '*s* ASSERTS that *P*' and '*P* is part of *s*'s position' and 'P is part of *a*'s position'.
   (also: *concur*)
5. '*s* ARGUES that *P*' entails:
   '*s* ASSERTS that *P*' and '*P* is a conclusion drawn from an argument within *s*'s position'.
   (also: *contend*)

It appears, then, that the following are likely to be factors of importance in the definition of assertive verbs: (a) prediction versus retrodiction; (b) public versus private assertion/implication; (c) confident versus tentative assertion; (d) informative versus argumentative assertion. It is also reasonable to assume that, since these distinctions are coded in the lexicon of assertive verbs, they may be of importance in the pragmatics of assertion. In any case, the contrasts which are relevant to assertive verbs, as to other illocutionary verbs, are often scalar rather than all-or-nothing. This is obviously true of distinctions like (b) and (c) above, and is perhaps surprising, in the view of the common presumption that assertions have a fairly clear-cut and uncomplicated task to perform, *viz* the conveyance of information from one person to another.

9.6 Conclusion

In the area of speech-act verbs, as in most other areas of the lexicon, the language make fuzzy category distinctions, whereas the realities to which these categories apply are often scalar or indeterminate. The implications of this, for speech-act theory, are:

(a) it is pointless to attempt a rigid taxonomy of illocutionary acts;
(b) it is, however, possible and illuminating to attempt a taxonomy of illocutionary verbs or illocutionary predicates; and
(c) it is reasonable to assume that on the whole, the dimensions of contrast which are significant for the definition of illocutionary verbs are also of relevance to the analysis of illocutionary activities.

The question which was often asked in earlier days of speech-act theory was 'How many speech acts are there?'[20] To which Wittgenstein's answer (to the question 'how many kinds of sentence are there?') that 'there are countless kinds' (1953, para. 23, *cf* Searle 1979:vii), is probably as sensible as any other reply. On the other hand, the question 'How many speech-act verbs are there in English?' is a question which permits a finite number as an answer. The different nature of the task of examining speech activity and examining speech-act verbs will be evident from this and preceding chapters. Speech activity can vary along many different dimensions, and an appropriate model for representing it is that of a means–ends analysis allowing continuous values, multiple goals, and goals of varying indirectness. It is also the case that speech-act activity does not often lend itself to segmentation into discrete 'acts' in the way assumed by speech-act theory. For all these reasons, the selection of a speech-act verb for reporting a speech act is bound to involve selection and simplification, including the imposition of 'categorical' structure on the data of conversation. The only case where real speech activity mirrors the categorical structure of illocutionary verbs is in the case of self-reporting utterances, especially performatives, where the speaker uses the metalanguage of speech-act verbs for describing his own discourse. The analysis of speech-act verbs can, therefore, be particularly necessary to the analysis of performative speech acts; but at the same time, it is clear that performatives are a totally special case which can in no way be regarded as the canonical form of speech activity.

Notes

1. Austin writes (1962:103): 'Our interest in these lectures is essentially to fasten on the second, illocutionary act and contrast it with the other two.' The same focus on illocutions is found in Searle, although Searle does not recognize (1969:23) Austin's distinction between locutionary and illocutionary acts.

2. Discussion of the different kinds of effects which might be designated 'perlocutionary' is found in Austin (1962:101–32) and Bach and Harnish (1979:16–18). A difficulty is that with some verbs such as *inform* and *tell* it seems unclear whether their meaning includes perlocutionary effects or not.

3. Here again there is uncertainty about the sense of some verbs. Does *persuade*, for example, always denote a linguistic act? Can one literally 'persuade' someone by brandishing a hatchet? Or is this merely a figure of speech?

4. 'Conclude' and 'reveal' occur in the list of illocutionary acts supplied by Bach and Harnish (1979:42).

5. Alongside Searle's five categories of illocutionary act, Austin's five categories of illocutionary force (1962:151) are: verdictives, exercitives, commissive, behabitives, and expositives. Searle's (1979 [1975a]) criticism of Austin's taxonomy, and his comparison of it with his own, bring out of the similarities as well as the contrasts between the two systems. Bach and Harnish (1979:41), in their turn, have categories corresponding to four of Searle's: constatives, directives, commissives, and acknowledgments. Searle's fifth category of declarations corresponds to what Bach and Harnish call 'conventional illocutionary acts'. A rather different taxonomy is that of Fraser (1974), who is concerned with 'vernacular performative verbs'.

6. *Cf* Searle's (1979 [1975a]) deep-structure analysis of performative sentences. The regularities that Searle observes are roughly parallel to those I note here.

7. Note that the distinction I drew in 5.2 between directive and impositive illocutions can also be applied to verbs. Thus *threaten* is impositive but not directive, while *invite* is directive but not impositive.

8. *Cf* the distinction drawn by Bach and Harnish (1979) between *communicative* and *conventional* illocutions, and by Fraser (1974) between *vernacular* and *ceremonial* performative verbs.

9. *Cf* Bach and Harnish's category of 'descriptives' and Fraser's category of 'stipulatives'.

10. *Threaten* denotes a conditional speech act, *ie* the sense of '*s*

threatened h with X' is roughly 's undertook to see to it that something unpleasant (X) would happen to h, if h did not do some act A desired by s'. This conditional nature of *threaten* links it to other verbs describing conditional speech acts, such as *promise* and *bet* (see Fotion 1981).

11. One should note the existence of some major exceptions to the complementizer patterns outlined in 9.2.2 above. (a) Assertive verbs (particularly in the passive) can occur with a following infinitive construction: *He was reported to be a Fascist*. (b) Assertive verbs, particularly with negation or interrogation, can occur with a following *wh*-clause: *Tom told them when Sheila would arrive*.

12. Example (b) in the preceding note has anticipated one exception to this: the apparent occurrence of assertive predicates with reported questions: 'Tom TOLD them WHEN Sheila would arrive.' But here the *wh*-clause describes a proposition from which one piece of information (represented by the *wh*-item *when*) has been omitted because it is presumably unknown not to the secondary, but to the primary speaker. In other words, *when Sheila would arrive* in the above example is not a reported question, but rather a reported statement about which the primary speaker poses a question.

13. The presuppositional nature of the propositional content of expressives is pointed out by Searle (1979 [1975a]:15). Fillmore's (1971) semantic analysis of verbs of judging (including expressive verbs such as *criticize* and *apologize*) also includes presuppositional elements.

14. In this respect as elsewhere (see note 2 above), *inform* and *tell* seem to be on the unclear boundary between illocutionary and perlocutionary verbs. The illocutionary analysis is supported by performatives such as *I tell you* and *I hereby inform you*. But one explanation of these might be that *tell* and *inform* are perlocutionary, but that they happen to describe perlocutions in which the effect follows relatively automatically from the utterance, and may therefore be taken for granted by the speaker. By the very fact of hearing a message, a person may become informed, but does not have to become persuaded.

15. Another category of speech-act verbs which does not appear in Fig. 9.5 is that containing *praise, denigrate, eulogize, deride*, and *ridicule*. These do not normally occur performatively, apparently for the following reason. Such 'affective' verbs appear to refer to speech activities of which the intended effect arises indirectly rather than directly from what is said. Thus *I hereby denigrate your parents* is rather like *I hereby tell you a joke*: the utterance is misconceived because *s* cannot make the utterance into a joke or a denigration merely by describing it as such. *Cf* Searle (1979 [1975a]:7).

16. A well-known case of the cultural relativity of performatives is the use of 'I divorce thee' as a performative. According to traditional Islamic law this is felicitous; in countries where other marriage laws obtain it is not.

17. Both *promise* and *thank*, however, have extended uses which are not

accommodated by the definitions in Table 9.2. *Promise* is sometimes (ironically?) used in reference to unpleasant events: *eg* in *You'll regret it, I promise you*, *promise* seems to denote a threat. Also, especially in letters of request, *thank* can be used anticipatorily: *eg: I thank you in anticipation for your help*. However, this seems an exceptional case arising from the fact that the writer of a letter does not obtain immediate feedback regarding the compliance of his correspondent. The addition of *in anticipation* or *in advance* makes it clear that the writer is aware of some infelicity in taking for granted that the reader will agree to the request.

18. Bach and Harnish (1979:42) specify two categories of assertives called 'predictives' and 'retrodictives'.

19. The marking ?*indicates that in my judgement [33a] and [34a] are not totally nonsensical. This is because it seems to me that one could, if required, make sense of them by reading into them an addictional covert speech act, so that [33a] would mean 'The economics experts predicted a future *report* that . . .', and [34a] would mean 'The economics experts reported an earlier *prediction* that . . .' These interpretations, although exceptional, would make the uses of *predict* and *report* in these sentences consistent with their definitions.

20. Austin (1962:150) hazards the estimate that there are somewhere between 1,000 and 9,999 different illocutionary forces. In a blatant resort to the Performative Verb Fallacy, he arrives at this figure by compiling 'a list of verbs' in the course of 'going through the dictionary . . . in a liberal spirit'.

Chapter 10

Retrospect and prospect

What I shall have to say here is neither difficult nor contentious; the only merit I should like to claim for it is that of being true, at least in parts.

[J. L. Austin, *How to Do Things with Words*, p 1]

I began by arguing for a research programme based on a distinction between semantics and pragmatics, between grammar and rhetoric, and between sense and force. I also argued that the dualism of grammar and rhetoric should be reinterpreted (in Halliday's terms, but not his understanding of them) as a threefold distinction between grammar (the ideational component), interpersonal pragmatics, and textual pragmatics. The canvas I roughed out in Chapters 1–3 was a large one, but in practice, most of this book has been an attempt to paint in the detail of one area – that of interpersonal pragmatics, since this is the area in which there has been most need to rethink issues, and to contest established positions. My aim, in pragmatics, has been to extend the model of Grice's Cooperative Principle, and to develop and illustrate an Interpersonal Rhetoric in which other principles and maxims – such as those of Politeness and Irony – play an important role in the description of pragmatic force. The influence of Artificial Intelligence has been evident in my reinterpreting of conversational implicature as common-sense inferencing, within a problem-solving framework. If there is one idea of importance in this investigation, it is the notion that illocutionary force can be translated into the problem-solving paradigm of means–ends analysis, and that pragmatic interpretation can also be formulated as problem-solving within a different paradigm – that of hypothesis formation and testing. Within this same general framework for studying communicative linguistic behaviour, 'indirect speech acts' have appeared as problem-solving strategies of the same kind as 'direct speech acts', except that the means–ends analysis is more complex and oblique. Performatives, on the other hand, have been shown to be specialized and atypical: since they define themselves as having a specific illocutionary force, they are abnormally categorical, and by no means a suitable yardstick for the general run of conversational behaviour. Thus I have placed in a 'complementarist' perspective issues which have been some of the main debating points in pragmatics, and have attempted to show how they may be resolved within a general paradigm for the integration of the formal study of language with the pragmatic study of language use.

The list of topics I have not attempted to cover in this book, even though they might be considered essential to my case, remains a large one. The following are particularly important omissions.

1. I have not done justice to the TEXTUAL RHETORIC. For example, there is much to be said about the Processibility Principle (see *pp* 64–6) in relation to the burgeoning literature on given–new articulation and on theme and focus. Also, there is much to be said about the Expressivity Principle and aesthetic aspects of communication, such as the iconic use of textual form.[1] Through such studies we will come closer to bringing linguistics into engagement with 'rhetoric' in the pedagogical sense of 'the effective use of the formal resources of the language in textual composition'.[2]

2. My presentation of the complementarist paradigm has remained informal. It awaits FORMALIZATION in terms of explicit mathematical models. If the view I have taken is correct, quite distinct models will be appropriate to semantics and to pragmatics. I believe that semantic categories, for example, will be appropriately formalized in terms of fuzzy logic,[3] whereas for pragmatics, an appropriate model will be that of linear programming.[4] This branch of mathematics has so far been typically applied to decision-making in business management, but might well be applied more widely to human goal-oriented behaviour and to the making of decisions in communicative contexts.

3. A fully fledged pragmatic theory would not only be formalized, but would yield hypotheses capable of empirical TESTING. Generally in interpersonal pragmatics we base descriptions on observations by native speakers who are members of the speech community being examined. Many of these observations are relative judgements of values on some scale – *eg* a scale of politeness, of relevance, of acceptability – and in principle can be objectively confirmed by informant tests. The important point, however, is that all other pragmatic variables, except the one being tested, should be held constant. In particular, one cannot easily make

comparisons of socio-pragmatic factors such as politeness across the boundaries of speech communities. In Textual Rhetoric, similar informant tests may be carried out: for example, in judging the acceptability of sentences with different degrees of end-weight (see *p* 65). The methodology of pragmatic testing is so far undeveloped, but is not in principle more problematic than other types of linguistic informant testing.

4. A different kind of confirmation of pragmatic hypotheses can be sought by analysis of CORPUS DATA. Such hypotheses will be in the nature of things probabilistic, since pragmatic principles and maxims can be overruled. In the simplest cases, it will be predicted that conformity to a given maxim is (considerably) more likely than nonconformity. But it is always possible that if corpus findings contradict the hypothesis, this can be explained as due to the influence of competing maxims.

5. I have not attempted much in the way of cross-linguistic comparisons of communicative behaviour, but this is a fascinating area of study in which much research remains to be done, and which has obvious applications to language teaching. Statements such as 'the Japanese are more modest than the British' or 'the British are more tactful than Americans' only make sense if we relativize them to pragmalinguistic strategies such as strategies of indirectness, and the norms observed in the performance of these strategies in different speech communities. The transfer of the norms of one community to another community may well lead to 'pragmatic failure', and to the judgement that the speaker is in some way being impolite, uncooperative, etc. (see Thomas 1981, 1983). But there is no absolute sense in which this can be true. My expectation is that the general paradigm presented in these chapters will provide the framework in which contrastive studies of pragmalinguistic strategies can be undertaken.

6. Another area I have left largely unexplored is the extension of this paradigm, which has been largely restricted to individual utterances or exchanges, to the study of connected discourse, *ie* to DISCOURSE ANALYSIS. I have given the impression (*eg* in the discussion of the Maxim of Relation in 4.3 and 4.4) that in a 'well-conducted' conversation, the goals of the interlocutors more or less coincide. The function of the CP is to ensure that one participant cooperates with the other in fulfilling the assumed goal of the discourse; while the function of the PP is to ensure that this cooperation persists even where the personal goals of *s* and *h* can be supposed to be in conflict. But I have also insisted that pragmatic principles such as the CP and the PP are observed only *to a certain extent*. A more realistic picture of discourse, then, will acknowledge that neither the CP nor the PP are inviolable, and

that these principles compete with other principles, and with private illocutionary goals. In the dynamics of a two-sided discourse between equals, the goals of the participants A and B will be 'negotiated', such that at least the following outcomes will be possible:

[1] A adopts B's goal
[2] B adopts A's goal
[3] A and B agree on a common goal intermediate between A's original goal and that of B
[4] A and B fail to agree on any goal.

The metaphor of 'negotiation'[5] (or, if one prefers the common market-place version, 'haggling') is quite appropriate here, since the four outcomes listed correspond to the four possible outcomes of a bargaining encounter:

[1] A accepts B's price
[2] B accepts A's offer
[3] A and B agree on an intermediate price
[4] A and B fail to agree on a price, so that the transaction does not go through.

A model of discourse analysis which is highly instructive from this point of view is that of Edmondson (1981, esp. Ch. 6). But one can criticize some other models of discourse analysis from the same point of view as that which applies to semanticist and pragmaticist approaches to illocutionary force. In the past, the influence of grammatical models has led to a tendency to compartmentalize and hierarchize units of discourse, as if they were constituents in an immediate constituent analysis.[6] The same tendency has been evident in earlier models of text analysis.[7] I suggest that this is an error corresponding to that of treating speech acts as discrete and mutually exclusive categories (see 8.1, 8.2). If one thinks of discourse analysis as interpersonal pragmatics projected into the time dimension, then the fault of 'overgrammaticization' can be observed here not only in the paradigmatic rigidity of a set of mutually exclusive categories, but also in the syntagmatic rigidity of a segmentation of discourse into discrete non-overlapping units.

Whatever the outcome of further research in these areas, my hope is that this investigation will stimulate others to come closer to an understanding both of the nature of language, and of the use we make of it in communication.

Notes

1. A first attempt to explore this area in terms of Textual Rhetoric is to be found in Leech and Short (1981: Ch. 7).
2. Again, for a first effort in this direction, see Leech, Deuchar, and Hoogenraad (1982: Ch. 12).
3. On fuzzy logic and fuzzy set theory, see McCawley (1981: 360–94).
4. On linear programming, see Kim (1971), esp. Chapter 4.
5. On the concept of negotiation in discourse, see Candlin and Lotfipour-Saedi (1981).
6. See Edmondson's (1981: 67–73) criticisms of Klammer (1973), Sinclair and Coulthard (1975), and other discourse models influenced by grammatical segmentation and hierarchy.
7. Earlier approaches to textlinguistics, including those influenced by the rigidity of grammatical models, are surveyed in de Beaugrande and Dressler (1981: 14–30).

References

AKMAJIAN, A., and HENY, F. (1975), *An Introduction to the Principles of Transformational Syntax*, Cambridge, Mass.: MIT Press.

ALSTON, W. P. (1964), *Philosophy of Language*, Englewood Cliffs, NJ: Prentice-Hall.

ANDERSON, S. (1971), *On the linguistic status of the performative–constative distinction*, Bloomington: Indiana University Linguistics Club.

ARGYLE, M., and DEAN, J. (1965), 'Eye-contact, distance, and affiliation', *Sociometry*, **28**, 289–304.

AUSTIN, J. L. (1962), *How to Do Things with Words*, Cambridge, Mass.: Harvard U.P.

BACH, K., and HARNISH, R. M. (1979), *Linguistic Communication and Speech Acts*, Cambridge, Mass.: MIT Press.

BAILEY, C.-J. N., and SHUY, R. W. (eds), (1973), *New Ways of Analyzing Variation in English*, Washington, DC: Georgetown U.P.

BARRETT, R., and STENNER, A. (1971), 'On the myth of exclusive "or"', *Mind*, **79**, *pp* 116–21.

BEAUGRANDE, R. de, and DRESSLER, W. (1981), *Introduction to Text Linguistics*, London: Longman.

BEVER, T. G. (1970), 'The cognitive basis for linguistic structures', in J. R. Hayes (ed.), *Cognition and the Development of Language*, New York: J. Wiley, *pp* 279–352.

BEVER, T. G. (1976), 'The influence of speech performance on linguistic structure', in Bever, Katz, and Langendoen, op. cit., *pp* 65–88.

BEVER, T. G., KATZ, J. J., and LANGENDOEN, D. T. (1976), *An Integrated Theory of Linguistic Ability*, New York: Thomas Y. Crowell.

BEVER, T. G., and LANGENDOEN, D. T. (1976), 'A dynamic model of the evolution of language', in Bever, Katz, and Langendoen, op. cit., *pp* 115–48.

BLOOMFIELD, L. (1933/35), *Language*, New York: Holt, Rinehart and Winston 1933; London: Allen & Unwin, 1935.

BOLINGER, D. L. (1961), *Generality, Gradience, and the All-or-None*, The Hague: Mouton.

BOLINGER, D. L. (1965[1952]), 'Linear modification', *PMLA*, 67, 1117–44. Reprinted in *Forms of English*, Cambridge, Mass.: Harvard U.P., *pp* 279–307.

BOLINGER, D. L. (1977), *Meaning and Form*, London: Longman.

BOLINGER, D. L. (1980), *Language – the Loaded Weapon*, London: Longman.

BOUCHER, J., and OSGOOD, C. E. (1969), 'The Pollyanna Hypothesis', *Journal of Verbal Learning and Verbal Behavior*, **8**, 1–8.

BROWN, P., and LEVINSON, S. (1978), 'Universals in language usage: politeness phenomena', in Goody, E. N. (ed.), *Questions and Politeness: Strategies in Social Interaction*, Cambridge: Cambridge U.P., *pp* 56–289.

BROWN, R., and GILMAN, A. (1960), 'Pronouns of power and solidarity', in Sebeok, T. A. (ed.), *Style in Language*, Cambridge, Mass.: MIT Press, *pp* 253–76.

BUBLITZ, W. (1978) *Ausdrucksweisen der Sprechereinstellung im Deutschen und Englischen*, Tübingen: Niemeyer.

BUBLITZ, W. (1980), *Conducive Yes–No Questions in English*, Trier: Linguistic Agency University of Trier, Series A, Paper No. 70.

BÜHLER, K. (1934), *Sprachtheorie*, Jena: Fischer.

BURT, M. K. (1971), *From Deep to Surface Structure: An Introduction to Transformational Syntax*, New York: Harper & Row.

CANDLIN, C. N., and LOTFIPOUR-SAEDI, K. (1983), 'Processes of discourse', *Journal of Applied Language Study*, **1**, 2.

CARDEN, G. (1973), 'Disambiguation, favored readings, and variable rules', in Bailey and Shuy, op. cit., *pp* 171–82.

CARNAP, R. (1942), *Introduction to Semantics*, Cambridge, Mass.: MIT Press.

CHOMSKY, N. (1957), *Syntactic Structures*, The Hague: Mouton.

CHOMSKY, N. (1964), 'Current issues in linguistic theory', in Fodor, J. A., and Katz, J. J., *The Structure of Language*, Englewood Cliffs, NJ: Prentice-Hall, *pp* 50–118.

CHOMSKY, N. (1965), *Aspects of the Theory of Syntax*, Cambridge, Mass.: MIT Press.

CHOMSKY, N. (1976), *Reflections on Language*, New York: Pantheon.

CHOMSKY, N., and RONAT, M. (1979), *Language and Responsibility* (trans. from the French by J. Viertel), Sussex: Harvester Press.

CLARK, H. H. (1976) *Semantics and Comprehension*, The Hague: Mouton.

CLARK, H. H., and CLARK, E. V. (1977), *Psychology and Language: An Introduction to Psycholinguistics*, New York: Harcourt Brace Jovanovich.

CLARK, H. H., and HAVILAND, S. E. (1974), 'Psychological processes as linguistic explanation', in Cohen, D. (ed.), *Explaining Linguistic Phenomena*, Washington, DC: Hemisphere Publishing, *pp* 91–124.

CLARK, H. H., and HAVILAND, S. E. (1977), 'Comprehension and the given-new contract', in Freedle, R. O. (ed.), *Discourse Production and Comprehension*, Norwood, NJ: Ablex Publishing, *pp* 1–40.

COLE, P., and MORGAN, J. L. (eds), (1975), *Syntax and Semantics*, Vol. 3: *Speech Acts*, New York: Academic Press.

COMRIE, B. (1976), 'Linguistic politeness axes: speaker–addressee, speaker–referent, speaker–bystander', *Pragmatics Microfiche*, 1, 7.

CORSARO, W. A. (1981), 'Communicative processes in studies of social organization', *Text*, 1(1), 5–63.

CRYSTAL, D., and DAVY, D. (1969), *Investigating English Style*, London: Longman.

DIK, S. C. (1978), *Functional Grammar*, Amsterdam: North-Holland.

DOWNES, W. (1977), 'The imperative and pragmatics', *Journal of Linguistics*, 13, 77–97.

EDMONDSON, W. (1981), *Spoken Discourse: A Model for Analysis*, London: Longman.

FILLMORE, C. J. (1971), 'Verbs of judging: an exercise in semantic description', in Fillmore, C. J. and Langendoen, D. T. (eds), *Studies in Linguistic Semantics*, New York: Holt, Rinehart and Winston, pp 273–89.

FIRBAS, J. (1980), 'Post-intonation-centre prosodic shade in the modern English clause', in Greenbaum, Leech and Svartvik, op. cit., pp 125–33.

FOTION, N. (1981), 'I'll bet you $10 that betting is not a speech act', in Parret, Sbisà and Verschueren, op. cit., pp 211–24.

FRASER, B. (1971), 'An examination of the performative analysis', Bloomington: Indiana University Linguistics Club.

FRASER, B. (1974), 'An analysis of vernacular performative verbs', in Shuy, R. W. and Bailey, C.-J. N. (eds), *Towards Tomorrow's Linguistics*, Washington, DC: Georgetown U.P., pp 139–58.

FRASER, B. (1975), 'Hedged performatives', in Cole and Morgan, op. cit., pp 187–210.

FRAZIER, L. (1979), 'On comprehending sentences: syntactic parsing strategies', Bloomington: Indiana University Linguistics Club.

GAZDAR, G. (1979), *Pragmatics: Implicature, Presupposition and Logical Form*, New York: Academic Press.

GIVÓN, T. (1979), *On Understanding Grammar*, New York: Academic Press.

GOFFMAN, E., (1963), *Behavior in Public Places: Notes on the Social Organization of Gatherings*, Glencoe, Ill.: Free Press of Glencoe.

GOFFMAN, E. (1967), *Interaction Ritual: Essays in Face-to-Face Behavior*, Garden City, NY: Doubleday.

GOFFMAN, E. (1971), *Relations in Public: Microstudies of the Public Order*, New York: Basic Books.

GORDON, D., and LAKOFF, G. (1971), 'Conversational postulates', in *Papers from the Seventh Regional Meeting, Chicago Linguistic Society*, Chicago: Chicago Linguistic Society, pp 63–84.

GREENBAUM, S., LEECH, G., and SVARTVIK, J. (eds) (1980) *Studies in English Linguistics: For Randolph Quirk*, London: Longman.

GRICE, H. P. (1957), 'Meaning', *Philosophical Review*, 66, 377–88. Reprinted in Steinberg, D. D. and Jakobovits, L. A. (eds) (1971), *Semantics: An Interdisciplinary Reader in Philosophy, Linguistics and Psychology*, Cambridge: Cambridge U. P., pp 53–9.

GRICE, H. P. (1981), 'Presupposition and conversational implicature', in Cole, P. (ed.), *Radical Pragmatics*, New York: Academic Press, *pp* 183–98.

GRICE, H. P. (1975), 'Logic and conversation'. In Cole and Morgan, op. cit., *pp* 41–58.

HAKULINEN, A. (1975), 'Finnish "sitä" – an instance of the interplay between syntax and pragmatics', in Hovdhaugen, E. (ed.), *Papers from the 2nd Scandinavian Conference of Linguistics*, Oslo, *pp* 147–63.

HALLIDAY, M. A. K. (1970), 'Clause types and structural functions', in Lyons, J. (ed.), *New Horizons in Linguistics*, Harmondsworth: Penguin, *pp* 140–65.

HALLIDAY, M. A. K. (1973), *Explorations in the Functions of Language*, London: Edward Arnold.

HALLIDAY, M. A. K. (1978), *Language as Social Semiotic*, London: Edward Arnold.

HALLIDAY, M. A. K. (1980), 'Modes of meaning and modes of expression: types of grammatical structure, and their determination by different semantic functions', in Allerton, D. J. *et al.* (eds), *Function and Context in Linguistic Analysis*, Cambridge: Cambridge U. P., *pp* 57–79.

HARE, R. M. (1970), 'Meaning and speech acts', *Philosophical Review*, **79**, 3–24. Reprinted in Hare, R. M. (1971), *Practical Inferences*, London: Macmillan, *pp* 74–93.

HARNISH, R. M. (1976), 'Logical form and implicature', in Bever, Katz, and Langendoen, op. cit., *pp* 313–92

HARRIS, R. (1978), 'The descriptive interpretation of performative utterances', *Journal of Linguistics*, **14**, 309–10.

HARRIS, Z. S. (1951), *Structural Linguistics*, Chicago: University of Chicago Press.

HAWKINS, J. A. (1978), *Definiteness and Indefiniteness: A Study in Reference and Grammaticality Prediction*, London: Croom Helm.

HOLDCROFT, D. (1978), *Words and Deeds: Problems in the Theory of Speech Acts*, Oxford: Clarendon Press.

HORN, L. R. (1976), *On the Semantic Properties of Logical Operators in English*, Bloomington: Indiana University Linguistics Club.

HUDSON, R. A. (1975). 'The meaning of questions', *Language*, **51**, 1–31.

JAKOBSON, R. (1960), 'Linguistics and poetics', in Sebeok, T. A. (ed.), *Style in Language*, Cambridge, Mass.: MIT Press, *pp* 350–77.

KARTTUNEN, L., and PETERS, S. (1979), 'Conventional implicature', in Oh, C.-K. and Dinneen, D. A. (eds), *Syntax and Semantics*, Vol. 11: *Presupposition*, New York: Academic Press, *pp* 1–56.

KATZ, J. J., (1964). 'Analyticity and contradiction in natural language', in Fodor, J. A. and Katz, J. J. (eds), *The Structure of Language: Readings in the Philosophy of Language*, Englewood Cliffs, NJ: Prentice-Hall, *pp* 519–43.

KATZ, J. J., and FODOR, J. A. (1963), 'The structure of a semantic theory', *Language*, **39**, 170–210.

KATZ, J. J., and POSTAL, P. M. (1964), *An Integrated Theory of Linguistic Descriptions*, Cambridge, Mass.: MIT Press.

KEENAN, E. O. (1976), 'The universality of conversational postulates', *Language in Society*, **5**, 67–80.

KEMPSON, R. M. (1975), *Presupposition and the Delimitation of Semantics*, Cambridge: Cambridge U. P.

KEMPSON, R. M. (1977), *Semantic Theory*, Cambridge: Cambridge U. P.

KIM, C. (1971), *Introduction to Linear Programming*, New York: Holt, Rinehart and Winston.

KLAMMER, T. P. (1973), 'Foundations for a theory of dialogue structure', *Poetics*, **9**, 27–64.

KUHN, T. S. (1962), *The Structure of Scientific Revolutions*, Chicago: University of Chicago Press (2nd enlarged edn, 1970).

KUNO, S. (1973), *The Structure of the Japanese Language*, Cambridge, Mass.: MIT Press.

LABOV, W. (1972), 'Rules for ritual insults', in Sudnow, D. (ed.), *Studies in Social Interaction*, New York: Free Press, *pp* 120–69.

LABOV, W. (1973), 'The boundaries of words and their meanings', in Bailey and Shuy, op. cit., *pp* 340–73.

LAKATOS, I. (1970), 'Falsification and the methodology of scientific research programmes', in Lakatos, I. and Musgrave, A. (eds), *Criticism and the Growth of Science*, Cambridge: Cambridge U. P., *pp* 96–196.

LAKATOS, I. (1978), *Mathematics, Science, and Epistemology: Philosophical Papers*, Vol. 2, Worrall, J. and Currie, G. (eds), Cambridge: Cambridge U. P.

LAKOFF, G. (1971), 'On generative semantics', in Steinberg and Jakobovits, op. cit., *pp* 232–96.

LAKOFF, G. (1977), 'Linguistic Gestalts', in *Proceedings of the Thirteenth Annual Meeting of the Chicago Linguistic Society*, Chicago: Chicago Linguistic Society, 236–87.

LAKOFF, R. (1972), 'Language in context', *Language*, **48**, 907–27.

LAKOFF, R. (1973), 'The logic of politeness; or, minding your p's and q's', in *Papers from the Ninth Regional Meeting of the Chicago Linguistic Society*, Chicago: Chicago Linguistic Society, *pp* 292–305.

LARKIN, D., and O'MALLEY, M. H. (1973), 'Declarative sentences and the rule-of-conversation hypothesis', in *Papers from the Ninth Regional Meeting of the Chicago Linguistic Society*, Chicago: Chicago Linguistic Society, *pp* 306–19.

LEECH, G. (1969), *Towards a Semantic Description of English*, London: Longman.

LEECH, G. (1971), *Meaning and the English Verb*, London: Longman.

LEECH, G. (1974), *Semantics*, Harmondsworth: Penguin.

LEECH, G. (1977), Review of Sadock (1974) and Cole and Morgan (1975), *Journal of Linguistics*, **13**, 133–45.

LEECH, G. (1980), *Explorations in Semantics and Pragmatics*, Amsterdam: John Benjamins.

LEECH, G. (1980[1976]), 'Metalanguage, pragmatics, and performatives', in Leech (1980), *pp* 59–78 (originally published in Rameh, C. (ed.), *Semantics: Theory and Application*, Washington: Georgetown U. P.).

LEECH, G. (1980 [1977a]), 'Language and tact', in Leech (1980), *pp* 79–

117 (originally Linguistic Agency University of Trier, Series A, Paper No. 46, 1977).

LEECH, G. (1980[1977b]), 'Natural language as metalanguage', in Leech (1980), *pp* 31–58 (originally published in *Transactions of the Philological Society*, 1976–77, 1–31).

LEECH, G. (1981 [1974]), *Semantics*, 2nd edn, Harmondsworth: Penguin.

LEECH, G. (1981), 'Pragmatics and conversational rhetoric'. In Parret, Sbisà, and Verschueren, op. cit., *pp* 413–42.

LEECH, G., and COATES, J. (1980), 'Semantic indeterminacy and the modals', in Greenbaum, Leech and Svartvik, op. cit., *pp* 79–90.

LEECH, G., DEUCHAR, M., and HOOGENRAAD, R. (1982), *Grammar for the Present Day*, London: Macmillan.

LEECH, G., and SHORT, M. (1981), *Style in Fiction: A Linguistic Introduction to English Fictional Prose*, London: Longman.

LEVIN, S. R. (1976), 'Concerning what kind of speech act a poem is', in Van Dijk, T. A. (ed.), *Pragmatics of Language and Literature*, Amsterdam: North-Holland, *pp* 141–60.

LEVINSON, S. C. (1978), 'Activity types and language', *Pragmatics microfiche*, 3, Fiche 3-3, D.1–G.5.

LIGHTFOOT, D. (1978), *Principles of Diachronic Syntax*, Cambridge: Cambridge U. P.

LURIA, A. R. (1976), *Basic Problems of Neurolinguistics*, The Hague: Mouton.

LYONS, J. (1977), *Semantics*, Vols 1 and 2, Cambridge: Cambridge U. P.

MCCAWLEY, J. D. (1968), 'The role of semantics in a grammar', In Bach, E. and Harms, R. T. (eds), *Universals in Language*, New York: Holt, Rinehart and Winston.

MCCAWLEY, J. D. (1981), *Everything that Linguists have Always Wanted to Know about Logic* * *but were Ashamed to Ask*, Chicago: Chicago U.P.

MALINOWSKI, B. (1930), 'The problem of meaning in primitive languages', in 2nd and subsequent editions of Ogden, C. K. and Richards, I. A. (1923), *The Meaning of Meaning*, London: Routledge, 296–336.

MATTHEWS, P. H. (1976), Review of Sadock (1974), *General Linguistics*, 16, 236–42.

MILLER, G. A., and JOHNSON-LAIRD, P. N. (1976), *Language and Perception*, Cambridge: Cambridge U.P.

MILLER, G. A., and NICELY, P. (1955), 'An analysis of perceptual confusions among some English consonants', *Journal of the Acoustical Society of America*, 27, 338–52.

MILLER, R. A. (1967), *The Japanese Language*, Chicago: Chicago U.P.

MORRIS, C. W. (1938), Foundations of the theory of signs, Chicago: Chicago U.P.

MORRIS, C. W. (1946), *Signs, Language, and Behavior*, Englewood Cliffs, NJ: Prentice-Hall.

NEWELL, A. (1973), 'Artificial Intelligence and the concept of mind', in Schank, R. C. and Colby, K. M. (eds), *Computer Models of Thought and Language*, San Francisco: W. H. Freeman, *pp* 1–60.

NEWMEYER, F. J. (1980), *Linguistic Theory in America*, New York: Academic Press.

O'HAIR, S. G. (1969), 'Meaning and implication', *Theoria*, **35**, 38–54.

PALMER, F. R. (1977), 'Modals and Actuality', *Journal of Linguistics*, **13**, 1, 1–23.

PALMER, F. R. (1980), '*Can, will*, and actuality', in Greenbaum, Leech and Svartvik, op. cit., *pp* 91–9.

PARISI, D., and CASTELFRANCHI, C. (1981), 'A goal analysis of some pragmatic aspects of language', in Parret, Sbisà, and Verschueren, op. cit., *pp* 551–68.

PARRET, H., SBISÀ, M., and VERSCHUEREN, J. (eds), (1981), *Possibilities and Limitations of Pragmatics*, Amsterdam: John Benjamins.

POPPER, K. R. (1972 [1963]), *Conjectures and Refutations: The Growth of Scientific Knowledge*, 4th edn, London: Routledge (originally published 1963).

POPPER, K. R. (1972), *Objective Knowledge: An Evolutionary Approach*, Oxford: The Clarendon Press.

QUIRK, R. (1965), 'Descriptive statement and serial relationship', *Language*, **41**, 205–17.

ROMAINE, S. (1981), 'The status of variable rules in sociolinguistic theory', *Journal of Linguistics*, **17**, 93–119.

ROSCH, E. (1977), 'Human categorization', in Warren, N. (ed.), *Advances in Cross-cultural Psychology*, Vol. 1, New York: Academic Press.

ROSCH, E., and MERVIS, C. B. (1975), 'Family resemblances: studies in the internal structure of categories', *Cognitive Psychology*, **7**, 573–605.

ROSS, J. R. (1970), 'On declarative sentences', in Jacobs, R. A. and Rosenbaum, P. S. (eds), *Readings in English Transformational Grammar*, Waltham, Mass.: Blaisdell, *pp* 222–72.

ROSS, J. R. (1973), 'A fake NP squish', in Bailey and Shuy, op. cit., *pp* 96–140.

SACKS, H., SCHEGLOFF, E., and JEFFERSON, G. (1974), 'A simplest systematics for the organization of turn-taking in conversation', *Language*, **50**, 696–735.

SADOCK, J. M. (1974), *Toward a Linguistic Theory of Speech Acts*, New York: Academic Press.

SAUSSURE, F. de (1959 [1916]), *Course in General Linguistics*, New York: Philosophical Library (translated by Wade Baskin; Original French edition 1916).

SEARLE, J. R. (1969), *Speech Acts: An Essay in the Philosophy of Language*, Cambridge: Cambridge U.P.

SEARLE, J. R. (1979), *Expression and Meaning*, Cambridge: Cambridge U.P.

SEARLE, J. R. (1979 [1975a]), 'A taxonomy of illocutionary acts', in Searle (1979), 1–29 (originally published 1975).

SEARLE, J. R. (1979 [1975b]), 'Indirect speech acts', in Searle (1979), 30–57 (originally published in Cole and Morgan (1975)).

SEARLE, J. R. (1979 [1975c]), 'Speech acts and recent linguistics', in Searle (1979), 162–79 (originally published 1975).

SINCLAIR, J. MCH. (1980), 'Discourse in relation to language structure and semiotics', in Greenbaum, Leech, and Svartvik, op. cit., *pp* 110–24.

SINCLAIR, J. MCH., and COULTHARD, R. M. (1975), *Towards an Analysis of Discourse*, London: Oxford U.P.

SLOBIN, D. I. (1975), 'The more it changes . . . on understanding language by watching it move through time', *Papers and Reports on Child Language Development*, University of California, Berkeley, September 1975, *pp* 1–30.

SMITH, N., and WILSON, D. (1979), *Modern Linguistics: The Results of Chomsky's Revolution*, Harmondsworth: Penguin.

SPIELMANN, R. W. (1980), 'Performative utterances as indexical expressions – comment on Harris', *Journal of Linguistics*, **16**, 89–94.

STEINBERG, D. D., and JAKOBOVITS, L. A. (eds), (1971), *Semantics: An Interdisciplinary Reader in Philosophy, Linguistics and Psychology*, Cambridge: Cambridge U.P.

STENIUS, E. (1967), 'Mood and language-game', *Synthese*, **17**, 254–74.

THOMAS, J. A. (1981), 'Pragmatic failure', University of Lancaster: unpublished M.A. dissertation.

THOMAS, J. (1983), 'Cross-cultural pragmatic failure', *Applied Linguistics*, 4.2, 91–112.

THORPE, W. H. (1972), 'The comparison of vocal communication in animals and man', in Hinde, R. A. (ed.), *Non-Verbal Communication*, Cambridge: Cambridge U.P. *pp* 27–47.

TREVARTHAN, C. (1977), 'Descriptive analyses of infant communicative behaviour', in Schaffer, H. R. (ed.), *Studies in Mother–Infant Interaction*, New York: Academic Press, *pp* 227–70.

VELOO, V. P. (1980), 'Grammar and semantics of the verb in Malayalam', University of Lancaster: unpublished M.A. dissertation.

VENNEMANN, T. (1973), 'Explanation in syntax', in Kimball, J. P. (ed.), *Syntax and Semantics*, Vol. 2, New York: Seminar Press, *pp* 1–50.

VERSCHUEREN, J. (forthcoming), *What People say they do with Words*, The Hague: Mouton.

WIDDOWSON, H. (1975), *Stylistics and the Teaching of Literature*, London: Longman.

WILSON, D. (1975), *Presupposition and Non-Truth-Conditional Semantics*, London and New York: Academic Press.

WILSON, D., and SPERBER, D. (1981), 'On Grice's theory of conversation', in Werth, P. (ed.), *Conversation and Discourse: Structure and Interpretation*, London: Croom Helm, 152–77.

WINSTON, P. H. (1977), *Artificial Intelligence*, Reading, Mass.: Addison-Wesley.

WITTGENSTEIN, L. (1953), *Philosophical Investigations*, Oxford: Blackwell.

YNGVE, V. (1961), 'The depth hypothesis', in *Structure of language and its mathematical aspects, Proceedings of Symposia in Applied Mathematics*, **12**, 130–8.

Index